The DRAGON and the BEAST

The
DRAGON
and the
BEAST

Islamic Prophecies in Daniel & Revelation

Faith Jones

outskirts press
Denver, Colorado

The opinions expressed in this manuscript are solely the opinions of the author and do not represent the opinions or thoughts of the publisher. The author has represented and warranted full ownership and/or legal right to publish all the materials in this book.

The Dragon and the Beast
Islamic Prophecies in Daniel and Revelation
All Rights Reserved.
Copyright © 2012 Faith Jones
v5.0 r2.2

Cover Photo © 2012 JupiterImages Corporation. All rights reserved - used with permission.

thedragonandthebeast.org

Scripture taken from the NEW AMERICAN STANDARD BIBLE®, Copright 1960, 1962, 1963, 1968, 1971, 1972, 1973, 1975, 1977, 1995 by The Lockman Foundation. Used by permission www.Lockman.org.

This book may not be reproduced, transmitted, or stored in whole or in part by any means, including graphic, electronic, or mechanical without the express written consent of the publisher except in the case of brief quotations embodied in critical articles and reviews.

Outskirts Press, Inc.
http://www.outskirtspress.com

ISBN: 978-1-4327-8169-9

Outskirts Press and the "OP" logo are trademarks belonging to Outskirts Press, Inc.

PRINTED IN THE UNITED STATES OF AMERICA

Table of Contents

Preface ix

Introduction: About Islam.. xv
    A brief History of Islam, its holy books and doctrinal differences between Sunnis and Shi'as; the end time prophecies of the Hadith with its five major figures: As-Sufyani, Al Mahdi, Al Dajaal, the Prophet Jesus, and Satan

    Part One: The Beast from the East—Islamic Prophecies in Daniel

Chapter 1: As-Sufyani and Al Mahdi in the Statue
and the Four Beasts of Daniel 3
    The historical rise of Islam and the future conquests of As-Sufyani in Nebuchadnezzar's statue; the empire of As-Sufyani and Al Mahdi in the four beasts of Daniel

Chapter 2: Antiochus IV and As-Sufyani in the Ram and Goat ..17
    The rise of Alexander the Great and the Seleucids in the ram and goat of Daniel; details of Antiochus IV and Islam's As-Sufyani in Daniel 11

Chapter 3: Al Mahdi in the Ram and Goat.............................35
    The transgression of Israel under As-Sufyani; Al Mahdi as the Insolent King who arises when the transgressors have finished

**Chapter 4: The Prophecy of the Seventy Weeks:
The Prince to Come** 53
The seventieth week; the covenant, the many, the Prince of the Covenant, the Prince to Come and his people; the timeline of the seventieth week

Chapter 5: Could it Really Happen Soon? 75
The feasibility of As-Sufyani, the Prince to Come, and Islam as the beast kingdom; modern signs of the people of the Prince to Come

Part Two: The Dragon and the Beast—
Islamic Prophecies in Revelation

Chapter 6: Identifying the Seven churches of Revelation 103
The seven churches of Asia as a type of the end time Church, and the letters of Revelation as prophecies to it; the meaning of the document with seven seals

Chapter 7: The Seven Seals and Matthew 24—*Seals 1-3* 111
Seals 1-3 as interpreted by Matthew 24; their correspondence with the first three letters to the Church, and their parallels in Islamic prophecy

Chapter 8: Seals 4-5 131
Seals 4-5 as the beginning of Israel's distress described in Matthew 24; their correspondence with the fourth and fifth letters to the Church, and their parallels in Islamic prophecy

Chapter 9: The Sixth Seal 153
The sixth seal as interpreted by Matthew 24; its correspondence with the sixth letter to the Church and its parallels in Islamic prophecy; the 144,000 and the multitude of gentiles in heaven

Chapter 10: The Little Book: Zooming in on Israel Midway through the Week **165**
The meaning of the Little Book and interpretations of the topics it contains: the temple and the two witnesses, the dragon, the woman and the male child

**Chapter 11: The Little Book Continued—
The Beast out of the Sea** **191**
The beast out of the sea and its parallels with Al Mahdi

Chapter 12: The Seventh Seal—Trumpets 1-6 .... **211**
The seventh seal as interpreted by Matthew 24; its correspondence to the seventh letter to the Church; the trumpets as the prophetic tool of the two witnesses and their parallels to Islam's Al Dajaal; possible interpretations of trumpets 1-6

Chapter 13: The Seventh Seal Continued—Trumpet 7 .... **231**
The beast out of the earth as the Israeli government under the co-leadership of Al Mahdi (Antichrist) and the Prophet Jesus (false prophet); the chronology of the seventh trumpet events, including the campaign of the mark and the rapture of the Jewish Church

Chapter 14: The Second Coming of Christ—The Seven Bowls ... **249**
Possible interpretations of bowls 1-6; the seventh bowl destruction of the Antichrist's Jerusalem capital (the harlot); Armageddon; parallels between Christ's millennial reign and the reign of Satan in Islamic prophecy

Appendices
Appendix 1: Calculations of Sir Robert Anderson 273
Appendix 2: Overview of Daniel's Visions 277
*Appendix 3: Parallels of the As-Sufyani/Mahdi
  pair in Daniel, Revelation and Matthew* 279
*Appendix 4: Summary of the Letters and their
  Corresponding Seals* 283

Preface

There are so many books about end time prophecy it seems almost ridiculous to publish yet one more. The fact is I had no intention of writing a book. It started off as a way to get my thoughts about Revelation down on paper, hoping maybe my kids would read them some day. So there I was, re-studying Revelation for the umpteenth time, when I came to chapter thirteen's description of the Antichrist kingdom. I realized that I had to go back to Daniel's vision to refresh my memory regarding the lion, bear and leopard. I had read material that discussed the similarities between the last Islamic Imam and the Antichrist, but when I realized that these animals described an empire made up of the Middle East, I was absolutely convinced: what else could the false religion of the Antichrist be but Islam?

I realized that if this were the case, all the Islamic prophecies would have to be fulfilled in order to convince Muslims that the Antichrist was in fact their expected Imam. But they would also have to fit the Biblical prophecies about the end time. After doing a little research, I discovered a book that had compiled all of the important prophecies in Islamic eschatology, and I was astounded to see in them so many parallels with the characters and end time events of Daniel and Revelation.

In it, there were five main figures: 1) As-Sufyani, the tyrant who terrorizes the earth; 2) Al Mahdi, the chosen Imam of Allah who defeats him, conquers Israel and rules the world; 3) Al Dajaal, the antichrist who comes to wage war against Al Mahdi; 4) the Islamic Prophet Jesus[1] who arises to defeat Al Dajaal and rule over the earth with Al Mahdi, and 5) Satan, who with his demons, comes in the guise of a human being and demands worship.

Reading Daniel and Revelation in light of these prophecies, I was surprised to find that scripture also has five main figures, paralleling those of Islam: 1) Daniel's Despicable Person (the dragon of Revelation 12), who conquers the Middle East and sets up the Abomination of Desolation in Israel; 2) the Insolent King of Daniel (the beast out of the sea in Revelation 13) who sets himself up as Messiah, tramples the temple and rules over the earth; 3) the two witnesses of Revelation 17 who prophesy and fight against the beast out of the sea; 4) the false prophet, co-ruler with the beast out of the sea (together forming the beast out of the land in Revelation 13); and 5) Jesus Christ Himself who comes with the saints to set up the millennial kingdom.

There seems to be a general knowledge among Christians of an Antichrist who will persecute the Church and Israel at the end of the age. Most know he's mysteriously identified with the number 666, and many teach that he will arise from Western Europe. Yet remarkably, most churches seem to avoid discussing end time prophecy altogether because it's too messy. A lot of Christians I know have never even attempted to read Revelation or study prophecy because there are too many interpretations and it's too scary to think about all that stuff happening in our lifetime; many have given up even thinking that Christ will return within the next generation or two.

---

1 From this point on, I will use the term "Prophet Jesus" to refer to this person. Whenever I talk about the Lord Jesus Christ I'll use "Jesus."

For me, the book of Revelation was something I believed would happen, but its references to talking idols and marks on hands and foreheads were just so difficult to imagine, that I gave up trying to identify who the Antichrist could be, or when he might come. Now that I've studied Islam and compared its belief system and prophecies to Biblical scriptures, it seems like it should have been obvious all along. Not only do Daniel and Revelation point to Islam, but current events give us a glimpse of what is to come—the violence, the fanaticism, the oppressive nature of Islam—it's like having a curtain pulled back, and suddenly, what seemed like mythology can be understood in its modern context.

My intention in publishing this book wasn't to make written-in-stone predictions about how all of these prophecies will be fulfilled, but rather to demonstrate that they aren't as far-fetched—or as far off—as many people would like to believe. In-depth analysis of history, current events and Islam go beyond the scope of this book (not to mention my own knowledge), but I've tried to lay a sufficient foundation in the beliefs and history of Islam, since most Americans seem largely uninformed about them. Ultimately, my desire is to provide ideas that will encourage people to start thinking concretely about the end time and to see how current events might be leading up to them.

Writing this book has completely changed the way I see the world. After spending hours researching and writing about the final conflict between God and Satan, I would go about my daily life and feel like I was walking around in a dream, more aware of the spiritual warfare going on around us; I felt like Elisha's servant to whom was suddenly revealed the thousands of angels on horseback surrounding his camp at Dothan. This surreal experience really drove home to me how difficult it is to be Christians in this modern world while still keeping our eyes on heaven. After so much time of waiting for the Lord's return, the Church has lost the urgency that the first century Church thrived on. Gone are the fire, the passion and the signs and wonders that the apostles experienced on a daily basis. At the end of the age, we'll be forced to choose between compromise and the type of steadfastness that may demand the ultimate price. We know this is true about the future, but what we fail to see is that it's our spiritual reality even now—to either float through our lives without the power of the Holy Spirit, never fulfilling our God-given purpose on this earth, or to step out in faith and be the salt and light not only in the witness of the lives we lead, but in our high measure of love, compassion and even miracles. Comparing the present Church with the first century Church has emphasized to me how much we fall short of our mission today.

In order to be effective Christians, we must act on the fact that this life affects eternity. We need to look beyond the trappings of this life to see the eternal significance of everything we do—to see everything through God's eyes. The Bible gives us small glimpses of that reality, if in no other way than to show us that one ordinary person's life recorded in the Old Testament 3500 years ago, can still have an impact on thousands of people today. Although we can't understand the economy of heaven, we must trust by faith that our lives count toward the redemption of this world, otherwise Christ wouldn't have entrusted us with His work.

The fact is that Satan is the prince of this world, and the age old battle between him and God is going on right now, just like it has been from so long ago. Unfortunately, as Job teaches us, we're the battleground. Like Paul says, "our struggle is not against flesh and blood, but against the rulers, against the powers, against the world forces of this darkness, against the spiritual forces of wickedness in the heavenly places" (Eph 6:12). There are many places today where the Church suffers as it did in Paul's day. Yet even where it doesn't, the spiritual reality of this life is that we're fighting a battle for the Lord in our everyday struggles and sufferings—in all the choices we make, our striving to know the Lord and love our neighbor as ourselves and in every step of our quest to be made in His image. There's something beautiful and privileged about the part we play in the redemption of this earth. When we become overwhelmed, we need to remember this scripture in Revelation: "Now the salvation, and the power, and the kingdom of our God and the authority of His Christ have come, for the accuser of our brethren has been thrown down who accuses them before our God day and night. *And they overcame him because of the blood of the Lamb, and because of the word of their testimony, and they did not love their life even to death*" (12:10,11). This is the mystery of which Paul speaks when he says,"...the manifold wisdom of God might now be made known *through the Church* to the rulers and authorities in the heavenly places" (Eph 3:8-10). In other words, our job on this earth is to demoralize Satan and the demons by proving the power of faith, just as Job did. For this reason we must endure to the end, even if our end as individuals comes long before the Antichrist does.

As you read this book, you might disagree with my ideas, and frankly, by the time you read it, I may have changed my mind about some of them myself! It's the nature of prophecy that we be blind about certain parts of it until the time God chooses to disclose its fullest meaning. The most exciting moments of studying prophetic scripture come when we're willing to let go of the things we've believed in exchange for God's ongoing revelation. This can only come through the passage of time and prayerful study. If you can't agree with my ideas, then my sincere prayer is that you'll disagree with a strong enough passion to read other authors and delve into scripture to build support for your own interpretations and ideas; being in the word will always bear fruit.

I'd like to give one last thought regarding the Church and Islam. I think it's very important for Christians to understand that Islam is our enemy as much as any false doctrine is, but Muslims are God's precious creation, and of course Christ aches to have them understand that He came to free them from the bondage of sin. Our calling is not to fight in anger or violence against anyone (Muslims included), but to combat every falsehood that binds the minds and hearts of people everywhere; and the only weapon that can accomplish this is the love of Christ.

Introduction: About Islam

Most Westerners know very little about how and when Islam started and even less about what it teaches, so it seemed a good idea to discuss Islam's history and major doctrines. The information in this chapter is intended to lay a foundation for the rest of the book, so don't get too hung up on the names and dates. Although there are many sects in Islam, only the two major ones are discussed here—Sunni and Shi'a.

History

According to Islam, Muhammad was born in Mecca in 570 A.D. When he was about 40 years old, he was meditating and praying in a cave when the angel Gabriel came and gave him his first revelation. At this time the Arabian peninsula was pagan, worshiping gods related to the sun, moon and stars. Muhammad's tribe, the Quraish, were caretakers of the Kabaah, the cube-shaped temple where pilgrims came from miles around to worship the 360 stone gods that had fallen from heaven. One of these, Hubal (also known as Allah), was the Quraish's patron god and the principle god of Mecca.[1] Gabriel revealed to Muhammad that Allah was the only

---

1   Sam Shamoun, "Did the Meccans Worship Yahweh God? Revisiting the Issue of the

god, not one of many. But when Muhammad preached this to his fellow Meccans, they weren't happy; not only was he criticizing their religion, he was threatening to take away their livelihood. As he started to gain a small group of followers, the pagan Meccans began to persecute them; eventually, they were even barred from the Kabaah. Finally, he and his small band fled to Yathrib, a city that would later come to be called Medina.[2] This flight is called the *hegira*, and it's from this year that Islam restarted its calendar: 622 A.D. begins the Muslim year 1 A.H. After gaining a stronghold in Medina, Muhammad began making treaties with other tribes in the peninsula, in many cases converting them to Islam.

But Muhammad wanted Mecca and the Kabaah. He and his fellow Muslims would fight three battles against the Meccans, winning two of them despite being outnumbered three to one. In 630 Muhammad would enter Mecca peaceably but victoriously, and take over the Kabaah, destroying the idols inside it and barring all non-Muslims from entering.

Islam wasn't around very long before it had its main split into Sunnis and Shi'as, and they've pretty much been enemies ever since. It started in 632 when Muhammad died, leaving the now Muslim Arabian peninsula without a leader. He had no son, and disagreements arose among the Muslim community as to who should succeed him: his father-in-law Abu Bakr, or his cousin and son-in-law, Ali (married to his only child, Fatima). One group claimed that the prophet had chosen Ali, and came to call themselves *"Shi'atu Ali,"*

Ishmaelites and the Worship of the True God," pp. 6-7, http://www.answering-islam.org/shamoun/ishmael-baal.htm

2 Yathrib's population was half Jewish, but the Muslims would ultimately expel two of the three tribes living there and massacre the third, selling its women into slavery. The Muslims chose Yathrib because the pagans living there invited Muhammad to act as arbiter of their tribal disputes. After the hegira, it was renamed Madinat un-Nabi, meaning "the City of the Prophet." Un-Nabi was soon dropped, so its name in English is "Medina," meaning simply "the city." Ed Hotaling, *Islam without Illusions: its Past, Its Present and its Challenge for the Future*, pp. 35, 66-70, Syracuse University Press, 2003

(followers of Ali)—Shi'as for short. To this day they consider themselves to be the true followers of the prophet's family, since they acknowledge only those Imams related by blood to Muhammad.

The other group decided to elect Abu Bakr instead of Ali. This group would later call themselves *Sunnis* from *sunnah,* meaning "well trodden path," emphasizing their belief that they followed the main path of the Islamic community. Being the majority, the Sunnis controlled the leadership of the growing religion and empire, and as a result, the Shi'as were suppressed and often persecuted.

Ali eventually got his chance when the Sunnis chose him as their fourth Imam and Caliph over the empire. Unfortunately, Mu'awiyah, governor of Syria, refused to acknowledge him and rebelled, starting a dynasty of his own—the Umayyads. The rebellion continued when Ali's son Hussein stepped up to the Caliphate. While on his way to Kufa to make his claim, he was ambushed and killed at Karbala, along with nearly everyone in his small party. Among the captives was his son, through whom the Shi'as would continue to count their rightful Imams. Hussein was claimed as a Shi'a martyr, his death commemorated each year by Shi'a men parading through the cities cutting and flagellating themselves; sometimes the battle of Karbala is reenacted in period costume.

Holy Books

The Koran

The Koran can be compared to the Christian Bible in that it's considered to be God's revelation to mankind. But while the Bible was written by many men over about 1500 years, the Koran was received and dictated by Muhammad alone throughout his lifetime. Islam teaches that the Torah and Christian gospel were originally revealed by Allah to the Jewish prophets and Jesus, but the Jews and Christians later adulterated them,[3] therefore Muslims are generally discouraged or even forbidden from reading Judeo-Christian scriptures. Some are even taught that Christians are sorcerers who derive their magic from the Bible, and in some countries it's downright dangerous for a Muslim to be caught with a Bible.[4]

The clear purpose of the Koran is to correct the errors of Jews, Christians and Pagans. Something not generally known in the West is that the Koran is considered by Muslims to be a progressive revelation to Muhammad over his lifetime; thus later recitations are considered to abrogate—that is cancel out—earlier revelations. According to the Koran, Allah states:

"And for whatever verse we abrogate and cast into oblivion, We bring a better or the like of it; knowest thou not that God is powerful over everything?"
-- Sura 2:106

"And when We exchange a verse in place of another verse—and God knows very well what He is sending down—they say, 'Thou art a mere forger!' Nay, but the most of them have no knowledge."
-- Sura 16:101

A famous example of this abrogation is called the Verse of the Sword, in which the earlier verse stating "Let there be no compulsion in religion; truth stands out clear from error" (2:256) was replaced by "...fight and slay the pagans wherever ye find them, and seize them, beleaguer them and lie in wait for them in every stratagem (of war). But if they repent, and establish regular prayers

---

3   Joseph Alrasouli, "Muslim View of the Bible," p. 1, Giving an Answer, http://www.givingananswer.org/articles/ muslimviewofbible.html
4   Lynn Copeland, editor, *Into the Den of Infidels: Our Search for Truth,* Living Sacrifice Book Company, Bartlesville, OK, 2003, chapter 8: How I Came to Know God

and practice regular charity, [i.e. become Muslims] then open the way for them" (9:5). Although there's a great difference of opinion among Muslim scholars as to which verses supersede which, most are agreed that the Verse of the Sword supersedes most of the previous verses regarding jihad. Some believe it abrogates as many as 111 verses.

According to Reverend Richard P. Bailey's study on the doctrine of Jihad, Muhammad's teaching went through a four-stage progression: 1) the command of non-retaliation while he and his followers were being persecuted in Mecca (during which time 90 of the 114 Koranic suras or chapters were given); 2) permission to fight defensively shortly after his migration to Medina; 3) the command to fight defensively during his battles with the Meccans; 4) and finally, after the conquest of Mecca in 630 (and still in force today), the obligation of the faithful to fight offensive wars against all non-Muslims. In fact, according to several verses of the Koran, the refusal to fight when physically able is considered "perverse rebellion" punishable by Allah; for this reason the faithful are forbidden to even pray for them or stand by their graves (Koran 9:84).[5]

The Koran is not organized chronologically, so it's impossible to know by reading it which verses take the place of which; it's said that over one third of the 114 suras of the Koran contain abrogated verses;[6] this must be kept in mind whenever the Koran is quoted.

The Hadith

During his life, the prophet Muhammad had many "companions," close followers who were discipled by him. They hung on

---

[5] Answering Islam, Rev. Richard P. Bailey, Jihad: "The Teachings of Islam from its Primary Sources—the Quran and Hadith", p. 19, http://www.answering–islam.org/Bailey/jihad.html

[6] Tourist Gems of Uzbekistan, Rustam Mirzaev, "The History of Osman's Koran", p. 3, http:// www.sairamtour.com/news/gems/50.html

his every word, and asked many questions to clarify his teachings. They remembered his *sunnah* (what he said and did), sharing them with the faithful through their *hadiths* (oral reports) which were eventually written and compiled into various volumes. In order to demonstrate its authenticity, each *hadith* had its own list of narrators going all the way back to the prophet himself. Collectively, this body of work is referred to as the *Hadith*. Muslims derive their doctrine, prophecies and examples for practical application of Islam from both the Koran and the Hadith, giving them equal importance. In other words, "whatever Muhammad said, did, condoned or condemned [according to Hadith]...is the perfect example for all human beings...whatever Muhammad did or said therefore becomes the basis from which to model all life and belief."[7]

Not all hadiths hold equal authority, however; in fact, some are even determined to be forgeries by each sect's authorities. Sunni authorities come from one of four major schools of law responsible for interpreting the Koran and Shari'a law, each one being named for the Imam considered to be its founder.[8] In order to determine which hadiths were authentic, Sunni scholars developed the "science of Hadith," a strict system of principles applied to the hadiths and their *usnads* (chains of narrators), in order to determine their status: false, weak or authentic and reliable. The highest body of authorities in the science of Hadith is termed Al Hufaz.[9]

Shi'as on the other hand, have two schools: the minority *Akhbari* school, which believes all of the Hadith is reliable; and the majority Usuli school, which holds that the authenticity of each hadith must

---

[7] Susan Crimp and Joel Richardson, editors, *Why We Left Islam*, preface, New York, NY, WND Books, inc., 2008
[8] They are Hanafi, Maliki, Shafi'i and Hanbali, *Sunni Islam*, New World Encyclopedia, http://www.newworldencyclopedia.org/entry/Sunni, p. 2
[9] The Muhammadan Reality, Grand Muhaddith of Morocco, Shaykh Abdullah ben Sadek, Ph.D, *Jesus, Al Mahdi and Moshaikh (Anti-Christ)*, translated by Shaykh Ahmad Darwish, p. 4, , http://www.muhammadanreality.com/ ImamMahdiSignsfor the Savoir.htm

be determined.[10]

While both the Koran and the Hadith are employed by Sunnis and Shi'as, most of the information about the end time comes from the Hadith. Most Shi'as accept only those narrations declared acceptable by the Usuli scholars. Among other things, this means they must be transmitted by members of Muhammad's family (called *Ahl al-Bayt*) and their supporters; of course Sunnis and Shi'as differ as to who they believe qualify as the Prophet's family. In addition to the Prophet's Hadith, Shi'as have a body of hadiths that Sunnis don't study or consider to be authoritative—the sunnah of their historical Imams, which they also put on the same level as scripture. Just as it's important to know which Koranic verses have not been abrogated, it's important to know which hadiths are considered valid or authentic; this is determined by Islamic scholars, who may differ depending on whether they are Sunni or Shi'a.

Doctrinal Differences between Sunnis and Shi'as

Sunnis still make up the majority of Muslims in the Middle East (about 1.19 billion[11]), while Shi'as constitute about 210 million.[12] The Sunni/Shi'a schism runs along doctrinal lines remarkably similar to Protestants and Catholics. Like Protestants, Sunnis trust that God's total revelation is found in their holy books, and they believe that no individual has special authority or ability to interpret them. Instead, the consensus of the community determines what is or is not an authentic Islamic practice.[13] Historically, the Caliph (prince) held the highest religious and political power, but Sunni Islam has

---

10 Wikipedia, Usuli, citing Momen, Moojan *An introduction to Shi'i Islam: the history and doctrines of Twelver Shi'ism*, p. 127, Oxford: G. Ronald, 1985
11 Jeffry Goldberg, "How Iran Could Save the Middle East", p. 2, The Atlantic, (July/Aug 2009), http://www.theatlantic.com/doc/200907/israel-sunni
12 ibid.
13 New World Enclopedia, "Ijma", p. 1, http://www.newworld encyclopedia.org/entry/Ijma%27

no hierarchical structure within the religion. The term *Imam* is used to refer to a man of high character in the community who's elected to lead the faithful in prayer and isn't required to have any formal training.[14]

In contrast, Shi'ite belief can be better compared to Catholic doctrine, holding that there is an office divinely created to guide the faithful, passed down through succession from the first leader. For the Catholic, this office is filled by the Pope who succeeded the Apostle Peter;[15] for the Shi'a, it's filled by the Imam, passed down by hereditary succession from Muhammad. Both Catholics and Shi'as believe that these leaders' teachings are infallible, and as such, they're included in the greater religious "tradition," holding equal authority with their holy books.[16] Unlike Catholics, however, Shi'as go so far as to believe that the Imam himself is free from sin and error by a special gift of Allah. This is why the Imam is so critical to Shi'as: only he is specially chosen and equipped to interpret the laws and traditions found in the Koran and Hadith.[17]

Sunni and Shi'a Views of Al Mahdi

Perhaps the most pivotal difference between Sunnis and Shi'as revolves around their beliefs regarding the end days and the identity and role of the last Imam of the age—Al Mahdi. There appears to be no official Sunni doctrine regarding Al Mahdi, thus there are several schools of thought regarding him. Since he's not mentioned

---

14   Global Security, Military, "Sunni Islam", http://www.globalsecurity.org/military/intro/islam-sunni.htm
15   New Advent Catholic Encyclopedia, "The Pope", p. 12 http://www.newadvent.org/cathen/12260a.htm
16   New Advent Catholic Encyclopeida, Infallibility, "Proof of the Church's infallibility", p. 3-4, http://www.newadvent.org/cathen/07790a.htm; Shiite Encyclopedia, http://www.alkafeel.net/english/shiite/Shi'a1.html
17   About.com, Agnosticism/Atheism, "Syria: Shi'a Islam", p.1, http://atheism.about.com/library/FAQs/Islam/ countries/ bl_SyriaIslamShi'a.htm

in the Koran or the oldest collections of hadiths, some say that the prophecies concerning him in the later books are false, and there will be no Mahdi at all. Others believe he will be merely a political or religious figure that people won't recognize until after his death. Still others believe in all the signs accompanying his appearance as reported in the Hadith. For these Muslims, he'll be the last Imam, the one who "closes" the religion, as Muhammad opened it, and he'll hold the religious position once held by the prophet Muhammad himself. Nevertheless, he's not considered to be divine.

The Shi'as hold a very different doctrine regarding Al Mahdi. The largest Shi'a sect, is the "Twelvers," so called because Shi'ite prophecies say that the last Imam of the age—the religious and political leader of the world—will be the twelfth Imam descended from Ali. According to Shi'ite belief, the twelfth Imam was born Muhammad al Muntazar, son of Hussan Askari, in 869 and was conferred with the office of Divine Leadership at the age of five. In order to secure his safety from the Sunnis, he was hidden on earth for 65 years (known as the "lesser occultation") during which time he was the spiritual leader of the Shi'as. In 939, he's believed to have been miraculously taken off the earth alive (called the "greater occultation"), and in his absence, the Usuli School of jurisprudence was formed and charged with the task of determining the proper interpretations of Shari'a law and the Koran (including esoteric levels of meaning which Sunnis do not give to it), until Imam Mahdi returns.[18] *Ayatollah* ("Sign of God") is the title given to high ranking Usuli Twelver Shi'a clerics who are considered experts in Islamic ethics, jurisprudence and philosophy. (Most Americans became familiar with this title when the Iranian Ayatollah Khomeini began his Islamic Revolution in 1979).

Shi'a Islam also asserts that Al Mahdi isn't divine. Nevertheless,

---

18   GlobalSecurity.org, Military, *Twelfth Imam/Hidden Imam/Imam Mahdi*, http://www.globalsecurity.org/military/intro/imam-mahdi.htm

their descriptions of him certainly appear to ascribe to him a divine messiahship: he's a "source of the existence and the remaining of the world" while hidden behind the "veil of occultation;" he'll reappear as the "executor of the divine will and command and will represent the Prophet Muhammad in both name and the real meaning of the word;" his reappearance signifies "the manifestation of *walayat,* the mastership of the Prophet," who was "first and last in degree of perfection in the arcs of descent and ascent, and who is in the highest possible stage of communion with the Absolute."[19] He's considered present on the earth spiritually, and many pray to him for special favors or protection;[20] many ascribe miraculous events to him and claim to have seen and spoken with him, and that he delivered them from times of crisis. Folklore says that every Shi'a meets the twelfth Imam once in his life without knowing it.[21]

In addition to their beliefs about the Imam, Shi'as have two major doctrines that separate them from Sunnis: *taqiyah*, hiding one's religious identity, and *mutah*, temporary marriage. Condemned by the Sunnis as cowardly, but encouraged by Shi'a Islam, *taqiyah* allows for a Muslim to hide his religion or deny certain practices for three reasons: when his life is in danger because of his beliefs; when disclosure of his religion would risk dishonor to the women in his family; or when it could leave him destitute.[22] This doctrine played a significant role in Shi'a Islam because of the extreme persecutions suffered under the Sunnis. As a result, this position as the underdog has become a part of the Shi'ite identity; this explains their emphasis on the idea of redemption through suffering and martyrdom for the truth.[23]

---

19 Ibid.
20 "Ahmadinejad and Mahdi", http://www.youtube.com/watch?v+j2dde95hxT8
21 Global Security, Military, "Twelfth Imam/Hidden Imam/Imam Mahdi," http://www.globalsecurity.org/military/ intro/Imam-mahdi.htm
22 About.com, Agnosticism/Atheism, "Syria: Shi'a islam", p.2 http://atheism.about.com/library/FAQs/islam/countries/bl_SyriaIslamShi'a.htm
23 Ibid.

Mutah is a marriage contract with a predetermined length of time that can be renewed; it can last anywhere from one day to as long as a lifetime. It became unacceptable to the Sunnis and was banned by the second Caliph, but the Shi'as still have the practice. If a couple agrees to a *mutah* (even if one party is coerced), the sexual act is not considered to be fornication or rape, and any resulting child is considered to be legitimate.[24] It must be pointed out that many Sunnis consider the Shi'as to be heretics because of such unorthodox beliefs.

Islamic Eschatology: The Prophecies of the Hadith

Because they both hold to the Hadith of Muhammad, Sunnis and Shi'as share many prophecies regarding the end time; below are paraphrases of some of the germinal prophecies considered to be authentic by both sects. Volumes of the hadiths are not like the Koranic verses which are always arranged the same regardless of translation. In essence their compilers are like editors, choosing whatever hadiths they want, and compiling them in whatever manner they choose. Because of this, hadiths must be referenced according to the compiler, book and page number of each individual collection. Most English books and articles I've read don't give specific references for the hadiths that they quote, or cite its chain of narrators, since most non-Muslims aren't familiar enough with Islam for it to be meaningful. What's probably more important is knowing that the prophecies have been declared authentic by the authorities of each sect; the source I've chosen is Sunni, but indicates that all the prophecies in it are also accepted by Shi'as. It's called *Al Mahdi, Jesus and the Anti-Christ*, compiled by the Grand Muhaddith of Morocco, Shaykh Abdullah ben Sadek, Ph.D. (1914-1993), and translated by Shaykh Ahmad Darwish. It also contains

---

24   Ibid.

authentic hadiths taken from a collection compiled by Imam Nawawi (1233-1278 A.D.) called *The Gardens of Righteousness*.[25]

As-Sufyani and Al Mahdi

As-Sufyani, so called because he's a descendant of Abu Sufyan, will come with 360 men and go to Damascus in Syria. There he'll raise an army of 30,000 men from the Kalb tribe with which he'll conquer Syria, then the cities of Kufa and Kurkisa in Iraq. He'll then enter Khorasan [a land area that included parts of Iran, Afghanistan, Tajikistan, Turkmenistan and Uzbekistan], and kill the "followers of Muhammad's family"—100,000 in Baghdad alone—brutally slaughtering men, women and children.

At around the same time, a fierce civil war will break out in "Muhammad's nation," caused by the death of a Caliph. Three sons of different Caliphs will attempt to gain command of the kingdom, but they'll merely end up killing each other. During this civil war, devoted Muslims on pilgrimage to Mecca in the month of Ramadan will be searching for an Imam, and will find a pilgrim—a civil war refugee from Medina—and drag him away from the Kabaah against his will to name him as Al Mahdi (the "Guided One"). He'll be a direct descendant of Muhammad, and his skin will be "the color of an Arab," and his body "like that of Israel." On his right cheek is a mole, and on his shoulder, he has another large brown mole surrounded by hair; this is the sign of the prophet.

Shuayb, the son of Salih will raise an army, and come under three black banners to Khurasan to fight As-Sufyani, defeating him in that battle. At around this same time, Al Mahdi will be on his way to Syria under the black banner of Muhammad. Shuayb will send him his

---

25 All was downloaded from The Muhammadan Reality, http://www. muhammadanreality.com/ ImamMahdiSignsforthesavoir.htm

allegiance and go out to join him. When As-Sufyani finds out that Al Mahdi is on the move, he'll send an army against him; but an earthquake will kill the troops in the desert between Mecca and Medina.

Thus Al Mahdi will come against As-Sufyani with an army of 12,000 to 15,000 men. Armies from numerous countries and tribes, including Al Abdal from Syria, will gather on the shores of the Sea of Galilee to pledge their allegiance to him. From there, As-Sufyani will launch his attack: seven banners will come out against Al Mahdi and under each one will be a man "seeking the kingdom for himself." With the support of Allah, he'll defeat the armies of As-Sufyani, capturing and killing him.

After defeating As-Sufyani, he'll conquer Istanbul, then go to Jerusalem where he and his men will make their stand in the Dome of the Rock Mosque [on the Temple Mount] against the army of Al Dajaal. Under Al Mahdi, all Muslims will be unified. He'll bring peace, justice, rain and prosperity to the earth.

Apart from the army being swallowed up by an earthquake, there will be two signs authenticating the appearance of Al Mahdi: the moon will eclipse on the first night of the month of Ramadan, and the sun will eclipse midway through. He'll come at a time when there are many earthquakes, famines and wars.

Both Shi'ite and Sunni eschatology include As-Sufyani, a tyrant who triggers the coming of Al Mahdi. This man is to be a direct descendant of Sakhr ibn Harb, also known as Abu Sufyan, who lived from 560-650 A.D. He was a member of the same tribe as Muhammad, but cheiftan of a different clan, the Banu Abd-Shams (Muhammad was from the Hashims). He was one of the most powerful leaders of Mecca and a protector of the pagan religion and way of life, a staunch enemy of Muhammad and his newly founded monotheistic Islam; however, when Muhammad conquered Mecca, Sufyan converted to Islam. While Sunnis accept him as a companion of Muhammad, the Shi'as consider him to be a hypocrite, believing that he converted only to retain political power in Mecca.[26] From their perspective, this makes sense, given that he was the father of Mu'awiyah who, if you'll remember, was the Syrian governor who rebelled against Ali by establishing the Umayyad dynasty in Syria; it was Sufyan's grandson who would kill Muhammad's grandson, Hussein, at the battle of Karbala, giving the Shi'as their first martyr.

The Hadith appears to have no explanation for why As-Sufyani slaughters large numbers of Muslims throughout the Middle East. The Shi'as interpret his invasions of Iraq and Khorasan (made up largely of Afghanistan and Iran) to be against the Shi'ite population, particularly since at least one hadith says he kills those of the "followers of Muhammad's family," one of the names by which they designate themselves.

Both sects agree that Al Mahdi will be a direct descendant of Muhammad through his daughter Fatima; but here the similarities end. According to Sunnis, he's born in Medina and elected by the community in Mecca while on pilgrimage. For Shi'as, he reappears and unveils himself at the Mosque of the Last Imam in Iraq. We don't know for sure whether Al Mahdi will be Shi'a or Sunni, but Revelation depicts the beast empire as standing on the feet of Persia, which is the historical center of Shi'a Islam, just as Iran is its center today. It's the only country to have Shi'a Islam as the state religion, and is the seat of the Shi'a Ayatollah, who rules as Supreme Leader of the country. The Shi'a belief in a Mahdi who is the "Imam of the age," "Lord of Time," and authority over the East, West and

---

26 Wikipedia Free Encyclopedia, Abu Sufyan Ibn Harb, http://en.wikipedia.org/wiki/Abu_Sufyan_ibn_Harb

the universe itself, provides the perfect set up for the Antichrist as he's described in Revelation 13. According to some scholars, these messianic doctrines surrounding the Shi'a Mahdi are fundamentally Persian, originally stemming from Zoroastrianism, which predated Islam.[27]

Regardless of which sect Al Mahdi comes from, what's astounding is that according to both Biblical scriptures and the Hadith, he will somehow manage to unify the Islamic world. In order to do this, both Shi'a and Sunni will have to be satisfied that he is Allah's chosen one—quite a tall order. Yet unification between the sects isn't unprecedented in history. At least twice in the past the two sects have come together: the first in 1931 when the Khilafat Movement brought them together in defense of the Caliphate following the fall of the Ottoman Empire after World War I. The second was in the *fatwa* (opinion) recognizing Shi'a Islamic law as the fifth school of Islamic law; it was issued by the rector of Al-Azhar's University in Egypt, the chief center of Sunni learning in the world. In 1959, the university also authorized the teaching of courses of Shi'a jurisprudence as part of its curriculum.[28]

Despite being given such messianic status by Shi'as, Al Mahdi is not called "Messiah;" instead, Islam reserves that title for the Prophet Jesus because he rescues Al Mahdi from the false Messiah, Al Dajaal.

Al Dajaal

Al Dajaal ("the Liar") will appear somewhere between Syria and Iraq, and on his forehead will be written "kafir," which means

---

27 About.com, Agnosticism/Atheism, "Syria: Shi'a Islam", p. 1, http://atheism.about.com/library/FAQs/ Islam/countries/bl_SyriaIslamShi'a.htm

28 Wikipedia.org, "Shi'a-Sunni relations", p. 8, http://en.wikipedia.org/wiki/Sunni-Shi'a_relations, referencing Nasr, Vali, *The Shi'a Revival* , p. 107, Norton, 2006

"unbeliever." He'll come for 40[29] and travel all over the Middle East causing destruction and bloodshed everywhere he goes. He'll call people to obey him, deceiving them with his power to make it rain. Those who reject his call, he'll strike by drought and famine, but whoever believes in him, he'll provide with food and water. He'll deceive people to the point where they believe water is fire, and fire is water. Muslims are therefore warned that if he commands them to jump into the water, they should jump instead into the fire. Followed by 70,000 Jews from Isfahan,[30] he will go to Jerusalem to fight against Al Mahdi.

The Sunnis have Al Dajaal arriving after Al Mahdi to besiege him in Jerusalem. Because he's leading Jews from Isfahan, some Sunnis believe Al Dajaal will himself be Jewish. Because some Shi'a Imams predicted that Al Mahdi will rule according to David and speak Hebrew, some Sunnis believe that the Shi'as will mistake Al Dajaal for Al Mahdi.[31]

In contrast to the Sunnis, the Shi'as say that Al Dajaal will come to mislead the Christians and Jews, "several hours" before Al Mahdi discloses himself in Iraq (12followershia interprets this as being within a year of his reappearance[32]). Thus, some will correctly fol-

---

[29] The narrator of the hadith was uncertain whether the 40 referred to days, months or years.

[30] The Shi'as add Christians to the throng. Isfahan is Iran's third largest city, found in Isfahan province with a population of over 4.5 million people. Despite the fact that many have emigrated, Iran still has one of the largest populations of Jews of any Muslim majority country, with unofficial 2009 estimates at 20,000-25,000. According to recent U.N. figures, there are 300,000 Christians living in the country, the majority of whom are ethnic Armenians, with estimates for Chaldean Christians at 10,000-20,000 between two Chaldean archdioceses. (U.S. Department of State: Diplomacy in Action, "Iran", p. 1, http://www.state.gov/g/drl/rls/irf/2009/127347.htm)

[31] Discovering Islam, excerpts from Ibn al-Hashimi, "Shi'a's Imam Mahdi is likely to be the Dajjal (Anti-Christ)", pp. 1, 2, http://www.discoveringislam.org/Shi'a_mahdi_anti-christ.htm

[32] 12followerShi'a video The Last Promise, part 2: Sufyani, Khurasani with the black flag, Al Mahdi and Persia, http://www.youtube.com/watch?v=FLh5eX37jT0

low him and the Prophet Jesus against As-Sufyani, while some will follow Al Dajaal; the Shi'as interpret the 70,000 from Isfahan as being Christians, Jews and many Muslim women.

The Prophet Jesus

The Muslims will continue to fight until Jesus descends at sunrise in the Mosque of Jerusalem (some hadiths say Damascus). He'll kill Al Dajaal, and before the Day of Judgment, the Muslims will kill the Christians and the Jews. When they hide behind a rock or tree it will call out: "O Muslim, there is an unbeliever hiding behind me, come and kill him."

Al Mahdi will ask the Prophet Jesus to lead the people in prayer, but he'll defer to Al Mahdi, saying: "We are princes over each other, which is Allah's gift to this nation." So Prophet Jesus will submit to him as the Imam, standing behind him as he leads the people in prayer. Then the Caliphate will be handed over to Prophet Jesus who will go to those who were loyal to Allah during Al Dajaal's deception, and tell them their status in heaven. He'll destroy all of the crosses, correct the falsehoods of Christianity and lead the worshipers to Mount Tur (Sinai).

Allah will then bring Gog and Magog to the Sea of Galilee to drink all its water. Prophet Jesus and his companions will return from worshiping on Mount Sinai to discover all the corpses of the armies of Gog and Magog—so many that there will be no place to walk. The Prophet Jesus will then ask Allah for help, and he'll send birds of carrion to take away the bodies, then send rain to cleanse and water everything.

The specific time period of this huge slaughter of Christians and Jews isn't given in the Hadith, only that it takes place before the Day of Judgment. It makes sense to put it here, given that it's a battle involving Muslims against Christians and Jews. It seems unlikely that it would happen when Al Mahdi conquers Jerusalem, since he'll be seen as a savior from the persecution of As-Sufyani.

Neither the Sunnis nor the Shi'as believe that Jesus was divine and they interpret the doctrine of the Trinity as polytheism. As far as the crucifixion, they maintain that Jesus was replaced with a look-alike on the cross (possibly Judas Iscariot), then taken to a lower heaven where he awaits his descent for Al Mahdi. According to Muslim eschatology, the Jews are expected to reject Jesus yet again, and so they'll deserve the severe persecution they receive when they won't convert to Islam. Similarly, the Koran states that the Prophet Jesus will eradicate the errors of Christianity when he comes; he's the one that technically receives the "Caliphate" or the position of king (perhaps commensurate with the modern role of president). This hints at a political theocracy similar to that of Iran: while the president is charged with ensuring that the constitution be implemented, in practice, his powers are circumscribed by the clerics and the Supreme Leader (the Ayatollah), who confirms the president's election, and makes decisions regarding security, defense and major foreign policy issues.[33]

The Muslim Rapture

At this time Allah will send a wind from Syria that will take the soul of every devoted Muslim, leaving their bodies behind. Only the wicked will remain alive on earth.

---

33   In Depth Iran: Who holds the power?, http://news.bbc.co.uk/2/shared/spl/hi/middle_east/03/iran_power/ html/president.stm

Introduction: About Islam

Satan

After Allah takes away the souls of the devoted ones, Satan will come with his demons, disguised as a human being. He'll demand of those left behind that they obey him and worship idols. He'll claim to be Allah, and will give those who obey him plenty to eat and drink and their lives will be comfortable until the Day of Judgment.

While the rapture of the Church is described in scripture as being a physical "catching up" of the faithful, in that of Islam, the body is left behind. Because of this, any massive death during the end days could be interpreted by them as being the rapture.

Judgment day

At the sound of the first trumpet blow, everyone will fall to the ground. Then Allah will send rain and the trumpet will sound again. The people will stand up to be judged, "and he'll take from them those to be sent to the fire--999 out of 1000."

__The Term "Antichrist"__

Now that you have some background in Islam's history, doctrines and eschatological prophecies, we can begin to explore the Biblical scriptures for evidence that Islam is the false religion of the Antichrist. But before we start, I want to address the term "antichrist." This word is found only in John's first two letters to the Church. In I John 2, he warns against the Gnostics as being "antichrists" because they denied that Jesus came, died and resurrected in the flesh—"anti" (against), "Christ" (Messiah). According to John, "Who is the liar but the one who denies that Jesus is the Christ?

This is the antichrist, the one who denies the Father and the Son." Along these same lines, Paul warns the Colossians not to be deceived by any man who builds a religion around visions of angels he has seen, "inflated without cause by his fleshly mind."[34]

John explains that these are the forerunners of the Antichrist "who is coming," the one Paul calls "the man of lawlessness" and "the son of destruction" (II Thessalonians 2:3). These references, along with the visions of Daniel and Revelation, are where the Church gets its teaching that the final instrument of Satan's rebellion will be a specific man referred to as the Antichrist. Thanks to John, we know that this man's false religion will consist of denying Jesus' physical death and resurrection, as well as denying the Trinity. Muslims can call the Prophet Jesus "Messiah," but it's an empty title; the true teaching of Islam denies that Jesus was the son of God, and that He died and resurrected for the atonement of sin.

---

34 Colossians 2:18. The Greek word translated as "worship" in the NAS is *threskeia*, which refers to "religion in its external aspect," according to Vine's Dictionary (Macdonald Publishing Company, McLean, VA) p. 954

Part One:
The Beast from the East:
Islamic Prophecies in Daniel

1

As-Sufyani and Al Mahdi in the Statue and the Four Beasts of Daniel

Typology in the Old Testament

Much of the interpretation of end time prophecies is based on the scriptural idea of "typology." In the New Testament, Christ and the apostles taught that the people, events and religious rites of the Old Testament looked forward to and foreshadowed Christ's life and mission, making them "figures" or "types" of the events and spiritual truths they point to.

There are many Christ "types" in the Old Testament. For example according to Romans 5:14, Adam is a type of Christ: while the sin of one man, Adam, brought death to all humanity, the sacrifice of the new Adam, Christ, brought resurrection to all humanity. Another Christ type is the bronze snake on the pole, through which God brought healing to the Hebrews dying of snake bites during the Exodus (Num 21:6-9): the snake is the sin which kills, the bronze snake typifies Jesus becoming sin for our sake, lifted up for the salvation of man (John 3:13, 14). Other types of Christ are found in the rock struck by Moses in the wilderness (I Cor 10:4), the Passover lamb (1 Pet 1:19, Is 53:7; John 1:29, Acts 8:32), Isaac and the ram (Heb 11:17-19), Abel (Heb 12:24) and manna from heaven (John 6:32).

Of course we also know through scripture that Satan is prince of this earth, and that he'll rebel against God as the man of wickedness in the latter days; just as the Old Testament is full of beautiful types of Christ and His victory, it's also filled with types of Satan and this final conflict. In fact, every book of the Bible speaks about the latter days either in type or direct prophecy. Every people or kingdom that came against the Israelites in some way prefigured the final Antichrist kingdom that we await: Egypt and its enslavement of the Jews; Babylon in its persecution of Daniel and his friends for refusing to worship the golden image; Persia, in Haman's attempt to destroy the Jews; and in Antiochus IV of the Greek empire, who desecrated the temple, murdered thousands of Jews and forbade them to practice their religion. For this reason it's not surprising to see in Revelation references to some of these historical types: Jerusalem is called Babylon because it will be the capital of the Antichrist's false religion; the plagues of Exodus are poured out on the beast kingdom; and Jezebel, who killed hundreds of God's prophets, is a false prophet referred to in the letter to Thyatira.

As the kingdoms that ultimately destroyed Israel, Assyria and Babylonia are the quintessential types of the Antichrist's future kingdom. As such, prophecies about their impending destruction of Israel often contain prophecies about the end time as well. Some of these are marked by phrases like "in the latter days," "in the Day of the Lord" or "in that day," while others are identifiable only by their parallels with apocalyptic scriptures. For example, Ezekiel 14:21 describes God's "four severe judgments" against Jerusalem as being the sword, famine, beasts and plague, all of which occur in the seven seals of Revelation.

Typology in Daniel

The entire book of Daniel points to the end time. Daniel himself and his friends, steadfast in their loyalty to God, are types of the faithful remnant of future Israel, whose severe persecution is typified in both the lion's den and the fiery furnace. Like the other prophets of the Old Testament, Daniel's visions intertwine with events that happen closer to his lifetime; but while some of these events happened in our past, ultimately, Daniel's prophecies merge into the time of the future Antichrist's kingdom and the restoration of Israel. Because John's visions in Revelation reference Daniel's visions, we must understand his prophecies before we can look at Revelation, and so it's here we begin. In this chapter, we'll look at how the statue of Nebuchadnezzar and the related vision of the four beasts point to As-Sufyani and Al Mahdi as those who re-establish the Islamic Empire.

Nebuchadnezzar's Statue and Daniel's Four Beasts

In 722 B.C., the northern kingdom of Israel was conquered by Assyria, which in turn was conquered by Babylonia in 612. The southern kingdom of Judah paid tribute as Babylonia's vassal, but secretly allied with Egypt against it, causing Nebuchadnezzar to destroy Judah in 586. Daniel and his friends were taken hostage to Ninevah and proved to be loyal to God even in the face of severe persecution. In Chapter 2, Daniel is called to interpret the king's dream, but first he told him what it was:

Daniel 2:31-35: ***The Dream***
"You, O king, were looking and behold, there was a single great statue; that statue which was large and of extraordinary splendor was standing in front of you and its appearance was awesome.

³²The head of that statue was made of fine gold, its breast and its arms of silver, its belly and its thighs of bronze, ³³its legs of iron, its feet partly of iron and partly of clay. ³⁴You continued looking until a stone was cut out without hands and it struck the statue on its feet of iron and clay and crushed them. ³⁵Then the iron, the clay, the bronze the silver and the gold were crushed all at the same time and became like chaff from the summer threshing floors; and the wind carried them away so that not a trace of them was found. But the stone that struck the statue became a great mountain and filled the whole earth."

Daniel 2:38-45 *The Interpretation*

³⁸You [Nebuchadnezzar] are the head of gold, ³⁹and after you there will arise another kingdom inferior to you, then another third kingdom of bronze, which will rule over all the earth. ⁴⁰Then there will be a fourth kingdom as strong as iron; inasmuch as iron crushes and shatters all things, so like iron that breaks in pieces, it will crush and break all these in pieces. ⁴¹And in that you saw the feet and toes, partly of potter's clay and partly of iron, it will be a divided kingdom; but it will have in it the toughness of iron, inasmuch as you saw the iron mixed with common clay. ⁴²And as the toes of the feet were partly of iron and partly of pottery, so some of the kingdom will be strong and part of it will be brittle. ⁴³And in that you saw the iron mixed with common clay, they will combine with one another in the seed of men; but they will not adhere to one another, even as iron does not combine with pottery, ⁴⁴and in the days of those kings the God of heaven will set up a kingdom which will never be destroyed and that kingdom will not be left for another people; it will crush and put an end to all these kingdoms, but it will itself endure forever. ⁴⁵Inasmuch as you saw that a stone was cut out of the mountain without hands and that it crushed the iron, bronze, clay, silver and gold, the great God has

made known to the king what will take place in the future; so the dream is true and its interpretation is trustworthy.

The statue represents four major ancient empires that controlled the region. Daniel links the first with Nebuchadnezzar himself, thus the next would be Persia then Greece (Alexander the Great). Since historically the Roman Empire came after Greece, many Church scholars have interpreted the legs as Rome. They then interpret the feet (the Antichrist kingdom) to be a revival of the Roman Empire. This theory appeared to be confirmed when the European Union was formed, consisting of ten countries, thought to be the ten toes of Nebuchadnezzar's statue. Now that the Union consists of 27 countries, this theory isn't so compelling.

But the biggest problem with interpreting Rome as the iron legs is that *Rome never conquered Babylonia or Persia, as the statue depicts*; both were controlled by Parthia throughout the period of the Roman Empire. Also problematic is that the statue doesn't show the Ottoman Empire between Rome and its supposed revival. This is because according to verses 40-41, the feet aren't a revival at all, but rather, combined with the legs, form the fourth empire that is standing when Christ comes. In fact, only Islam fits the details of the statue, being the only historical entity to have conquered the entire geographical area depicted by the statue, all of which has remained Muslim to this day (except for Israel and the Balkans).

After interpreting Nebuchadnezzar's dream, Daniel has a vision himself, one that's remarkably similar in its interpretation:

Daniel 7:2-14
[2]...I was looking in my vision by night and behold, the four winds of heaven were stirring up the great sea. [3]And four great beasts were coming up from the sea, different from one another. [4]The first was like a lion and had the wings of an eagle. I kept looking

until its wings were plucked and it was lifted up from the ground and made to stand on two feet like a man; a human mind was also given to it. ⁵And behold, another beast, a second one, resembling a bear. And it was raised up on one side, and three ribs were in its mouth between its teeth; and thus they said to it, "Arise, devour much meat!" ⁶After this I kept looking, and behold, another one, like a leopard, which had on its back four wings of a bird; the beast also had four heads and dominion was given to it. ⁷After this I kept looking in the night visions, and behold, a fourth beast, dreadful and terrifying and extremely strong; and it had large iron teeth. It devoured and crushed and trampled down the remainder with its feet; and it was different from all the beasts that were before it, and it had ten horns. ⁸While I was contemplating the horns, behold, another horn, a little one, came up among them and three of the first horns were pulled out by the roots before it; and behold, this horn possessed eyes like the eyes of a man, and a mouth uttering great boasts. ⁹I kept looking until thrones were set up and the Ancient of Days took His seat…¹⁰and the books were opened. ¹¹Then I kept looking because of the sound of the boastful words which the horn was speaking; I kept looking until the beast was slain and its body was destroyed and given to the burning fire….¹³and behold, with the clouds of heaven, one like the Son of a Man was coming and He came up to the Ancient of Days and was presented before Him. ¹⁴And to Him was given dominion, glory and a kingdom that all the peoples, nations and men of every language might serve Him. His dominion is an everlasting dominion which will not pass away; and his kingdom is one which will not be destroyed.

Daniel 7:17-18, 23-25
¹⁷These great beasts, which are four in number are four kings who will arise from the earth. ¹⁸But the saints of the Highest One

will receive the kingdom and possess the kingdom forever, for all ages to come.²³…The fourth beast will be a fourth kingdom on the earth, which will be different from all the other kingdoms and it will devour the whole earth and tread it down and crush it. ²⁴As for the ten horns, out of this kingdom ten kings will arise; and another will arise after them and he will be different from the previous ones and will subdue three kings. ²⁵And he will speak out against the Most High and wear down the saints of the Highest One and he will intend to make alterations in times and in law; and they will be given into this hand for a time, times, and half a time.

At this point it becomes obvious that these visions are somehow connected, with Nebuchadnezzar's dream serving as a Rosetta Stone for interpreting the vision of the beasts. Both visions describe a kingdom that conquers all at once the geographical areas of ancient Babylonia, Persia and Greece, and endures until the latter days. Yet there's an important difference between the visions too. While Daniel states that the first kingdom in the statue is ancient Babylonia, verse 17 of the beasts vision indicates that all four kings would arise in Daniel's future, thus excluding ancient Babylonia, which stood on the eve of its destruction at the time of the vision. The best explanation for this is that the first three beasts represent the three periods of the historical rise of Islam in the Middle East as they correspond to the ancient empires: the Arab Abbasids with their capital in ancient Babylonia; the dynasties of the Iranian Intermezzo and the Safavids of Persia; and the Turkish Ottomans, who took over the empire of the Byzantine Greeks. There was significant overlap between periods, with all three empires existing at once, just as depicted in the statue and the four beasts. It's this geographical area (corresponding to Alexander's empire) that remains Islamic, ready to be conquered by As-Sufyani and Al Mahdi (the legs/feet and the fourth beast).

The Lion and the Golden Head

The lion was the symbol of ancient Babylonia, represented in the statue by the golden head of Nebuchadnezzar. His seven year humiliation and subsequent restoration is symbolized by the lion standing on two feet and being given the mind of a man (see Dan 4:28-37). Babylonia is depicted as an eagle with great wings in Ezekiel 17, signifying great political power and military might. When Daniel's lion has its wings plucked off, it can only mean military defeat, which came at the hands of Medo-Persia under Cyrus the Great.

Similarly, the Islamic Empire during the Arab period was both a lion and a golden head. The Rashidun Caliphs (the first four after Muhammad) would take only 30 years to conquer the entire Middle East. Starting with the area of ancient Babylonia, they defeated the Sassanids and expanded from Saudi Arabia to include all of Iraq, Iran, Syria, Lebanon, Jordan, Egypt, Israel and eastern Turkey. Shortly afterwards, the Umayyads took over the empire, adding Spain, northern Africa and Khorasan. However, in 750 A.D., Al-Abbas of the Abbasid dynasty plucked off the wings of the Umayyads, and moved the capital from Damascus to Baghdad, marking the beginning of the "Golden Age of Islam." Under the Abbasids, thanks in large part to the accomplishments of the Persian Sassanid Empire before it, Baghdad would become "...the capital of one of the most enlightened empires in history, the world's most accomplished civilization...," lasting for five hundred years.[1] While Europe languished in the Dark Ages, the *Bayt al-Hikma* or "House of Wisdom" was translating into Arabic ancient Greek texts of math, astronomy and

---

[1] Ed Hotaling, *Islam without Illusions: its Past, its Present and its Challenge for the Future* (Syracuse: Syracuse University Press, 2003), p. 103

philosophy, with Muslim scholars expanding on them and making their own contributions in geography and medicine. These works were later passed on to Europe, leading directly to the renaissance of the fourteenth century, and even to the European Enlightenment of the eighteenth century.[2] However, eventually the Turkish slaves purchased for the Abbasids' armies would begin their own dynasties. Beginning in Persia, they would move west into Anatolia, acknowledging the Abbasids in name only. Finally, in 1519, the Turkish Ottomans would officially bring them to an end.

The Bear and the Arms/Chest

The bear raised up on one side and the two arms are the kingdoms of Media and Persia, which were united by Cyrus. The three ribs in the bear's mouth were Persia's conquest of Lydia (western Turkey), Babylonia and Egypt.

During the Islamic "Persian" period, the Abbasids continued to hold religious authority in Baghdad, but in actuality Iran would be ruled by a series of overlapping native Persian dynasties. This period from 821 to 1055 was known as the "Iranian Intermezzo" because it was a bridge between the Abbasids' decline and the Seljuks' conquest of Iran. These dynasties (in particular the Buyids) are credited for reviving the Iranian national spirit, culture and language in an Islamic context. This revitalization served to ensure the Persianization of the Seljuks and the Mongol Timurids who would later rule in Iran.

Later, as the Timurids declined, the militant Shi'a Safavids would become the first native dynasty since the Sassanid Empire to establish a unified Iranian state. Ruling from 1501 to 1722 (with a brief revival from 1729-1736), they would conquer all of Iran and

---

2   Ibid., pp. 104-105

most of Khorasan and Iraq.³ The image of the bear on one side most likely represents the supremacy of Shi'a Islam, established under the Safavids as the state religion of Iran; to this day it remains the center of Shi'a Islam.

The Leopard and the Belly/thighs

Among Daniel's beasts, the leopard is the Macedonian or Greek empire of Alexander the Great. After his death, his kingdom would be divided into various satrapies, which would come to be controlled by four of his generals (the four heads of the leopard): Cassander (Macedonia), Lysimachus (Thrace), Ptolemy (Egypt) and Seleucus (Syro-Babylonia). The birds' wings (though not of an eagle) are again related to political strength and military prowess. There are only two pairs, one for the Seleucids and one for the Ptolemies, who struggled for dominance over the empire.

The "Greek" period of Islamic rule in the Middle East consisted of the Ottoman Empire (1299-1923), which starting as a small area, eventually took over what was left of Greek Byzantium.⁴ In 1453, it conquered Constantinople, renaming it Istanbul and making it their new capital. Although they failed to take Khorasan and most of Iran, the Ottomans took the Safavid capital of Tabriz in 1514, and in 1534, they captured Baghdad. With his illusions of invincibility and divinity crushed, the Persian king, Shah Ismail I, would abdicate his throne, leading to ten years of civil war.

The four powers that had a share of the geographical

---

3   They would also conquer Azerbaijan, Armenia and the Caucasus, but this is land outside the boundaries of the ancient Alexandrian Empire.

4   In fact, several historians, such as Edward Gibbo, Dimitri Kitzikisand, and Speros Vryonis have asserted that the Ottomans were in essence a continuation of the Byzantines under a Turkish Islamic veneer. (Stone, Norman, "Turkey in the Russian Mirror," pages 86-100 from *Russia War, Peace and Diplomacy,* edited by Mark & Ljubica Erickson, Weidenfeld & Nicolson: London, 2004 pages 92-93)

Alexandrian kingdom during the expansion of the Ottomans were the Turks (the Ottomans and various other Turkish dynasties), the Byzantine Greeks, the Mongols (especially the Timurids) and the Persians (most notably the Safavids). Although they would battle all three powers, the second set of wings would have to be assigned to the Byzantines, for the ultimate prize was Byzantium's capital, Constantinople, which no Muslim power had managed to conquer. Its conquest represented the defeat of Christianity by Islam, and greatly accelerated the empire's expansion. It's important to keep in mind that although the "Greek" period's Ottoman Empire didn't include all of ancient Persia, the Islamic Empire as a whole still included of all the land area held by the four kingdoms of ancient Greece.

The Fourth Kingdom

Because the borders of the first three empires were constantly changing, we're left to ponder the extent of the future fourth empire, formed by the conquest of the region by As-Sufyani and Al Mahdi. Although involving much of the same land, there were significant differences among the three. For example, the Arabs never captured Anatolia or the Balkans but held Spain; the Safavids never controlled anything west or south of Iraq; and the Ottomans never got Khorasan or all of Iran.

The only specific information we're given in the Islamic prophecies is that As-Sufyani conquers Iraq, Syria, and Khorasan (which includes part of Iran), and that Al Mahdi conquers Turkey and establishes himself in Jerusalem. Daniel 11:40-45 indicates that As-Sufyani also takes Egypt and Sudan, as well as "overflowing many countries" which are not mentioned by name. In short, it appears that the Ottoman Empire (leopard) is reunited under As-Sufyani, thus the fourth kingdom should include the Balkans and Turkey.

However, because the Arabs (lion) are named, it should also include Spain and Saudi Arabia, and because the Safavids (bear) are named, it should include Iran and Khorasan (Afghanistan, Tajikistan, Turkmenistan and Uzbekistan). Not surprisingly, this land area is largely included in Alexander's Empire, which as we'll see, is the focus of the remainder of Daniel.

In his interpretation of the statue, Daniel indicates that each successive empire is inferior to the one before it, each one becoming less valuable in terms of wealth, but more valuable in terms of making tools and weapons; the statue's legs/feet and the fourth beast are an iron empire that brutally crushes the rest. Interestingly enough, there's a short sura in the Koran entitled "Iron." It discusses the "beautiful loan to Allah"—the willingness to give up one's life, time and material wealth for the cause of Allah, linked by verse 10 to the fighting that the faithful performed throughout Arabia before the conquest of Mecca: "Not equal among you are those who spent and fought before the Victory...Those are higher in rank than those who spent and fought afterwards. But to all has Allah promised a goodly (reward)." (57:10)[5] It goes on to say in verse 25, "We [Allah] sent aforetime our apostles with clear signs and sent down with them the Book and the Balance of right and wrong, that men may stand forth in justice; *and we sent down iron in which is mighty war*, as well as many benefits for mankind, *that Allah may test who it is that will help* (Koran 57:25, emphasis mine). A famous eschatological passage from the Hadith also mentions iron, praising once again the courage of Muslims who go to war for the cause of Allah: "The Black Banners [of the prophet] will come to you from the East, their hearts are like iron. Whosoever hears about them, let them go crawling—even over ice—[to join themselves to Al Mahdi]."[6]

---

5 *The Meaning of the Holy Qur'an,* Abdullah Yusuf 'Ali, eleventh edition, Aman Publications, Beltsville, MD, 2006

6 The Muhammadan Reality, p. 14, http://www.muhammadanreality.com/ImamMahdiSignsforthesavoir.htm

Through Muhammad's example of "holy war" and in many later passages of the Koran, the message is clearly given to the Muslims that they are to use warfare to spread Islam, and that in so doing, they will be rewarded—"those who believe and adopt exile and fight for the Faith in the cause of Allah, as well as those who give them asylum and aid, these are (all) in very truth the Believers; for them is the forgiveness of sins and provision most generous" (8:74). This is the doctrine of jihad or Holy War, which demands the death or subjugation of those refusing to convert. Considering such a commission, and in light of what we know about Islamic terrorism, the Islamic Empire fits much better than Rome (a relatively pluralistic society) the "iron" strength and shattering nature of the religiously dominated fourth kingdom.

The Feet and Toes/Ten Horns—Iron Mixed with Clay

Some might suggest the weakness of the empire is due to the split between Shi'a and Sunni. However, verse 43 describes this division as being at a more fundamentally human level than religious or political factions could account for: "iron mixed with common clay, combining with one another *in the seed of men...*" The seed of men are their children, who traditionally take on the religion of their fathers. If clay is the flesh of humanity and iron is Islam, is it possible that this is a reference to coerced conversions within the fourth Empire? After all, unlike the Middle East, Islam didn't "stick" to Georgia, Armenia, Spain, Greece, Macedonia or the other Balkans when the Ottomans were forced to leave. This could explain how Rome becomes one of the beast's heads in Revelation.

In Daniel's vision, we're told that there are ten horns on the iron beast before the eleventh horn grows out of it. This last horn out of As-Sufyani's fourth kingdom is Al Mahdi, the Antichrist himself (compare Dan 7:9-14 and Rev 13:6-7, 19:20). Because he's a military/political/religious leader, consistency demands that the ten horns existing before him be the same type of leaders. According to Daniel, he subdues or "humbles" three kings, so it's not surprising to see that in the Hadith, one of his generals arrives under three banners, while As-Sufyani comes under seven (tribal banners were used in battle by the Arabs to organize their troops). Since Revelation 17:12-14 says these ten won't be crowned until Al Mahdi comes to power (compare Rev 12:3 with 13:1), it seems likely that they're generals in As-Sufyani's campaigns who side with Al Mahdi and are made rulers over various regions in his empire.

His attempt at making alterations in times could be that he restarts the calendar, as Muslims did with Muhammad's *hegira*, or it could be the imposition of the Islamic calendar onto secular life. Changes in law could be the imposition of Shari'a law.

2

As-Sufyani in the Vision of the Ram and Goat

Daniel has one more vision, the rest of the book consisting of the angel's explanations and prophecies concerning it. Throughout these, we continue to see the As-Sufyani/Mahdi pair:

Vision/Prophecy	As-Sufyani's kingdom	Mahdi
The Ram and Goat	Horn out of the horn	Insolent King
Seventy weeks	Time of the Prince to Come	Time of the One Who Makes Desolate
Chapters 11 &12	Despicable Person	Time of the Great Distress

Vision of the Ram and Shaggy Goat: Ancient Greece

Daniel 8:5-8
⁵...**Behold a male goat was coming from the west over the surface of the whole earth...and it had a conspicuous horn between his**

eyes. ⁶And he came up to the ram that had the two horns...and rushed at him in his mighty wrath. ⁷And I saw him come beside the ram...and shatter his two horns...he hurled him to the ground and trampled on him and there was none to rescue the ram from his power. ⁸Then the male goat magnified himself exceedingly. But as soon as he was mighty, the large horn was broken and in its place there came up four conspicuous horns toward the four winds of heaven.

Daniel 8:21; 11:4
²¹And the shaggy goat represents the kingdom of Greece and the large horn that is between his eyes is the first king.¹¹:⁴ But as soon as he has arisen, his kingdom will be broken up and parceled toward the four points of the compass, though not to his own descendants, nor according to his authority which he wielded; for his sovereignty will be uprooted and given to others besides them.

Here the book of Daniel begins its focus on Alexander's Empire, specifically the Seleucid division. The ram is said to be Medo-Persia which overthrew Babylonia in 539 B.C. The goat is Greece, its large horn being Alexander the Great who conquered Persia in 330 B.C. Gabriel explains how his empire would be divided into four parts, one of which was the Syro-Babylonian[1] Seleucid Empire, after Seleucus, the general who conquered it. The historical rise of the Seleucid dynasty is detailed in Daniel 11. The career of the Despicable Person in verses 21-35, matches that of Antiochus IV, the empire's eighth king, even to the setting up of the Abomination of Desolation and the Maccabean war (11:32). But if we look more closely we see that, starting at verse 37, the narrative of the Despicable Person loses its

---

[1] The Seleucids were known both as Syrian and Babylonian kings. Although the empire included Persia, part of Turkey and the Levant, it had two capitals: Antioch in Syria, and Seleucia-on-the-Tigris in Babylonia, thus the designation of "Syro-Babylonian."

parallel with Antiochus IV, and merges into a series of events that as yet have not come to pass, especially as they flow into chapter 12. This is because, as stated in 8:17 and 19, the ram and the goat are about the latter days; thus in typical Old Testament prophecy style, the story starts with the Seleucids, then melds into the end days. First we'll look at the vision of the ram and the goat and chapter 11 from the historical perspective of the Seleucids and Antiochus, then we can compare it to what we know about As-Sufyani.

The History of the Seleucids

Daniel 8:9
⁹Out of one of [the horns] came forth a rather small horn which grew exceedingly great toward the south, toward the east, and toward the Beautiful Land.

Daniel 11:5
⁵ "Then the king of the South will grow strong, along with one of his princes who will gain ascendancy over him and obtain dominion; his domain will be a great dominion indeed.

Daniel 8:9 and 11:5 are parallel passages relating the rise of Seleucus I (Nicator) from being a general in the army of Ptolemy (who received Egypt) to his place as emperor of Syro-Babylonia. Verses 6-31 continue the history of his dynasty and its conflicts with the Ptolemies, verses 10-19 discussing Antiochus III, and the capture of Panium; this battle in 198 B.C. transferred Coele-Syria (the area in northern Israel) and Judea (the Beautiful Land of verse 16) from Egypt into Seleucid hands. As a reward to those who supported the Seleucids—the "violent ones" among Daniel's people in verse 14—Antiochus III granted Judea an exemption from his policy of Hellenization. In addition, he gave them autonomy in their temple worship, even giving them funds to pay for certain temple activities.² Verses 17-18 continue the career of Antiochus III, describing the marriage alliance between his daughter Cleopatra and Egypt's Ptolemy V, and his defeat by Rome at the Battle of Magnesia. When his son, Seleucus IV Philopator, came to the throne he sent Heliodorus to rob the temple treasury in order to pay the tribute exacted by Rome (verse 20). According to some, Heliodorus poisoned Philopator after his brief reign of 12 years.

The Career of Antiochus

Daniel 11:21
²¹And in his place a despicable person will arise, on whom the honor of kingship has not been conferred, but he will come in a time of tranquility and seize the kingdom by intrigue.

After Seleucus Philopator's assassination in 175 B.C., his brother, Antiochus IV (he called himself *Epiphanes*, meaning "manifestation of God") usurped the throne with help from the king of Pergamum; ultimately he would earn the nickname *Epimenes* ("madman"), a pun on *Epiphanes*.

²²And they will be flooded away before him and shattered and also the prince of the covenant. ²³And after an alliance is made with him, he will practice deception and he will go up and gain power with a small people. ²⁴In a time of tranquility he will enter the richest parts of the realm and he will accomplish what his fathers never did, nor his ancestors; he will distribute plunder, booty and possessions among them and he will devise his schemes against strongholds, but only for a time.

---

2   Wikipedia, "Acra (fortress)", p. 2, http:/en.wikipedia.org/wiki/Acra_(fortress), quoting Josephus' Antiquities of the Jews, 12:138-146

Verses 22-24 are difficult, since Daniel doesn't identify the "they," the prince, or the ones who make an alliance with Antiochus. The translation is even more difficult because ancient Hebrew didn't have paragraph distinctions, making it hard to know how the verses should be grouped. There are no records of any battles Antiochus fought in order to gain power over the kingdom,[3] leading some to believe that verse 22 begins his campaigns against Egypt. This would make the Prince of the Covenant the Ptolemaic King, Philometor. The problem with this interpretation is that the Prince of the Covenant must be Jewish, because the Hebrew word for "prince" here is *nagid*, a term reserved for Jewish leaders in Israel. Furthermore, verse 20 indicates that Israel becomes a vassal state under the suzerainty of the Seleucids, the same type of arrangement Judah and Israel once had with Assyria and Babylonia. Under such a covenant, the king of the conquered country becomes the prince of the suzerain, paying him tribute in exchange for protection. This makes the Prince of the Covenant a high priest, and those who are flooded away his contingency.

This is precisely what happened four years after Antiochus took the throne of the empire in 175. Onias, the high priest of Israel, had been replaced with his Hellenist brother Jason,[4] who determined to make Jerusalem a Greek city. He had renamed it Antioch and taken advantage of Antiochus' generosity to build a gymnasium, a central part of Hellenist culture. According to the Jewish Encyclopedia, however, the small Tobiad faction, even more zealous Hellenists than Jason, believed he catered too much to the traditionalists by maintaining the autonomy of the temple originally granted by Antiochus III.[5] Verses 22-24 describe how Antiochus betrayed

---

3   Edwyn Robert Bevan, *Antiochus IV and the Conquest of Egypt*, p. 126, http://vinyl2sentex.net/~tcc/Bevan/AntIV-Egypt.htm, p. 1
4   Jason's Hebrew name was Jeshu; his use of this Greek name reflects his Hellenist loyalties.
5   Jewish Encyclopedia, "Menelaus," http://www.jewishencyclopedia.com/view.

Jason by removing him and installing the Tobiad, Menelaus, as the new Prince of the Covenant in 171; it was around this time that Antiochus was preparing to go to battle against Egypt over Coele-Syria. Menelaus' installation resulted in the polarization of Judea between the Oniads, who supported Jason and the Ptolemies, and the Tobiads, who supported Menelaus and the Seleucids. These two factions would come into play when Jason returned in an attempt to reclaim control of Judea.

Verses 25-30 describe the two campaigns that Antiochus fought against the Ptolemies from 170-169. Antiochus went up against Pelusium in the Sinai peninsula and managed to capture the young king Philometor; in his place, his regents crowned his brother Euergetes. Antiochus, claiming to be the rightful king's protector, played on the loyalties of Philometor's armies to capture the fortress and lower Egypt (all except Alexandria, which remained loyal to Euergetes). He claimed Memphis as the new capital, and installed Philometor as a puppet king. Ultimately, Antiochus besieged Alexandria, but just at the critical point, he suddenly and mysteriously lifted the siege and evacuated Egypt.[6] Although failing to take the capital, he maintained the fortress of Pelusium, and left Egypt in a state of civil war between its vying brother kings. Verse 28 describes Antiochus in his first attack on Jerusalem in 169 when, according to 1 Maccabees 1:24, he attacked Judea and plundered the temple.

Daniel 8:10-11

[10]And it grew up to the host of heaven and caused some of the host and some of the stars to fall to the earth and it trampled them down. [11]It even magnified itself to be equal with the Commander

---

jsp?artid=460&letter=M

[6] Edwyn Robert Bevan, *The House of Seleucus, Vol II*, Chapter 23, "Antiochus IV and the Conquest of Egypt", p. 131, http://vinyl2.sentex.net/~tcc?Bevan/AntIV-Egypt.htm, p. 5

of the host and it removed the regular sacrifice from Him and the place of His sanctuary was thrown down.

Daniel 11:29-31

²⁹At the appointed time, he will return and come into the South but this last time it will not turn out the way it did before. ³⁰For ships of Kittim [Cyprus and other coastal territories of Rome] will come against him; therefore he will be disheartened and will return and become enraged at the holy covenant and take action; so he will come back and show regard for those who forsake the holy covenant. ³¹And forces from him will arise, desecrate the sanctuary fortress, and do away with the regular sacrifice. And they will set up the abomination of desolation.

Philometor and Euergetes would ultimately reconcile and rule from Alexandria as joint-kings. In 168, Antiochus advanced on Memphis, then Alexandria, but was stopped by Rome who sent an envoy to demand that Antiochus evacuate Egypt. During this time a rumor had spread that Antiochus was dead, so Jason returned to Jerusalem to fight Menelaus with a small army. The Tobiads appealed to Antiochus for help. According to II Maccabees 5, an angry Antiochus sent an army which burned the city, killed 40,000 Jews and sold 40,000 more into slavery. Reversing his father's policy, he sent an edict to Judea forbidding the Jews to practice their religion. Upon pain of execution, they were ordered to ignore the Sabbath and feasts, stop the sacrifices in the temple, stop reading the Torah and cease from circumcising their sons.[7] According to Josephus, those who continued to observe their faith were flogged and crucified, and around their necks were hanged their wives and circumcised sons.[8] Torah scrolls were burned and in 167 BC, Antiochus

---

7   Septuagint, 1Maccabees 1:41-45
8   Josephus, *Antiquities*, 12:255-256

erected an idol (presumably Zeus) in the temple, sacrificing a pig upon the altar.[9] Daniel 8:11 describes the temple system taken over by Antiochus through his proxy, Menelaus.

Daniel 11:32b
[32b]...the people who know their God will display strength and take action.

The Maccabees arose in reaction to the temple's desecration, launching a three year war against the Seleucids that resulted in the rededication of the temple in 164 BC, an event memorialized by Hanukkah.

The Vision of the Ram and the Goat: Antiochus as a Type of As-Sufyani

Before the Abomination of Desolation

The shaggy goat is clearly stated to be Greece, and the small horn can only refer to the Seleucid dynasty and Antiochus IV. Yet the vision also parallels the Islamic prophecies regarding As-Sufyani, who will come to hold all the land area once controlled by the Seleucids:

- Like Seleucus, he becomes a Syro-Babylonian king (conquering Syria and Iraq), establishing his political and military seat in Syria
- Just as Seleucus started off as a small power, As-Sufyani starts off as a small "horn" with only 360 men, then grows larger with the 30,000 man army he raises in Syria.

---

9   Ibid., vv 47-54

- Just like Seleucus, his campaign moves east (he invades Khorasan) before he goes to the Beautiful Land (he ends up in Jerusalem to fight against Al Mahdi). Based on certain hadiths, he will conquer Egypt first before going to Syria, paralleling even more closely Seleucus, who first grew great towards the south in Ptolemy's Egyptian army.
- Just like Antiochus IV, he seizes the kingdom when it hasn't been conferred on him, and he is certainly despicable—a violent tyrant who kills women and children.

From these parallels, it is apparent that Antiochus IV is a type of As-Sufyani, and as such, we would expect him to fulfill the other passages corresponding to Antiochus IV:

Daniel 8:10
[10]And it grew up to the host of heaven and caused some of the host and some of the stars to fall to the earth and it trampled them down.

Daniel 11:28
[28]Then he will return to his land with much plunder; but his heart will be set against the holy covenant, and he will take action and then return to his own land.

Historically, this describes Antiochus' first attack on Israel when he entered the city and plundered the temple. But if As-Sufyani were to do this, Israel's eyes would be opened to his true agenda before the appointed time. The explanation for this may lie in Daniel 11:28 which says that his "action" flows out of his *heart*. What's in a person's heart can be kept secret, thus what he does at this point, along with his motivation, aren't necessarily overt. In addition, the Hebrew word rendered "takes action" is simply "do," and can mean a variety of things, such as "make, appoint, govern or practice." This may indicate that he does something through the leadership of Israel at that time. This is a possible reference to the Christian persecution described by Jesus as occurring before the Abomination is set up: "They will deliver you to tribulation and will kill you and you will be hated by all nations on account of My name" (Matt 24:9). The letter to the church at Smyrna indicates that this tribulation will in fact be at the hands of the Jewish authorities.

After the Abomination of Desolation

Daniel 8:11
¹¹It even magnified itself to be equal with the Commander of the host and it removed the regular sacrifice from Him and the place of His sanctuary was thrown down.

Daniel 11:31
³¹And forces from him will arise, desecrate the sanctuary fortress, and do away with the regular sacrifice. And they will set up the abomination of desolation.

This would parallel Antiochus' open attack on Israel to take over both politically and religiously; As-Sufyani might even sacrifice a pig on the altar as the ultimate insult to Judaism.

While some interpret the phrase "thrown down" in Daniel 8:11 to be a physical destruction of the temple, this is unlikely, as it wasn't the case with Antiochus. Instead, he desecrated the temple itself (termed the *qodesh* by Ezekiel) and "brought low" the Temple Mount fortress (the *miqdash*) by building the Acra, a garrison believed to have been attached to the south wall of the Temple Mount. This prefigured As-Sufyani's battle against Al Mahdi in "the house of Jerusalem," and later, Al Mahdi's fight against Al Dajaal from the Dome of the Rock on the Temple Mount.

Daniel 11:32b-12:3

^{32b}... The people who know their God will display strength and take action. ^{33}And those who have insight among the people will give understanding to the many; yet they will fall by sword and by flame, by captivity and by plunder for many days. ^{34}Now when they fall they will be granted a little help and many will join with them in hypocrisy. ^{35}And some of those who have insight will fall, in order to refine, purge and make them pure, until the end time; because it is still to come at the appointed time. $^{12:3}$And those who have insight will shine brightly like the brightness of the expanse of heaven, and those who lead the many to righteousness, like the stars forever and ever.

We would expect those Jews who understand the significance of the Abomination of Desolation to take action against As-Sufyani, just as the Maccabees did against Antiochus, and this is precisely what we see in the woman of Revelation 12; but that will be discussed in more detail later. What needs to be pointed out here is that those who will have the most insight to the events of that day will be the Christians in Israel who according to 11:33, will be sharing the gospel. Stars are associated with Israel in several scriptures (Gen 15:5, Gen 37:9-10), and are specifically connected with the Messiah (Nu 24:17; Mt 2:2; 2 Pet 1:19; Rev 2:28, 22:16). It's "those who have insight" and "lead the many to righteousness" who are compared to stars in Daniel 12:3, making them recipients of the same promises and inheritance as faithful Israel. Correspondingly, the messengers to the Church are symbolized by the seven stars in Revelation 1:20.

The Rest of the Story

³⁷And he will show no regard for the gods of his fathers or for the desire of women, nor will he show regard for any other god; for he will magnify himself above them all. ³⁸But instead, he will honor a god of fortresses, a god whom his fathers did not know; he will honor him with gold, silver, costly stones, and treasures. ³⁹And he will take action against the strongest of fortresses with the help of a foreign god; he will give great honor to those who acknowledge him, and he will cause them to rule over the many and will parcel out land for a price. ⁴⁰And at the end of time, the king of the south will collide with him, and the king of the north will storm against him with chariots, with horsemen, and with many ships; and he will enter countries, overflow them and pass through. ⁴¹He will also enter the Beautiful Land, and many will fall; but these will be rescued out of his hand: Edom, Moab [Jordan] and the foremost of the sons of Ammon [Jordon]. ⁴²Then he will stretch out his hand against other countries and the land of Egypt will not escape. ⁴³But he will gain control over the hidden treasures of gold and silver and over all the precious things of Egypt; and Libyans and Ethiopians [Sudan] will follow at his heels.⁴⁴But rumors from the East and from the north will disturb him and he will go forth with great wrath to destroy and annihilate many. ⁴⁵And he will pitch the tents of his royal pavilion between the seas and the beautiful Holy Mountain; yet he will come to his end, and no one will help him.

At this point, the narrative begins to describe the future and As-Sufyani, since the details from verse 37 onward simply don't fit Antiochus or his career. First of all, Antiochus was famous for his support of the Greek gods (the gods of his father), in particular Zeus. Secondly, the mention of the king of the north colliding with him in verse 40 is puzzling when up to this point, Antiochus himself is the one referred to as king of the north (i.e., Syria). Historically, the only northern king who came against Antiochus was Mithridates I of Parthia, who during the Maccabean revolt, rebelled in the northeast, forcing Antiochus to leave a commander to handle Judea while he responded. He managed to take back Armenia, but died suddenly of disease in 164. This means that Antiochus couldn't have gone on the additional campaigns described in verses 41-45.

If instead the Parthian rebellion (which did in fact bring him to his end), is being described in verse 44, then who are the kings of the north and south in verse 40? Antiochus never went against Israel or Egypt again. Furthermore, we have to wonder who the king of the south is: why would Egypt be called this in verse 40, but two verses later, be called "Egypt"?

As further evidence that the rest of the story is not about Antiochus, verse 35 describes the "people with insight" as being purged "until the end of time," an apocalyptic phrase used again in verse 40 to describe the Despicable Person's encounters with the kings of the north and south. We're given the impression that this appointed end of time will follow shortly, and in fact we see that it comes in chapter 12. Verse 36 also mentions that this person will have control "until the [decreed] indignation is finished;" this is the same indignation linked to the vision of the ram and the goat in 8:19-27, which is said by the angel to "pertain to the appointed time of the end." Thus, while we are hard pressed to link this passage to Antiochus, it fits easily as a tribulation occurring in the end time. The characteristics and events of verses 37-45 fit As-Sufyani:

- He won't worship the pagan Allah of his fathers, instead, he'll honor the Muslim Allah, transformed by Muhammad into the One God of monotheistic Islam, the God of jihad (fortresses, or war).

- He'll honor Allah with the *zakat*, (one of the five pillars of Islam), an annual religious tax paid on crops, herds, merchandise and liquid assets.
- The king of the north in verse 40 might be the overthrown king of Syria retaliating against As-Sufyani, perhaps through the Abdal tribe's support of Al Mahdi. An alternative identity for the king of the south could be Saudi Arabia, attacking As-Sufyani as he continues to consolidate the former Alexandrian Empire. If this is the case, Egypt's civil war at the time of Antiochus could prefigure Saudi Arabia's, where according to the Hadith, three Caliphs fight for the kingdom but none wins it.
- Verse 44 would then describe the rumors of the armies from the east (Khorasan) marching to meet Al Mahdi at the shores of the Sea of Galilee; thus As-Sufyani pitches his royal pavilion in the Holy Land but comes to his end at the hand of Al Mahdi with no one to help him.

As to his disregarding the "desire of women" in verse 37, some have interpreted this as homosexuality and others as ruthlessness. However, in Antiochus' case, some point to the strictly religious context of the passage as being women's *religious* objects of desire, perhaps Dionysus, Tammuz/Adonis, or Nanaia/Artemis/Aphrodite, the goddess whose temple Antiochus plundered in his eastern campaign.[10]

However, as nothing else following verse 36 appears to apply to Antiochus, there must be an explanation that fits As-Sufyani and his religion. In his book *Why I Left Jihad*, Walid Shoebat posits that this is a reference to the maltreatment of women in Islamic nations where women have very little input in either religion or society. They're not permitted to hold positions of religious leadership, and

---

10 Ibid.

in some places they're either not permitted in the mosque at all, or they're segregated from the men. In the secular realm, Shari'a law places very strict limits on women. Their treatment reflects the attitude of many Islamic states that women are less intelligent and capable than men. For example, at least two women must testify in order to be counted as eyewitness testimony. In Saudi Arabia, a woman is required to be a ward of her father, brother or husband, and if she lacks one of these, then she becomes a ward of the state. Women can't leave their homes without a male, can't drive and must wear the hijab in public.[11] Finally, husbands are allowed by law to beat their wives (based on certain Koranic verses), and fathers have full control of their daughters to give them in marriage, ban them from social life or even kill them, often with complete impunity.[12]

Certainly this attitude disregards the desire of women, yet is it really what the passage refers to? Read it again without the reference to the desire of women:

[36]Then the king will do as he pleases, and he will exalt and magnify himself above every god and will speak monstrous things against the God of gods; and he will prosper until the indignation is finished, for that which is decreed will be done. [37]And he will show no regard for the gods of his fathers...nor will he show regard for any other god; for he will magnify himself above them all. [38]But instead, he will honor a god of fortresses, a god whom his fathers did not know; he will honor him with gold, silver, costly stones, and treasures.

The purpose of verses 36 and 37 is to describe what gods the

---

11 *Why we left Islam: Former Muslims Speak Out,* compiled and edited by Susan Crimp and Joel Richardson, WND Books, Inc., Los Angeles, CA, 2008, p.99
12 Ibid., p. 103

Despicable Person will *not* worship:

1. he will set himself above every god, and show no regard to any god (gentile)
2. he will speak monstrous things against the God of gods (Jehovah)
3. he will show no regard for the gods of his fathers (pagan gods of his ancestors)

The purpose of verse 38 is to describe the god he will worship:

1. Instead, he will honor a god of fortresses (war) whom his fathers did not know

Given the context of verses 36-38, it makes no sense to interpret the "desire of women" as something unreligious in nature. So what would the "desire of women" equate to in the modern Middle East? According to the *Mideast and North Africa Encyclopedia*, women of all the major religions in the Middle East have created their own religious rituals as a result of their limited access to religious education, hierarchy, places of worship and rituals. These include visits to neighborhood shrines and other holy sites dedicated to female figures (such as shrines to Mary, Rachel's tomb and the shrine of Zaynab), some of which are guarded by women and visited only by women.[13] In particular, Shi'a women have turned the tombs of Muslim saints into places of worship and refuge.[14] In North Africa, Egypt, Sudan, Yemen and the countries around the Persian Gulf, women also take part in spirit possession and healing cults, called Zar. In these cults, the ritual masters are often women

---

13 Mideast and North Africa Encyclopedia, "Women's Religious Rituals," Answers.com, pp 1-2, http://www.answers.com/topic/women-s-religious-rituals
14 Oxford Islamic Studies Online, "Women—Sufism and Shrines," p.4, http://www.oxfordislmicstudies.com /article/opr/t243/e370

who heal the afflicted by using trances and dance to pacify evil spirits.[15] Finally, there is Sufism, a sect of Islam that has generally been more open to women, allowing them to participate in their orders and rituals (although they're frequently in separate groups with female leadership).[16]

What this could mean is that As-Sufyani is strictly Sunni, rejecting not only all non-Islamic religious groups (verses 36-37), but also those non-mainstream Muslim sects who give greater access to women, including Shi'ism and Sufism. Such a stance would fit the profile of Wahhabism, which rejects religious ceremonies at tombs and shrines as a form of polytheistic saint worship, to the point of attacking those sites considered to be holy even to Sunni Islam.[17] Remember that in the Hadith, the prophecies regarding As-Sufyani's ruthless attacks focus on countries having larger populations of Shi'a Muslims, prompting the Shi'as to interpret them as specific attacks against them. In addition, at least one hadith emphasizes his violence against women, describing him ripping out their bellies.

---

15 Mideast and North Africa Encyclopedia, "Women's Religious Rituals," Answers.com, pp 1-2, http://www.answers.com/topic/women-s-religious-rituals

16 Oxford Islamic Studies Online, "Women—Sufism and Shrines," p.4, http://www.oxfordislmicstudies.com /article/opr/t243/e370

17 Dore Gold, The Fight for Jerusalem: Radical Islam, the West, and the Future of the Holy City, p. 21, Regnery Publishing, Inc., 2007

3

Al Mahdi in the Ram and the Goat

The Transgression and the Indignation

Daniel 8:12,13
¹²And on account of transgression, the host will be given over to the horn, along with the regular sacrifice…¹³…How long will the [sacrifice be given over to the horn] while the transgression causes horror, so as to allow both the holy place and the host to be trampled?

Daniel 11:36
³⁶Then the king will do as he pleases and he will exalt and magnify himself above every god, and will speak monstrous things against the God of gods; and he will prosper until the indignation is finished, for that which is decreed will be done.

Daniel says that the horn (As-Sufyani) will set up the Abomination of Desolation and control Israel because of "the transgression," and that he will prosper until the "indignation is finished." The word used here is *peshah*, meaning "rebellion, sin, transgression," and is applied to Israel's rebellion against God's covenant with Israel. In that covenant, God gives His expectations for each party: Israel is to worship Jehovah alone, and follow all of His commandments and statutes, and God gives blessings to them according to their obedience and faithfulness. However, when they transgress the covenant, God in His indignation, punishes them for their disobedience and idolatry. All the interactions we see in the Old Testament, whether they deal with individuals or Israel as a people, flow from this covenant, and every tragic event that happens to Israel is a consequence of transgressing the covenant.

In Deuteronomy 28, as the new generation of Israel is brought out of the wilderness to take possession of the Holy Land, Moses gives the people a list of the blessings and curses promised to come upon them based on their commitment to keeping the covenant:

The Blessings

Deuteronomy 28:1-13
¹Now it shall be if you will diligently obey the Lord your God, being careful to do all His commandments which I command you today, the Lord your God will set you high above all the nations of the earth. ²And all these blessings shall come upon you and overtake you, if you will obey the Lord your God. ³Blessed shall you be in the city and in the country. ⁴Blessed shall be the offspring of your body and the produce of your ground and the offspring of your beasts...⁷The Lord will cause your enemies who rise up against you to be defeated before you...⁹The Lord will establish you as a holy people to Himself, as He swore to you, if you will keep the commandments of the Lord your God and walk in His ways. ¹⁰So all the peoples of the earth shall see that you are called by the name of the Lord; and they shall be afraid of you. ¹¹And the Lord will make you abound in prosperity...¹²He will open for you His good

storehouse, the heavens, to give rain to your land in its season and bless all the works of your hand; and you shall lend to many nations, but you shall not borrow. ¹³The Lord shall make you the head and not the tail, and you only shall be above and you shall not be underneath...

The Curses

Deuteronomy 28:15-66
¹⁵But it shall come about, if you will not obey the Lord your God, to observe to do all His commandments and His statutes with which I charge you today, that all these curses shall come upon you and overtake you. ¹⁶Cursed shall you be in the city and in the country. ¹⁷Cursed shall be your basket and your kneading bowl. ¹⁸Cursed shall be the offspring of your body and the produce of the ground... ²⁰The Lord will send upon you curses, confusion and rebuke, in all you undertake to do, until you are destroyed and until you perish quickly, on account of the evil of your deeds because you have forsaken Me. ²¹The Lord will make the pestilence cling to you until He has consumed you from the land where you are entering to possess it. ²²The Lord will smite you with consumption and with fever and with inflammation and with fiery heart and with the sword and with blight and with mildew and they shall pursue you until you perish...²⁵The Lord will cause you to be defeated before your enemies...²⁶And your carcasses shall be food to all the birds of the sky and to the beasts of the earth...²⁷The Lord will smite you with the boils of Egypt and with tumors and with the scab and the itch from which you cannot be healed. ²⁸The Lord will smite you with madness and blindness and bewilderment of heart ²⁹and you shall grope at noon as the blind man gropes in darkness and you shall not prosper in your ways; but you shall only be oppressed and robbed continually with no one to save you...³⁶The Lord will

bring you and your king whom you shall set over you, to a nation which neither you nor your fathers have known, and there you shall serve other gods, wood and stone. ³⁷And you shall become a horror, a proverb and a taunt among all the peoples where the Lord will drive you...the alien who is among you shall rise above you higher and higher, but you shall go down lower and lower. ⁴⁹The Lord will bring a nation against you from afar, from the end of the earth as the eagle swoops down, a nation whose language you shall not understand, ⁵⁰a nation of fierce countenance, who shall have no respect for the old, nor show favor to the young... ⁶²Then you shall be left few in number whereas you were as the stars of heaven for multitude, because you did not obey the Lord you God...⁶⁴Moreover, the Lord will scatter you among all peoples from one end of the earth to the other end of the earth; and there you shall serve other gods, wood and stone, which you or your fathers have not known. ⁶⁵And among those nations you shall find no rest and there shall be no resting place for the sole of your foot; but there the Lord will give you a trembling heart, failing of eyes and despair of soul. ⁶⁶So your life shall hang in doubt before you; and you shall be in dread night and day, and shall have no assurance of your life.

Assyria, Babylonia, and Rome all fulfilled the prophecy of driving Israel from their homeland, and even modern history has witnessed the Jews' persecution and expulsion by their host countries throughout the world. In the Old Testament, God's indignation is manifested by both punishments of nature (plagues, famine, etc.) as well as by His "rods"—the foreign nations with whom Israel "plays the harlot." Always, God saves for Himself a remnant and waits until Israel turns back to Him to renew the covenant. No matter how many times Israel transgresses, God always remains faithful to His end of the contract: He forgives, rebuilds, restores. God has given

Israel back its land and blessed it, but just like the Hellenistic Jews, whose faithlessness to God's covenant caused them to turn their country and temple over to Antiochus, those who support compromise with Islam and As-Sufyani will be the transgressors who open the door to his persecution. Thus will the "final period of God's indignation" be made manifest by the rod of Islam.

In Daniel's prayer of chapter 9, he confesses the transgression that caused the Babylonian exile, and thus acts as a type of the remnant who will be in Israel at the time of the final indignation:

Daniel 9:8-11
8Open shame belongs to us, O Lord, to our kings, our princes and our fathers, because we have sinned against You. 9To the Lord our God belong compassion and forgiveness, for we have rebelled against Him...11indeed all Israel has transgressed Your law and turned aside, not obeying Your voice; so the curse has been poured out on us, along with the oath which is written in the law of Moses..."

In response to Daniel's prayer, Gabriel prophesies the restoration of Israel from its exile in Babylon, but goes on to describe the future cycle of transgression and indignation, which culminates in Israel's desolation during last seven years of the age. The transgression spoken of in 8:12 as leading to the little horn's control of Israel and the temple is no different than the transgression that brought on God's punishment by the hand of Assyria and Babylonia: relying on other countries to protect them instead of the Lord (Hos 7:11-13), and turning to the false religions of those countries around them, despite continuing the outer trappings of the worship of Jehovah (Hos 8:11-14, Amos 5:21-27, Jer 7). Only when Israel recognizes her sin at the Day of Atonement and repents, will Christ Himself bring the final restoration of Israel in the New Jerusalem.

In a series of chapters in Isaiah that are clearly latter day prophecies, God Himself tells us this about Judah: "You have not heard, you have not known, even from long ago your ear has not been open, because I knew that you would deal very treacherously; and you have been called a transgressor from birth. For the sake of My name I delay My wrath, and for My praise I restrain it for you, in order not to cut you off. Behold, I have refined you, but not as silver; I have tested you in the furnace of affliction for My own sake, for My own sake I will act; For how can My name be profaned? And my glory I will not give to another" (Isaiah 48:8-11). Then, beginning with verse 12, God proceeds to do an interesting thing: in speaking words of comfort and encouragement to the faithful remnant, and promising the ultimate defeat of Babylon as the false religion, He lays down the doctrine of the Trinity, almost as if in direct response to the denials of Islam, the false religion of their future transgression (echoes of this passage are found in Revelation 1, spoken by the risen Christ):

Isaiah 48:12-49:7
¹²Listen to Me, O Jacob, even Israel whom I called; I am He, I am the first, I am also the last. ¹³Surely My hand founded the earth, and My right hand spread out the heavens; when I call to them, they stand together. ¹⁴Assemble, all of you and listen! Who among them has declared these things? The Lord loves him; he shall carry out His good pleasure on Babylon, and His arm shall be against the Chaldeans. ¹⁵I, even I have spoken; indeed I have called him, I have brought him, and He will make his ways successful. ¹⁶Come near to Me, listen to this: from the first I have not spoken in secret, from the time it took place I was there. And now the Lord God has sent Me and His Spirit ⁴⁹:¹...The Lord called Me from the womb; from the body of My mother He named Me. ²And He has made My mouth like a sharp sword; in the shadow of His hand He

has concealed Me...⁵And now says the Lord, who formed Me from the womb to be His Servant, to bring Jacob back to Him in order that Israel might be gathered to Him (for I am honored in the sight of the Lord, and My God is My strength), ⁶He says, "It is too small a thing that You should be My Servant to raise up the tribes of Jacob and to restore the preserved ones of Israel; I will also make You a light of the nations, so that My salvation may reach to the end of the earth." ⁷Thus says the Lord, the Redeemer of Israel, its Holy One, to the despised One, to the One abhorred by the nation, to the Servant of rulers, "Kings shall see and arise, Princes shall also bow down; because of the Lord who is faithful, the holy One of Israel who has chosen You."

Continuing to prophesy about Israel's restoration, God says in 51:12, "I, even I, am He who comforts you," bringing to mind those passages where Jesus called the Holy Spirit "the Comforter" (John 14:16,26; 15:26; 16:7).

When the Transgressors have Finished

Al Mahdi as the Insolent King

Daniel 8:23-25
²³And in the latter period of their rule [the Alexandrian Empire], *when the transgressors have run their course*, a king will arise insolent and skilled in intrigue. ²⁴And his power will be mighty, but not by his own power. And he will destroy to an extraordinary degree and prosper and perform his will. He will destroy mighty men and the holy people. ²⁵And through his shrewdness, He will cause deceit to succeed by his influence; and he will magnify himself in his heart, and he will destroy many while they are at ease. He will

even oppose the Prince of Princes. But he will be broken without human agency. (Italics mine)

Daniel 8:23-25 is usually considered to be an interpretation of the horn and his activities in Daniel 8:9-12. However, if read carefully, it actually appears to describe two different periods: the first during the time of the transgressors, when the area of the Alexandrian Empire is controlled by the horn (As-Sufyani); and the second when the transgressors have finished, at which time the Insolent King (Al Mahdi) takes over (later we're told that each period lasts for three and half years). Other details also support that the horn and the Insolent King are the As-Sufyani/Mahdi pair:

1. While the activities of the horn center on the desecration of the sacrifice and temple, the Insolent king passage makes no mention of them.
2. The horn establishes the kingdom, while the Insolent King rules during the "latter part" of the kingdom—i.e., the second 3 ½ year period.
3. The horn magnifies himself, but the Insolent King isn't mighty by his own power. This corresponds to the beast of Revelation 13, who arises after the dragon and isn't mighty on his own: his power, throne and authority come from the dragon.

He will Oppose the Prince of Princes: Assyria and Babylonia as Types

Verse 25's "Prince of princes" is generally interpreted as being Christ. Yet this can't be the correct interpretation, since the passage clearly categorizes the Prince as a human agency that doesn't break the king: "He will even oppose the Prince of Princes. *But* he will be broken without human agency."

This passage is easily explained however, if we recognize that the Prince of Princes is As-Sufyani, against whom Al Mahdi will battle and not be broken; in fact, it's As-Sufyani who will come to his end "with no one to help him" (Dan11:45). The title "Prince of princes" in Arabic is *Amir ul-Umara,* used as a military rank equivalent to "Supreme Commander." In addition, Daniel and Revelation indicate that As-Sufyani will control many kings through conquest, making him suzerain over many "princes." In a similar way, Hosea and Isaiah identify Ancient Assyria as suzerain over many kings:

Hosea 8:9-10
9For [Israel] has gone up to Assyria like a wild donkey all alone, Ephraim has hired lovers. 10Even though they hire allies among the nations, now I will gather them up; and they will begin to diminish because of the burden of the king of princes.

Isaiah 10:5-8
5Woe to Assyria, the rod of My anger and the staff in whose hands is My indignation, 6I send it against a godless nation and commission it against the people of My fury to capture booty and to seize plunder and to trample them down like mud in the streets. 7Yet it does not so intend nor does it plan so in its heart, but rather it is its purpose to destroy, and to cut off many nations. 8For it says, "Are not my princes all kings?"

In their conquests of Israel, both Assyria and Babylonia prefigure the end time Islamic Empire. More specifically though, the Assyrian Empire prefigures As-Sufyani, while Babylonia, the seat of the false religion, typifies Al Mahdi. This typology is carried through in that, as Assyria was destroyed by Babylonia, As-Sufyani will be destroyed by Al Mahdi. This can be seen in two prophecies given by Isaiah.

As-Sufyani—the Destroyer

Isaiah 33:1-16

¹Woe to you O destroyer, while you were not destroyed; and he who is treacherous while others did not deal treacherously with him. As soon as you shall finish destroying, you shall be destroyed. As soon as you shall cease to deal treacherously, others shall deal treacherously with you. ²O Lord, be gracious to us; we have waited for Thee. Be Thou their strength every morning, our salvation also in the time of distress. ³At the sound of the tumult peoples flee…⁷Behold, their brave men cry in the streets, the ambassadors of peace weep bitterly. ⁸…He has broken the covenant, he has despised the cities, he has no regard for man. ¹⁰"Now I will arise," says the Lord, "Now I will be exalted, now I will be lifted up. ¹¹You have conceived chaff, you will give birth to stubble; My breath will consume you like fire ¹²and the peoples will be burned to lime, like cut thorns which are burned in the fire. ¹⁴Sinners in Zion are terrified; trembling has seized the godless. Who among us can live with the consuming fire? Who among us can live with continual burning? ¹⁵He who walks righteously and speaks with sincerity, he who rejects unjust gain, and shakes his hands so that they hold no bribe…¹⁶he will dwell on the heights; his refuge will be the impregnable rock."

The Destroyer is not explicitly named as Assyria, but is interpreted as such because of the reference to a broken covenant. Historically, this is Sennacherib's covenant with Hezekiah of Judah, but it also points to Israel's future covenant with As-Sufyani. While this passage speaks of Assyria's destruction by Babylonia, it also contains an undercurrent of prophecy about Satan himself, as well as Zion's judgment by fire (Rev 8:7-8, 18:18). Both this passage and Daniel 11 allude to the sin of the transgressors— briberies, deceit and actions for unjust gains.

Al Mahdi—King of Babylonia

Isaiah 14:12-20
[12]How you have fallen from heaven O star of the morning, son of the dawn! You have been cut down to earth you who have weakened the nations! [13]But you said in your heart, "I will ascend to heaven; I will raise my throne above the stars of God, and I will sit on the mount of assembly in the recesses of the north. I will ascend above the heights of the clouds; I will make myself like the Most High." [15]Nevertheless you will be thrust down to Sheol to the recesses of the pit. [16]Those who see you will gaze at you, they will ponder over you saying, 'Is this the man who made the earth tremble, who shook kingdoms, [17]who made the world like a wilderness and overthrew its cities, who did not allow his prisoners to go home?' [18]All the kings of the nations lie in glory, each in his own tomb. [19]But you have been cast out of your tomb like a rejected branch, clothed with the slain who are pierced with the sword, who go down to the stones of the pit like a trampled corpse. [20]You will not be united with them in burial because you have ruined your country, you have slain your people.

As with the Destroyer, this prophecy seems to serve double duty: as a message to ancient Babylonia and as a message to Satan himself in his final rebellion through Al Mahdi. Both this passage and Revelation describe the king's arrogance and desire to be worshiped above God; both describe his military prowess—that none will be able to defeat him; both describe his death and burial being not that of mortal kings, but rather as being thrown into the pit.

Isaiah 13 and Revelation 14:8, 17:5 and 18:2-4 make a clear link between Babylon and the Antichrist kingdom, and throughout the Old Testament the religion of Babylon is held up as THE false religion—the starting point of mankind's rebellion after the flood. Originating in Babylon (Genesis 10), the Baals became so entrenched in the early civilizations of the Middle East, that even the Greek conquerors merely overlaid them with their own pantheon. In fact, despite their Greek roots, the Seleucids admired the religion and culture of the Middle East and had no real desire to eradicate them. They even identified themselves as Babylonian kings and prided themselves on being the restorers of the Babylonian Empire. Their reign consisted of imposing a thin veneer of Greek language, architecture and social institutions upon an otherwise eastern culture and religion,[1] as they supported eastern art, literature, science and temples.[2] Even Antiochus IV, who was brought up in Rome, was connected only superficially to the Greek religion. According to native records, the idol placed in the temple by Antiochus was acknowledged to be Baal Shamayim: "The Greek name of the idol was Zeus Olympus (or, the Romans called him Jupiter Capitolinus), but it was clearly the old Mesopotamian Sun god."[3] Likewise, the first Olympic games celebrated at Tyre included sacrifices made to Heracles, the Greek name ascribed to the Phoenician's patron god Melkarth.[4]

Islam as Babylon

Islam also has its share in Babylon. The Quraish's patron god, Hubal, is acknowledged in the Koran to have been imported from Moab, and there is evidence that the name is derived from the

---

1 "Syria Becomes the New Babylon," pp. 2-3, Associates for Scriptural Knowledge, http:www.askelm.com/ people/peo016.htm
2 "Syria Becomes the New Babylon," p. 4, citing Tarn, *Hellenistic Civilisation*, pp. 118-119. Associates for Scriptural Knowledge, http:www.askelm.com/ people/peo016.htm ,
3 "Syria Becomes the New Babylon", pp. 4-5
4 *House of Seleucus, Vol II*, Chapter 23: "Antiochus IV and the Conquest of Egypt"

same root as the Hebrew *Ha Baal*, "the Baal."⁵ In Mecca, *Allah*, the general term for god, was intimately associated with Hubal, who was given the distinction of being called "Lord of the Kabaah." From the *allahs* of the various Arab tribes, Muhammad eventually succeeded in building a bridge to the idea of Allah as one God, supreme over all. Remarkably, Muslims today come to that same Kabaah to perform the same rites before Allah that their Pagan ancestors performed before their idols, only they're given different meanings, as illustrated in the chart below.

Pagan and Islamic Pilgrimage Rites at the Kabaah

Rite	Pagan significance	Islamic significance
Circumambulating the Kabaah seven times	Revolution of heavenly bodies, linked to one of Hubal's daughters	Reminder that Allah is the center of everything and the source of all meaning in life
Throwing stones at pillar	Stoning sun demons at autumnal equinox to expel the heat of summer	Reenacting Abraham throwing stones at Satan for trying to dissuade him from sacrificing Ishmael⁶

---

5 Sam Shamoun, "Did the Meccans Worship Yahweh God?: Revisiting the Issue of the Ishmaelites and the worship of the true God," p. 4, http://www.answering-islam.org/Shamoun/ishmael-baal.htm

6 Although the Koran doesn't name which son Abraham nearly sacrificed, Muslims generally hold that this incident didn't happened to Isaac, but rather Ishmael, through whom they trace the ancestry of Muhammad. They believe that the Torah and the New Testament have been adulterated by Jews and Christians respectively, and so they pick and choose what they believe to be true.

Making sacrifices	Animal and sometimes humans sacrificed to astral deities[7]	Sheep sacrificed as reminder of Abraham's substitute for Ishmael[8]
Kissing the black stone	The black stone represented Hubal; kissing it was act of worship[9]	• Sent from Allah for Adam's altar (found by Abraham while digging Kabaah's foundation), or given to Abraham by Gabriel to keep track of circumambulations.[10] • Act removes people's sins (turned from black to white from absorbing sins[11]) or emulates Prophet, who kissed it making circumambulations
Running between the hills of Safa and Marwah	Worship of idols Isaf and Na'ila, placed on the hills	Reenacts Hagar's search for water in the wilderness.
Shaving the head	Gratitude upon returning safely from journey	Three locks of hair are cut after running between hills.[12] No Islamic explanation given.

These rites are so unchanged that if a pre-Islamic Arab were to see pilgrims at the Kabaah today, he would assume the pilgrims were of his own religion—right down to the 99 names of Allah, suspiciously familiar as names of other idols in their pagan Arabian pantheon.[13]

Isaiah 14:17 mentions that the king of Babylon doesn't let his prisoners go home, and this was true of both the Assyrian and Babylonian kings, who deported large portions of a conquered state, either selling them or taking them as slaves to their own kingdoms. In the case of Al Mahdi, we're told in Revelation 13:15 that in his kingdom, those who don't worship him will be killed, and in Revelation 18:13 the merchants of the earth weep over the destruction of Babylon because there will be no one to buy their goods, among which are "slaves and human lives."

The Koran gives only four optional treatments for those defeated in war: being set free (generally reserved for those who convert), decapitation, being held as prisoner for ransom, or being sold into slavery. While enslavement of conquered peoples may seem a far-fetched notion in this modern day, it's not beyond credibility for

---

7 In fact, the Hadith tells the story of how Muhammad's father was to be sacrificed and how it was avoided. See Salih Suruç, "How did the event in which the Holy Prophet (PBUH)'s Father, Abdullah, was pledged as a sacrifice materialize?" http://www.questionsonislam.com/index.php?s=article&aid=10424

8 Council on Islamic Education, "Hajj intro for People of Other Faith", p. 1, http://www.islamicity.com/ mosque/hajj/hajjintro.htm

9 According to Sam Shamoun, Wellhausen believes that the black stone represented Hubal until the idol of human form was imported from Mesopotamia, "Did the Meccans Worship Yahweh God..." p.8

10 Bayt al-Hikmah, Virtual Library of Witness-Pioneer, "The Significance of the Black Stone," http://www.witness-pioneer.org/vil/Articles/ibadah/significance_of_the_black_stone.htm.

11 Black Stone of Mecca-Crystalinks, http://www.crystalinks.com/blackstone.html

12 Jamiluddin Morris Zahuri, "A Pilgrimage", http://www.zahuri.org/Pilgrimage.html.

13 Sam Shamoun, "Did the Meccans Worship Yahweh God?: Revisiting the Issue of the Ishmaelites and the worship of the true God," p. 18, quoting Walker, *Foundations of Islam*, p. 43. http://www.answering-islam.org/Shamoun/ishmael-baal.htm

the Islamic Empire. Recently, some Muslim scholars have reopened the issue of slavery. In 2003, a high-level Salafi Saudi jurist, Shaykh Saleh Al-Fawzan, issued an opinion stating that "slavery is a part of Islam. Slavery is part of jihad, and jihad will remain as long as there is Islam."[14] Another prominent Saudi government official cleric, Shaikh Saad Al-Buraik, recently called for Palestinians to end normal relations with Jews, saying, "Muslim Brothers in Palestine, do not have any mercy neither compassion on the Jews, their blood, their money, their flesh. Their women are yours to take, legitimately. God made them yours. Why don't you enslave their women? Why don't you wage jihad? Why don't you pillage them?"[15] Other clerics, including Shaykh Fadhlalla Haeri of Karbala and Dr. Abdul-Latif Mushtahari of Al Azhar University (chief center of Sunni Islamic learning in the world) support the idea of slavery in the context of war fought against non-Muslims.[16]

Even now, selling girls for sex slaves is a fairly common practice in countries like Iran, where fathers have complete rights over their daughters and aren't prosecuted for the crime. Sadly, such girls, if ever escaping their plight, are imprisoned or executed for sexual immorality.[17] In Tehran alone, there has been an estimated 635 percent increase in the number of teenage prostitute girls, and thousands of Iranian women and girls have been sold into sexual slavery internationally, often to other Arab countries.[18] In fact, the

---

14 Wikipedia, "Islam and Slavery," p. 14, citing Shaikh Salih al-Fawzaan, "Affirmation of Slavery," p. 24 of "Taming a Neo-Qutubite Fanatic Part I," http://www.salafipublications.com/sps/downloads/pdf/GRV070005.pdf, accessed 2/17/2007

15 Primary Document, "Saudi Telethon Host Calls for Enslaving Jewish Women, http://old.nationalreview.com/ document/document042602.asp, from the orginal tape at http://media.islamway.com/arabic/images/ lessons/burek/monkey.rm

16 Wikipedia, "Islam and Slavery," p. 14-15, citing "the Elements of Islam," 1993, and "You Ask and Islam Answers", pp. 51-52

17 Jihadwatch, "Iraq: Girls sold as sex slaves, then prosecuted for prostitution and other "crimes," http://www.jihadwatch.org/2010/05/iraq-girls-sold-as-sex-slaves-then-prosecuted-for-prostitution-and-other-"crimes"

18 Donna M. Hughes, "Islamic Fundamentalism and the Sex Slave Trade in Iran," p.1-3 http://www.uri.edu/ artsci/wms/hughes/iran_sex_slave_trade. (The period for this

head of Iran's Interpol bureau believes that the sex slave trade is one of the most profitable activities in Iran today, being conducted with the full knowledge and participation of the ruling fundamentalists, including mullahs, judges and the police.[19] This sex slave trade is facilitated even further by the attitudes of Iranian officials, who vacillate between denying the existence of prostitution in Iran, and suggesting that the government establish brothels and use the doctrine of *mutah* (temporary marriage) to legitimize prostitution; their rationale is that it would curb the rise of AIDS.[20] Both slavery and the doctrine of *mutah* would explain the allusion to sexual immorality of the beast kingdom in Revelation 9:21.

In looking at the typology of Daniel and the Old Testament prophets, then, it can be said that when As-Sufyani comes, he will be the new Assyrian, reviving the Assyrian Empire (Iraq and Syria); the new Seleucid, reviving the Seleucid Empire (Syro-Babylonia); and a new Caliph, reviving the Islamic Empire. But in the end, the last antichrist kingdom will be a revival of Babylon, and the last king of Babylon will be Al Mahdi.

---

increase isn't stated in the article.)
19 Ibid., p. 4
20 Ibid.

4

The Prophecy of the Seventy Weeks: The Prince to Come

Daniel 9:24-27

[24]Seventy weeks have been decreed for your people and your holy city, to finish the transgression, to make an end of sin, to make atonement for iniquity, to bring in everlasting righteousness, to seal up vision and prophecy and to anoint the most holy place. [25]So you are to know and discern that from the issuing of a decree to restore and rebuild Jerusalem until Messiah the Prince, there will be seven weeks and sixty-two weeks; it will be built again, with plaza and moat, even in times of distress. [26a]Then after the sixty-two weeks, the Messiah will be cut off and have nothing, [26b]and the people of the prince who is to come will destroy the city and the sanctuary and its end will come with a flood[1]; [26c]even to the end there will be war; desolations are determined. [27a]And he will make a firm covenant with the many for one week, but in the middle of the week, he will put a stop to sacrifice and grain offering; [27b]and on the wing of abominations will come one who makes desolate, even until a complete destruction, one that is decreed, is poured out on the one who makes desolate.

---

1   Although "flood" is often used in scripture as a metaphor for armies, it could be a literal flood in this context—see Zechariah 14:8 and Ezekiel 47:1-5

This passage is perhaps the most controversial in Biblical prophecy, having three major schools of interpretation: Preterism, Historicism and Futurism. Preterists believe that the seventieth week was fulfilled in the time of ancient Rome, the Abomination of Desolation and the Great Tribulation occurring at Titus' destruction of Jerusalem in 70 A.D. This interpretation is easily dismissed, since in Matthew 24 Jesus clearly links the Abomination of Desolation to the end time, and describes His second coming as being a literal event occurring immediately after the Great Tribulation.

Historicists use the more accurate translation of *gabar* in verse 27 as "makes strong a covenant," to mean that the Prince confirms an existing covenant, rather than making a new one.[2] This contributes to their mistaken interpretation of the Prince to Come as Christ Himself, in His role of confirming God's covenant during His earthly ministry. They contend that "Messiah the prince (*nagid*)" of verse 25 is the same "Prince (*nagid*) to Come" of verse 27.[3] The seventieth week is allegorized to be the last week of the old covenant or the first week of the new, the midpoint being His death, when He "stopped" the sacrifice by rendering it ineffective. Israel's rejection of Christ resulted in the continuation of an ineffective sacrifice for 40 more years, which they see as the Abomination of Desolation bringing on its heels the "desolations" of 70 A.D. under Titus.[4] Thus as the people of the Prince to Come, the Jews are understood to be the ones who destroyed their own city and sanctuary by rebelling against Rome. However, Historicists teach that the ultimate destruction referred to in verse 27b of the prophecy is still future, being *decreed* during the Roman period, but not *fulfilled*. They

---

2   William H. Shea, "Antiochus Epiphanes and the Little Horn," http://specialtyinterests.net/ antiochus_epiphanes.html
3   Willima H. Shea, "Antiochus Epiphanes and the Little Horn," pp. 36-42, http://specialtyinterests.net/ antiochus_epiphanes.html. The poetic form is AB-A-B: Messiah Nagid (AB) in verse 25, Messiah (A) in verse 26, and Nagid (B) in verse 26.
4   Ibid.

ascribe a "prophetic year" to each day of Daniel's prophecies and see the first half of the week as the 1260 year rule of the Catholic Church over Europe (538-1798). The Antichrist will therefore be a revival of the Catholic Church's rule over the earth.

Finally, there are the Futurists, who hold that the high priest Onias was the Prince of the Covenant shattered by Antiochus IV in Daniel 11:22. Since they believe the people of the Prince to Come were the Romans of 70 A.D., they teach that the Prince to Come is the Antichrist out of a revived Roman Empire (i.e., Western Europe) who'll make a seven year peace treaty with Israel, only to break it half way through the term.

In order to accurately interpret the seventy week prophecy, we must start by breaking it down into its various topics, looking for clues in the text and the historical types that Daniel has provided.

The Week

Gabriel states that for the Jews and Jerusalem there are "seventy periods of seven"—seventy "weeks" of years—to seal up vision and prophecy. He describes events occurring during this 490 year period but, just like the rest of Daniel's prophecies, he ultimately focuses on the last seven years, the time of the last antichrist empire. He breaks down the 490 years into 3 periods: 7 weeks (49 years), 62 weeks (434 years) and 1 week (7 years). The forty-nine years covered the period from Artaxerxes' decree to rebuild the city of Jerusalem in 445 B.C., until its completion under Nehemiah in 396;[5] then 434 more years passed until Christ's

---

5 There was a decree regarding the rebuilding of the temple under Cyrus, and a decree in the seventh year of Artaxerxes to allow Jews to return to Jerusalem with items necessary for the temple. It is obvious that those returning must have begun rebuilding the city, but in Nehemiah we read of the distress they were having because of the broken wall. It was not until the twentieth year of Artaxerxes that the decree went out to build the wall, which would have been in 445 B.C. (Arthur Bloomfield, *The End of Days*, pp. 62-64, Bethany Fellowship, inc, Minneapolis, MN,

triumphal entry, after which He was crucified.[6] Because these first 483 years were literal, consistency demands that the last "week" be literal too, unlike the allegorized week in the Historicists' view. The purpose of prophecy is to reveal God's plan; to have a week laid out in His own mind that's unrecognizable to us defeats this purpose. In contrast, if we take the week to be literal, then according to Daniel, it will be clearly identifiable by the confirmation of a covenant at its beginning, the Abomination of Desolation at its midpoint and the coming of the One Who Makes Desolate in the second half. This second half is described in Daniel 12:1-3 as beginning after the Despicable Person of chapter 11 comes to his end, and is paralleled in Revelation 12:

Daniel 12:1, 6-7
[1]Now at that time Michael, the great prince who stands guard over the sons of your people, will arise. And there will be a time of distress such as never occurred since there was a nation until that time; and at that time your people, everyone who is found written in the book, will be rescued.[6]"...How long will it be until the end of these wonders?" [7]...Time, times and half a time; and as soon as they finish shattering the power of the holy people, all these events will be completed.

Revelation 12:7,9,13-14;13:1,5
[7]And there was war in heaven, Michael and his angels waging war with the dragon. [9]And the great dragon was thrown down...[13]And when the dragon saw that he was thrown down to the earth, he persecuted the woman who gave birth to the male child. [14]And

---

1961).
6 See Appendix 1 for the detailed calculation made by Sir Robert Anderson in *The Coming Prince*, pp. 122-128, Kregel, Grand Rapids, 1967, as quoted by Tomas S. McCall and Zola Levitt, *Satan in the Sanctuary, an Israeli Controversy: The Temple, Fantasy or Tomorrow's reality?*, pp. 85-88, McCall & Levitt, 1983

the two wings of the great eagle were given to the woman, in order that she might fly into the wilderness to her place where she was nourished for a time and times and half a time... [13:1]**And I saw a beast coming up out of the sea...** [5]**and there was given to him a mouth speaking arrogant words and blasphemies; and authority to act for forty-two months was given to him.**

Although the first 69 weeks were consecutive, there's obviously been a long gap between the 69th and 70th, because the city and temple needed to be restored before the Antichrist comes. Israel was restored as a modern state in 1948, now we await the building of the third temple.

It's tempting to interpret some of the seventy weeks prophecy as having been fulfilled in Christ's first coming, especially the "making atonement for iniquity," and "bringing in everlasting righteousness." But the book of Daniel isn't about the Church—that's reserved for John. All his prophecies are about the Jews and Jerusalem, so the transgression spoken of here isn't the sin of mankind through Adam, but rather Israel's transgression against the covenant. Christ's first coming didn't put an end to this transgression, nor has Israel made atonement for its iniquity by receiving Jesus' sacrifice. Despite the re-establishment of Israel, the curse that God promised is still in force: "Moreover, the Lord will scatter you among all peoples, from one end of the earth to the other end of the earth; and there you shall serve other gods, wood and stone, which you or your fathers have not known. And among those nations you shall find no rest and there shall be no resting place for the sole of your foot; but there the Lord will give you a trembling heart, failing of eyes and despair of soul" (Deut 28:64,65). The "gods which you or your fathers have not known," "made of wood and stone" fit the descriptions of Antichrist's false religion in Daniel 11:37-38 and Revelation 9:20. The atonement of verse 24 will be made when Israel sees Him in the clouds and all mourn Him (Zech 12:10, Matt 24:30, Rev 14:14); then Christ will bring in everlasting righteousness in the millennial kingdom, anointing Jerusalem and the temple.

The Princes

In the book of Daniel, *sar*, the more common term for prince, is used approximately 18 times, while *nagid* is used only three times: 1) the Messiah *Nagid* (9:25), 2) the *Nagid* who is to Come (9:26), and 3) the *Nagid* of the Covenant (11:22). It's reasonable to believe that Daniel intentionally used *nagid* in these three contexts because of its unique significance in scripture. In I Samuel 9:16, the Lord commanded Samuel to anoint Saul as *nagid,* in contrast to the people's request for a *melek*, the usual term for a king. According to Jeong Bong Kim and D.J. Human, "...The use of nagid is distinguished from melek...to provide divine legitimacy for Saul's leadership which turned into kingship (I Sam 11:15)."[7] They go on to make a connection between the idea of the *melek* as king and the *nagid* as shepherd king, an example of which they give from II Samuel 5:1-2, "For some time, while Saul was king [*melek*] over us, it was you [David] who led out Israel and brought it in. The Lord said to you: It is you who shall be shepherd of my people Israel, you who shall be *nagid* over Israel." Supporting this idea is God's use of a flock and shepherd to describe his own relationship with Israel (Ps 80:1; Mi 7:14; Ezek 34:12; Jer 31:10). The prophets also used the metaphor for the Messiah, who would lead Israel perfectly in the ways of the Lord (Ezek 34:23, 37:24) and to curse prophets and leaders who were leading the people astray (Ezek 34:2-10; Jer 49:19; Zech 10:2,

---

7   "Nagid: A re-examination in the light of the royal ideology in the ancient near east," p. 9, http://www.scielo.org.za/scielo.php?pid=S0259-94222008000300018&script=sci_arttext

11:15-17). Originally then, this term was introduced to refer to a leader having a religious role in addition to political and military roles.

So, in Daniel, Messiah *Nagid* (9:25) is clearly Christ, but who is the *Nagid* to Come? The Historicists argue that he is also Christ. Yet 9:26 treats them as if they were two distinct individuals; to interpret them as the same person simply doesn't make sense. In addition, the Historicists say that the *Nagid* of the Covenant is also Christ, and that the Despicable Person is Roman; but this flies in the face of 11:1-21, which clearly connects both of them to Greece and the Seleucids.

The futurists on the other hand, would say the *Nagid* to Come is the Antichrist himself. Yet from Daniel it's clear that As-Sufyani is the one who sets up the Abomination of Desolation, not Al Mahdi, who would be the One Who Makes Desolate during the second half of the week. Furthermore, intrinsic in the term *nagid* is the idea of a Jewish ruler over Israel, and Al Mahdi is Arabic, a direct descendant of Muhammad.[8]

We've already seen that Antiochus was suzerain over Israel. As a type of As-Sufyani, we must therefore look at the *nagids* that he covenanted with in order to understand the identity of the *Nagid* to Come. Jason would be a type of the *Nagid* of the Covenant (Dan 11:22) because he was the first prince under the suzerainty of Antiochus IV. He represents the Israeli leader who will covenant with Syria. But Jason was later replaced by Menelaus, the type of the future *Nagid* to Come, who will confirm that covenant (9:26, 27) and cause great tribulation in Israel.

---

[8] This is true; however, he may also have some Jewish blood or appear to be Jewish, since the Islamic prophecies say "his body is like Israel."

Jason as the Nagid of the Covenant

Daniel 11:22
²²And they will be flooded away before him and shattered and also the prince of the covenant.

Jason was responsible for initiating the Hellenization of Judea, yet he was supported by the Oniads for having maintained the temple traditions. We might expect the future *Nagid* of the Covenant to be like him in many ways, covenanting with As-Sufyani, but making possible the temple worship. Like Jason, he'll be replaced, possibly to return later to fight against his replacement. In fact, just as with Antiochus, this could be what precipitates As-Sufyani's attack on Israel and the establishment of the Abomination of Desolation.

Menelaus as the Nagid to Come

¹¹:²³And after an alliance is made with him, he will practice deception and he will go up and gain power with a small people.

The word used for alliance in 11:23 is *chabar*, meaning to "join together," as in sewing together two pieces of the tabernacle tent or the priestly garments. Other examples are: Psa 94:20 ("Can a throne of destruction be allied with You?"); Eccl 9:4 ("For whoever is joined with all the living there is hope..."); Hos 4:17 ("Ephraim is joined to idols..."). Two of the four times it's used in the sense of a political agreement, it refers to having a single purpose, or even a brotherhood, as in II Chronicles 20, where it refers to an alliance between Judah and Israel for the purpose of building ships to go to Tarshish, or the unity of the tribes of Jerusalem in Psalms 122:3. In Daniel 11:6, it indicates an alliance strengthened through marriage.

The idea of *chabar* is reflected in Antiochus' relationship with Menelaus in contrast to that of Jason. With Jason as the *Nagid* of the Covenant, Antiochus had a partner in changing the socio-political life of Israel, but not the temple; in Menelaus however, he had a devoted partner in Hellenizing every aspect of Judea. Under him came the corruption of the religious system as well as the civic system, since the priests were in charge of the courts. As such, Menelaus is the type of the *Nagid* to Come who confirms the covenant between Israel and Syria; he's the Shepherd that eats the flock and leads it astray. (Zech 10:2, 11:16-17).

Daniel 9:27 tells us only about the religious side of the *Nagid* to Come, which is that he'll stop the continual sacrifices and offerings. This fact appears to contradict what we're told in Daniel 11:31, that the Despicable Person will stop the sacrifices. Which is it? According to the types of Antiochus and Menelaus, both men will be responsible: while Antiochus sent his troops to punish Judea and establish the Abomination of Desolation, it was Menelaus who sent for him and led him into the temple.[9]

Thus, according to the typology of Daniel, it would appear that the *Nagid* of the Covenant in Daniel 11:22 will be a modern Israeli leader who will have a relationship with Syria. At some point, he will be replaced by the *Nagid* to Come, a man with an even closer alliance with Syria and As-Sufyani.

The Covenant

Because the book of Daniel is a cohesive work using consistent terminology, other passages can shed light on the covenants of 9:27 and 11:22, specifically Daniel 11:30 and 11:32, which make a distinction between the "holy covenant" and the "covenant":

---

9   II Maccabees 5:11, 15

The Holy Covenant

³⁰Therefore he will be disheartened and will return and become enraged at the holy covenant and take action...so he will come back and show regard for those who forsake the holy covenant.

The Covenant

³²And by smooth words, he will turn to godlessness those who act wickedly toward the covenant but the people who know their God will display strength and take action.

From these passages we see that the Despicable Person is opposed to the *holy covenant*, while the godly people (i.e., those who keep the *holy covenant*) are opposed to the *covenant*. Clearly they are not the same, as the Historicists claim, but are diametrically opposed to one another. It would seem then, that neither 9:27 nor 11:22 refers to the *holy* covenant between God and Israel, but rather a political treaty. However, unlike what the Futurists contend, it isn't between Israel and the Antichrist (Al Mahdi), but rather with As-Sufyani. If this is right, then we'd expect to see a covenant between his scriptural types and Israel; this is in fact the case. Assyria made treaties with both Israel and Judah which it later broke. In addition, the Seleucids had a covenant with Judea regarding their religious autonomy, which Antiochus eventually broke. The covenant between As-Sufyani and Israel is also discussed in the end time prophecy of Isaiah, who speaks of a covenant that gives Israel a false sense of security:

Isaiah 28:14-18
Therefore hear the word of the Lord, O scoffers, who rule this people who are in Jerusalem, ¹⁵Because you have said, "We have made a covenant with death and with Sheol we have made a pact.

The overwhelming scourge will not reach us when it passes by, for we have made falsehood our refuge and we have concealed ourselves with deception." ⁱ⁶Therefore thus says the Lord God, "Behold, I am laying in Zion a stone, a tested stone, a costly cornerstone for the foundation, firmly placed. He who believes in it will not be disturbed, ¹⁷and I will make justice the measuring line and righteousness the level: then hail shall sweep away the refuge of lies, and the waters shall overflow the secret place. ¹⁸And your covenant with death shall be canceled and your pact with Sheol shall not stand; when the overwhelming scourge passes through, then you become its trampling place."

Jeremiah also speaks of the "ambassadors of peace," the prophets of ancient Samaria, "who prophesied by Baal and led my people Israel astray...committing adultery and walking in falsehood (Jer 23:13-14). They speak a vision of their own imagination, not from the mouth of the Lord. They keep saying to those who despise Me, "The Lord has said 'You will have peace...Calamity will not come upon you'" (Jer 23:16-17). "...And they have healed the brokenness of My people superficially, saying, 'Peace, peace,' but there is no peace" (Jer 6:14).

It seems reasonable that the covenant and alliance associated with the Despicable Person in Daniel 11:22-23 involves peace with Syria and/or the Palestinians in modern Israel. While the details of such a covenant can't be known at this point, we do know that international pressure on Israel to make a peace treaty with Syria and the Palestinians is only intensifying. Such an agreement will have to involve giving over land, most likely the West Bank and even part of Jerusalem, to the Palestinians, and the Golan Heights to Syria. In fact, Syria has made such concessions a prerequisite to peace negotiations. As enticement, Syria could easily include some kind of protection from Hamas and Hezbollah; former Israeli Prime Minister

Olmert tried to accomplish just this in 2007 by offering Syria the Golan Heights.

One thing is for sure: it's hard to expect the temple to be rebuilt or sacrifices to resume without some kind of political agreement with the Palestinians. In the proverbial Catch 22, however, the Palestinians insist that no treaty will be signed unless they're given complete control of the Temple Mount. Right now the Islamic Waqf that administers the Mount has a very tight rein on the activities of Jews and Christians. A peace covenant with the Palestinians might therefore include some kind of agreement whereby the Muslims continue to control the Temple Mount, but Jews are granted limited autonomy over their own worship there, whether it be in a new temple, or a shared Dome of the Rock or Al Aqsa mosque (equally difficult to imagine). Some translations of 9:27 indicate that the sacrifices are stopped in violation of the covenant ("the *nagid* comes to make the covenant strong *but* halfway through the week stops the sacrifices") while others do not ("*and* halfway through he stops the sacrifices").

Unfortunately, Islamic prophecy doesn't help us out much. There's at least one hadith that mentions a seven year treaty, but it contradicts Daniel 9 and 11 in that it's made between Al Mahdi and the West, not As-Sufyani and Israel. Shaykh Abdullah ben Sadek gives no hadiths detailing As-Sufyani's relationship with Israel, peaceful or otherwise. However, there are hints of conquest. One hadith states that Al Mahdi will not come until As-Sufyani is "established," and another that says their battle will take place "in the house of Jerusalem." The Shi'as believe that the Zionists and the West will support As-Sufyani, but it seems highly unlikely, since by the time Al Mahdi comes midweek, he will have already turned on Israel. Remember too that historically, it was Rome (i.e. the West) who stopped Antiochus in his second Egyptian campaign.

If As-Sufyani starts off conquering in a way that looks like he's bringing stability and less oppressive governments to the Middle East, then it's plausible the West would support him and that Israel might trust him as leader of Syria; however, if he starts off his campaign as violently as the Hadith prophesies, this seems unlikely. At the rate things are going, Israel may end up making a treaty with Syria because they have no choice; with the "Arab Spring," they may lose their treaties with both Jordan and Egypt.

<u>The Many</u>

Although the covenant agreement will be with As-Sufyani, as indicated by the alliance of 11:23, Daniel 9:27 refers to the *Nagid* to Come as confirming that covenant with "the Many":

9:27a And he will make strong a covenant *with the many* for one week, but in the middle of the week, he will put a stop to sacrifice and grain offering.

We're not told who the many are. However, we have some clues:

11:33 And those who have insight among the people will give understanding to the many; yet they will fall by sword and by flame, by captivity and by plunder for many days.

11:34 Now when they fall they will be granted a little help and many will join with them in hypocrisy.

12:3 And those who have insight will shine brightly like the brightness of the expanse of heaven, and those who lead the many to righteousness, like the stars forever and ever.

Whoever "the many" are, they are unrighteous (12:3), don't

understand the implications of the covenant (11:33) and, out of hypocrisy (11:34), will join with those who are given understanding. Given all of these facts, it seems likely that "the many" consist at least in part of Jews, but could just as easily include any within Israel who support the covenant. But why would the *nagid* make a covenant with his own people (i.e., Israeli citizens)?

According to Daniel J. Elazar, the establishment of the office of *nagid/melek* is described as a covenanting in I Samuel 9, as was David's anointing in II Samuel 5:1-3. "First a relationship is established between God and David, which gives David a theo-political status (I Sam 16). Then that relationship is transformed into covenants between David and the people, with God acting as the guarantor…it seems that, despite the hereditary element introduced by David, his heirs had to be confirmed through covenants with the representatives of the people [i.e. tribal elders]…."[10] After the Babylonian exile, the high priest functioned more or less as king, thus he became the *nagid* who covenanted with the people to lead them.

The People of the Nagid to Come

For the most part, Daniel 9:26 is interpreted to be the destruction of the city and temple by the Roman Empire. This makes the Futurists expect the *Nagid* to Come to be from Rome (Western Europe). One problem with this interpretation is that it ignores the meaning of the Hebrew word *'am* ("people"). In this context, it would either be an ethnic designation (as in Daniel 9:24), or a political one, where the people are those ruled over by the prince. Even if we set aside the Jewish significance of the word *nagid*, from

---

10 Daniel J. Elazar, "Dealing with Fundamental Regime Change: The Biblical Paradigm of the Transition from Tribal Federation to Federal Monarchy under David," p. 15, Jerusalem Center for Affairs, http://www.jcpa.org/dje/articles2/regimechange.htm

an ethnic standpoint it couldn't be said that the prince's people are "Roman," because the Roman Empire and its capital were populated by many ethnic groups; in fact, technically, the armies that destroyed Jerusalem under Titus were Syrian—the 15th legion of Apollo.[11] As to the political sense of *'am* in this context, it's obvious that people living in 70 A.D. can't possibly be under the rule of a prince who comes 2000 years after them.

The fact is that just because 9:25 discusses the second temple, doesn't mean that verse 26b occurs at the time of the second temple. In reality, Titus' destruction of the city and temple are already covered in verse 26a which describes the state of the Messiah's kingdom in the simple phrase "the Messiah will be cut off and have nothing." Since the Messiah will reign over the earth from His throne in the temple of Jerusalem, this phrase says it all: He has nothing because the city is destroyed, the people are scattered and the second temple is razed to the ground. This means that the sanctuary in verse 26b is the yet future third temple.

Many say it can't be the third temple because if it's destroyed by the Prince's people, there would be nothing for the Antichrist to take over, nowhere to set up the Abomination of Desolation. But the Hebrew word *shachath* doesn't have to be translated as "destroy" in Daniel 8:24-25 and 9:26. It's translated as "corrupt" throughout the Old Testament, even in end time prophecies, to describe Israel's corruption by the idolatry of foreign nations.[12] In the Aramaic portion of Daniel, the word derived from it (*shchath*) is used in the sense of corruption three times, once in 2:9 and twice in 6:4 where it's stated that because Daniel was faithful, the king's men could find no corruption in him. Even in Daniel 8:24-25 *shachath* could be translated as corruption by Al Mahdi, and is even given as an alternative translation in the NAS:

---

11   "De Imperatoribus Romanis," p.2 , http://www.roman-emperors.org/titus.htm
12   See Deu 4:16,25; Deu 31:29; Psa 14:1, Prov 25:26; Exe 20:44; Eze 23:11

²⁴And his power will be mighty, but not by his own power. And he will *corrupt* to an extraordinary degree and prosper and perform his will; he will *corrupt* mighty men and the holy people.

²⁵And through his shrewdness He will cause deceit to succeed by his influence and he will magnify himself in his heart, and he will *corrupt* many while they are at ease.

This term "while they are at ease" is based on the word *shalvah*, which is defined as "security, abundance, peace, prosperity, quietness." The King James has it as "by peace he will destroy many." It seems difficult to physically destroy someone by peace; true, this could be a reference to a sneak attack, but spiritual corruption seems more likely since Al Mahdi must initially be seen as a savior from the tyranny of As-Sufyani.

Based on this interpretation, 26b and 26c tell what the Prince's people will do at or around the time of his arrival, not 2000 years before he comes (i.e., the Romans of 70 A.D.). The violent end of the city (or of the Prince himself, given as an alternate translation in the NAS) is the future *consequence* of their corruption:

²⁶ᵇand the people of the prince who is to come will *corrupt* the city and the sanctuary and its end will come with a flood; ²⁶ᶜeven to the end there will be war; desolations are determined.

Verse 27 then goes on to give details regarding how that end will be realized, telling us that Israel's leader will represent the many in supporting the covenant. It's only after the Abomination of Desolation is set up that the One Who Makes Desolate (Al Mahdi) will cause the desolations spoken of in verse 26c, bringing upon the city and temple the judgment of God in the seven trumpets and bowls of Revelation.

Translating *shachath* in 9:26 as "corrupt" makes much better sense than "destroy" because by spiritually corrupting the city and temple, especially through political channels, the *Nagid's* people will pave the way for his rise to power and whatever compromises the covenant will entail; this aligns with what Menelaus' people did during the time of Antiochus. After all, the main aim of Satan is to destroy the soul by deceit and corruption, and the goal of the beast kingdom is to usurp Christ's rightful place upon the throne of Jerusalem; the physical destruction of the temple and city don't accomplish this. One of the most powerful avenues for such deceit will be a political platform of peace.

The qodesh and the miqdash

Further support that the temple is corrupted and not destroyed, comes in the two different words translated as "sanctuary" in Daniel: *qodesh* and *miqdash*. There's disagreement over the significance of Daniel's use of these two words, but an article by one author points out that whenever Ezekiel is viewing the millennial temple, he uses *qodesh* to describe the inner court where the priests sacrifice upon the altar, along with the holy place and the Holy of Holies (Ezek 41:21, 23; 42:20: 44:27; 45:2); in contrast, he uses *miqdash*, to denote the whole complex upon the Temple Mount, including the outer gates, the court of the gentiles and the court chambers immediately within the outside wall (Ezek 43:21; 44:1,5,7,9,11,15,16; 45:3-4,18; 47:12; 48:8,10,21).[13] It seems reasonable that Daniel used these two different words intentionally and with purpose:

9:26b "The people of the prince who is to come will destroy [corrupt] the city and the *qodesh*."

---

13 "Ezekiel-Chapter 41: The Sanctuary Environs," http://prweb0.voicenet.com/~lelgee/ezekiel/ch41.html

11:31 "Forces from him will arise, desecrate the *miqdash* fortress, do away with the regular sacrifice and set up the abomination of desolation."

8:11-12 "[The small horn] magnified itself to be equal with the commander of the host, removed the sacrifice and the *miqdash* was thrown down. And...it will fling truth to the ground..."

8:13 "How long will the vision about the regular sacrifice apply...to allow both *the qodesh* and the host to be trampled?"

8:14 "For 2300 evenings and mornings then the *qodesh* will be vindicated."

The Romans destroyed the entire temple complex in Jerusalem. If the people of the *Nagid* to Come in 9:26b were the armies of Titus, we would expect Daniel to say they destroy the *miqdash*, just as he did in 9:17 regarding the Babylonian destruction; instead, he mentions only the *qodesh* or inner sanctuary of the temple.

On the other hand, if we interpret the people as being the *Nagid's* contingency—some of "the many" with whom he covenants—then 9:26 describes how they help the *Nagid* and As-Sufyani to corrupt the city and the temple; if this is the case, then 9:26b-27a parallel the activities of the horn out of the horn and the Despicable Person. In 11:31, these activities are described as *chalal*, "desecration," as in sinfulness or ritual impurity.[14] This same word is used in Daniel 11:32, where the Despicable Person corrupts by flatteries those who act wickedly towards the covenant.

If the people destroy the *qodesh* in 9:26, then the "throwing down" of the *miqdash* in 8:11 would have to be an act of physical

---
14   See Exo 31:14; I Chr 5:1; Eze 7:22, 7:24, 28:7; Jer 16:18

destruction. However, 13-14 speak of the *qodesh* as being "trampled" over a period of 2300 days, something that would not be true of a single act of destruction, but could certainly apply to corruption and desecration (see Isaiah 1:12). In addition, if the *qodesh* were physically destroyed, its restoration would be described as a reconstruction. But Daniel 8:14 states that at the end of the period, the *qodesh* will be "vindicated" (*tsadaq*), which means making something right in a moral or legal sense—"to cleanse, do justice or be turned to righteousness."[15]

Therefore, *shalak* is used figuratively in 8:11 for the "throwing down" of the *miqdash,* as well as in verse 12 for the "flinging to the ground" of truth. The people of the *Nagid* to Come will begin this process of corruption, which will ultimately allow As-Sufyani to desecrate the *qodesh* with the Abomination of Desolation, and profane the *miqdash* in his battle against Al Mahdi. This is exactly what happened with Antiochus: he desecrated the *qodesh* with the idol and pig sacrifice, but also profaned the *miqdash* by attaching the Acra to the outer wall of the temple complex. This explains how, in Revelation 11:2, the outer courts (the *miqdash)* are trampled by the gentiles for 42 months while the inner courts (the *qodesh*) remain intact, with both the altar and the religious courts functioning corruptly, just like other Old Testament prophecies describe.[16]

The Timeline of Daniel

Daniel gives us quite a bit of information to use in forming a timeline of the latter days:

---

15 Abingdon's Strong's Exhaustive Concordance of the Bible, (Nashville: Abington Press, 1984), word #6663, p. 130
16 See Ezek 11:1-12, 34:1-10; Is 28:7-8; Jer 5:26-28, 31, 6:13; Is 1:10-17, 23

- 2300 period during which the sacrifice, *qodesh* and host are affected
- 1260 days from the time the *Nagid* to Come confirms the covenant, to when the Abomination of desolation is set up
- 1260 days (time, times and half a time, or second half of the week) for the time of distress, during which the Insolent King rules
- 1290 days from the time the Abomination is set up until the seventh trumpet harvest of Revelation 14:16 (i.e., the end of the witnesses' ministry, which is 1260 days)
- 1335 days from the Abomination of Desolation until Christ's millennial kingdom is set up

The first issue is the 2300 time period mentioned in Daniel 8:13. The Hebrew doesn't actually use the term "days," but rather says, "2300 evening morning." The expression "from evening until morning" is consistently used to refer to the worship cycle of the temple services in Leviticus and Numbers and because the context here is the temple sacrifice, 2300 could be the number of sacrifices missed during the transgression. Since there were two sacrifices each day, evening and morning, the actual number of *days* referred to would be 1150. This was, in fact, the case with Antiochus. According to records kept by the priests of that day, from the point of his desecration, Antiochus controlled the temple for 2300 evening and morning sacrifices, i.e., 1150 days, as calculated using the Greek calendar that was employed during the reign of the Seleucids.[17] If we assume that control of the future temple also begins at the establishment of the Abomination, then 1150 days would fall short of the 1290

---

17   Fred P. Miller, "The 2300 Day Prophecy of Daniel 8,"pp.4-6, Moellerhaus Publications, http://www.ao.net/ ~fmoeller/ 2300.htm. From the time the idol was erected in the temple until the rededication was 3 years and 10 days. Using the 360 day year and assuming that two of the three years contained an intercalary month of 30 days each, Miller arrives at 1150 days: (3x360)+(2x30)+10=1150

stated in Daniel 12:11 to be the period from the Abomination to the vindication of the *qodesh*.

The other option, 2300 literal days (roughly six years and four months), would cover most of the 2520 days of the entire seventieth week, thus including all of Al Mahdi's rule as well as most of As-Sufyani's, even before the Abomination is set up. Since the holy one asks about the trampling of the temple *and* the host, we could go back to Daniel 8:10 as the first mention of the host being trampled, which definitely takes place before the Abomination is set up. This would be the persecution of the Jews and Christians under As-Sufyani's proxy, the *Nagid* to Come. This same 2300 day time period could also be applied historically to Antiochus if we consider his control of the temple to begin at the appointment of his proxy, Menelaus. Although the precise date of his installation is unknown, it was a little over six years from the time he took over the high priesthood until the Maccabees cleansed the temple.

The second issue is what period the 1290 days cover. We know from Daniel 12:7 and Revelation 13 that Al Mahdi's reign will last for 1260 days, but do the extra 30 days fall before or after this period? They must come before, since according to Daniel 12:11, the 1290 days begin at the time the Abomination of Desolation is set up—that is, before Al Mahdi is established. This makes perfect sense, since there must be a period during which As-Sufyani still controls the empire while the two battle it out. This is confirmed in Daniel 11:32-45, where As-Sufyani continues military action for some time after the Abomination of Desolation is set up. It's during this thirty day period that the Jews (the woman of the Revelation 12) are persecuted and Al Mahdi gathers support for his battle against As-Sufyani. This is further supported by the 42 month rule of beast out of the sea in Revelation 13, which is only established after the war with Michael (Dan 12:1) and the persecution of the Jews (Rev 12, Dan 11:31-35).

Sufyani's rule-----Abom. set up-------→Mahdi's rule--------7th trumpet--------→Christ's rule
(1260 days)   (30 days)   (1260 days)   (+45 days = 1335 days)
                         Persecution
                         and Battles

5

Could it Really Happen Soon?

<u>The Feasibility of As-Sufyani</u>

All of the types we've been discussing are interesting, but how realistic is it to expect that any of this could happen any time soon? The current "Arab spring" going on in the Middle East right now could easily serve as a catalyst to the rise of As-Sufyani. Instability is always a perfect breeding ground for the rise of tyrants, making governments subject to revolutions with their heroes and reactionaries. Think of the Islamic Revolution in Iran under Ayatollah Khomeini, who in turn influenced the founders of Hezbollah. Consider also the Iraqi dictatorship of Saddam Hussein, a leader of the revolutionary Ba'ath party whose ideology of Pan-Arabism and Arab socialism was directly opposed by Osama bin Laden, one of the founders of Al-Qaida. Given current events, and considering the violent fervor of Islamic extremism and the intense hatred between Sunnis and Shi'as, the scenario of a violent man growing to power in the Middle East seems completely within the realm of possibility.

Islamic prophecies describe two opposing tribes in Syria, one supporting As-Sufyani and one supporting Al Mahdi. This could be an allusion to the Sunni/Alawite Shi'a division within the country.

The minority sect that has controlled the military and government of Syria up until now are the Alawis, who are accepted by the Shi'as despite their belief in a system of divine incarnation (Ali being considered an incarnation of God), and certain shared practices with Gnostic Christianity.[1] In fact, their mysterious acceptance by Shi'as is most likely based on political convenience rather than religious commonalities: the Shi'as of Iran give financial support to both of Syria's proxies (Hamas and Hezbollah), in their pursuit to eliminate Israel. The Alawite sect gained power over Syria in 1966 and has used the ongoing war with Israel to justify an oppressive dictatorial "emergency rule" begun in 1963. As long as the conflict with Israel has continued, there's been a pretext for maintaining the police state and therefore Alawite control.[2] Some have feared that if the Alawite government were to sign a treaty with Israel, the Sunni majority of Syrian Muslims would accuse it of treason, possibly sparking a civil war. For these reasons, it's been speculated that as long as the Alawis control the government, there could be no peace agreement between Syria and Israel.[3] Especially if As-Sufyani is Sunni, he would have a source within Syria itself to draw on for a rebel militia against its government, since the majority of Syrian Muslims are Sunnis who deeply resent the Alawis, and might very well jump at an opportunity to overthrow them. It will be very interesting to see which Islamic countries support the present opposition armies in Syria and who will end up pulling the strings if Syria comes under a new regime. Such a shift would open up new possibilities of a peace treaty with Israel, and consequently a treaty between Israel and the Palestinians.

---

1   "Lebanon—Religious sects," p. 1, GlobalSecurity.org, http://www.globalsecurity.org/military/world/lebanon/religious-sects.htm
2   Michael J. Totten, No Peace without Syria, p4, http://www.commentarymagazine.com/blogs/index.php/totten/82001
3   Ibid.

Even if As-Sufyani doesn't arise from the current unrest in Syria, there's always the future possibility of war in the Middle East due to the growing lack of water because of drought and population increase.[4] In 1974, Iraq put troops on the Syrian border, threatening to destroy Syria's al-Thawra dam on the Euphrates because they needed more water, and the situation has only been worsening. Right now, Turkey controls water flowing to Syria and Iraq via their dams on the Tigris and Euphrates rivers, and has refused demands from the two countries that it increase the volume of flow.[5] A perfect opportunity for "seizing the kingdom by intrigue," may come if Iraq and Syria ever join forces against Turkey in order to procure more water for drinking, crops and hydroelectric power.

The Feasibility of the Nagid to Come

"The many" of Jason's day were the Hellenists, and the traditionalists who were tolerant of civic Hellenization as long as the temple could function intact. Just as David's covenant with God was confirmed in his covenants with the elders of Israel, Jason's covenant with Antiochus was confirmed in his "covenants" with the factions of Judea. It seemed to be the best of both worlds—autonomy of Judea's religious system for the traditionalists, but the Hellenization of its civic life with Antiochus' support. "The many" of the future could easily consist of the Palestinians and those actively pursuing peace with them and with Syria, as well as those who are willing to pay any price to rebuild the temple and revive the Sandhedrin and temple worship. Of course in modern Israel,

---

4   Larry West, Larry's Environmental Issues Blog, "Water Shortage in Iraq puts Millions of People at Risk," http://environment.about.com/b/2009/08/27/water-shortage-in-southern-iraq-puts-millions-of-people-at-risk, p.1
5   UPI.com, Energy Resources, "Turkey tells Iraq, Syria: No water", Sept. 4, 2009 http://www.upi.com/Science_News/ Resource-Wars/2009/09/04/Turkey-tells-Iraq-Syria-No-water/UPI-59381252095273/

there is neither king nor high priest, thus the question is raised as to who the *Nagid* to Come could be.

In the Israeli government today, there are two figure heads: the Prime Minister and the President. While the Prime Minister is the true political head of state, responsible for guiding foreign and domestic policy, the office of President consists of responsibilities affecting both the political and religious aspects of Israeli society—and his term is seven years. According to law, the president, who's considered to have a primarily symbolic role, may "neither intervene politically nor express personal views on issues that divide the public."[6] That being said, he has the potential to affect quite a bit both civically and religiously. From the political side, he 1) nominates the candidate for Prime Minister from the Knesset to be voted on by the cabinet, 2) selects a member of the Knesset to form the government (the executive branch), 3) appoints the President of the Supreme Court and judges to the secular civil courts, 4) appoints members to the Broadcasting Authority,[7] 5) appoints the Governor of the Bank of Israel, and 6) grants presidential pardons.[8] In addition, his signature is required on all laws not relating to his own powers, as well as on treaties that have been ratified by the Knesset. Finally, presidential consent is required to dissolve the Knesset at the request of the Prime Minister in cases where the government has lost its majority, preventing its effective functioning.[9] From the religious side, the president is responsible for appointing members to the Chief Rabbinical Council, and judges to rabbinical and Muslim courts, which decide on

---

6 Wikipedia, quoting the President of Israel's official website," The Function and Purpose of the Presidency," http://www.president. gov.il/Pages/default.aspx
7 According to the Israel Ministry of Foreign Affairs website, "Since its inception in 1967, Israel Television has been the country's principal and most influential channel of media communications."
8 Wikipedia, "President of Israel," citing paragraph 11a of the Basic Law: The Presidency, which was passed in 1964.
9 Wikipedia, "President of Israel," citing paragraph 29a of the Basic Law: The Government.

civil matters involving religious laws.

As for the possibility of a future president defying the law to be active politically, he would have a precedent in current President Shimon Peres of the Kadima party. Shortly after taking office in 2007, Peres (who as Foreign Affairs Minister of Israel was instrumental in negotiating the Oslo Accords in 1993) had a secret meeting in which he presented Palestinian Prime Minister and Finance Minister, Salam Fayyad with a plan to evacuate and transfer to the Palestinians 97% of the West Bank and several Arab Israeli cities located in areas that are internationally accepted as Israeli territory. Peres then presented the plan to top European Union Officials, Ehud Olmert (Prime Minister at the time, also Kadima), and top aides for Palestinian Authority President Mahmoud Abbas.[10] In addition, upon his inauguration, Peres created a stir when he publicly called on Israel to withdraw from the West Bank.[11] He has also been involved in religious politics, openly supporting Rabbi Yosef Sholom Elyashiv's call for Jews to stay off the Temple Mount.[12]

I'm not saying that the *Nagid* to Come will necessarily be the president of Israel, but it seems a reasonable possibility. Any treaty with Syria negotiated by the Prime Minister would have to be signed by the president, and if it includes the re-establishment of the temple worship, the president would be the one to legitimize a Sandhedrin court. It would be an amazing feat, but one he might only promise to the many for his seven year term, just as the *Nagid* to Come confirms the covenant with the many for seven years.

---

10 WorldNetDaily, "Peres holds secret meeting with Palestinian chief: Plan drafted by veteran politician would forfeit strategic West Bank," 8/21/2007, http://www.wnd.com/news/article.asp?ARTICLE_ID=57256

11 WorldNetDaily, "Rabbis: 'Peres must repent': New president slammed for policies 'that will spill Jewish blood'", http://www.wnd.com/news/article.asp?ARTICLE_ID=56762

12 Worldnetnews.com, "Rabbi Elysashiv: Don't go to Temple Mount," http://www.ynetnews.com/articles/0,7340,L-3787113,00.html

The Feasibility of Islam as the Beast Kingdom

Hopefully you've been convinced by now that Rome will not be the source of the Antichrist. While it's conceivable that Western Europe could form a coalition against the Middle East in order to protect its oil interests or its security against nuclear threat, it makes no sense that it would attack Israel, a NATO ally, and establish a religious regime, beheading those who don't submit to their false religion as described in Revelation 13:15 and 20:4. Even if it did, what would its false religion be? Islam on the other hand, is a religion that directly opposes the tenets of both Judaism and Christianity. And it's certainly anti-Christ, denying the Trinity, the divinity of Jesus and His crucifixion and resurrection.

Syria, Lebanon, the Palestinians—all have voiced their animosity toward Israel, and Hamas, which holds the majority of seats in the Palestinian Authority parliament right now, denies in its own charter the right for Israel to exist as a nation.[13] Surely they would be more likely than Europe to betray a treaty and take violent action against Israel, especially given the context of the Hudna of Hudaibiya, Muhammad's ceasefire with the pagan Meccans in 628. Most Western historians agree that this ten year treaty, broken after only two, was a military strategy which gave Muhammad time to strengthen his forces under peaceful circumstances, then make his move against Mecca, claiming breach of contract as justification. Whether Muslims blame the Meccans for the breach, or acknowledge that Muhammad was the first to break the treaty, the Hudaibiya treaty has come to be seen as an acceptable strategy even in modern times—the ultimate "ends justify the means;" after all, the life of Muhammad is a perfect example of how Muslims

---

13 "Hamas Charter: The Covenant of the Islamic Resistance Movement (Hamas)," 1988, MidEast Web Historical Documents, p. 2, http://www.mideastweb.org/hamas.htm

should live their lives, and Mecca's conversion to Islam was the outcome intended by Allah.[14]

This attitude was evidenced by PLO chairman Yasir Arafat who, after signing the Oslo Accords with Israel in 1993, defended his actions to outraged Arabs by saying, "I see this agreement as being no more than the agreements signed between our Prophet Muhammad and the Quraish in Mecca," and "we now accept the peace agreement, but [only in order] to continue on the road to Jerusalem." This wasn't the last time he would refer to the treaty of Hudaibiya.[15] Perhaps the leader of Syria who finally covenants with Israel will justify it in this way as well.

The Ultimate Goal of Islam

But if anyone doubts that Islam has the elimination of Israel and world domination as its goals, one need only listen to the rhetoric of both Sunni and Shi'ite leaders:

"A message to our brothers in Palestine: I have hope that Almighty Allah, as I have been pleased with the victory in Egypt, that He will also please me with the conquest of the al-Aqsa Mosque, to prepare the way for me to preach in the al-Aqsa Mosque. May Allah prepare the way for us to (preach) in the al-Aqsa Mosque in safety—not in fear, not in haste. May Allah achieve this clear conquest for us. O sons of Palestine, I am confident that you will be victorious."[16]

---

14 Daniel Pipes, "Al-Hudaybiya and]Lessons from the Prophet Muhammad's Diplomacy," Middle East Quarterly, September 1999, http://www.danielpipes.org/316/al-hudaybiya-and-lessons-from-the-prophet-muhammads, p. 3

15 Daniel Pipes, Middle East Quarterly, Sept. 1999, http://www.danielpipes.org/316/al-hudabybiya-and-lessons-from-the-prophet-muhammads

16 Big Peace, Al-Qaradawi Leads Friday Prayers in Cairo, Prays for the Conquest of Jerusalem http://bigpeace.com/amutarjim/2011/02/19/al-qaradawi-leads-friday-prayers-in-cairo-prays-for-the-conquest-of-jerusalem/

--Shaykh Yusuf al-Qaradawi,
Spiritual leader of the Muslim Brotherhood
February 18, 2011, following Mubarak's
relinquishment of the Egyptian government

"Allah has chosen you for Himself and for His religion, so that you will serve as the engine pulling this nation to the phase of succession, security, and consolidation of power, and even to conquests through da'wa [preaching] and military conquests of the capitals of the entire world. Very soon, Allah willing, Rome will be conquered, just like Constantinople was, as was prophesized by our Prophet Muhammad. Today, Rome is the capital of the Catholics, or the Crusader capital, which has declared its hostility to Islam, and has planted the brothers of apes and pigs [Jews] in Palestine in order to prevent the reawakening of Islam. This capital of theirs will be an advanced post for the Islamic conquests, which will spread through Europe in its entirety, and then will turn to the two Americas, and even Eastern Europe. I believe that our children or our grandchildren will inherit our Jihad and our sacrifices, and Allah willing, the commanders of the conquest will come from among them. Today, we instill these good tidings in their souls, and by means of the mosques and the Koran books, and the history of our Prophet, his companions, and the great leaders, we prepare them for the mission of saving humanity from the hellfire on the brink of which they stand."
--Hamas Member of Palestinian Parliament
and Cleric Yunis Al-Astal
Al-Aqsa TV (Hamas-Gaza) April 11, 2008

"We must declare that Palestine, from the Jordan River to the Mediterranean Sea, is an Islamic land, and that Spain—Andalusia—is also the land of Islam. Islamic lands that were occupied by the enemies will once again become Islamic. Furthermore, we will reach beyond these countries, which were lost at one point. We proclaim that we will conquer Rome, like Constantinople was conquered once, and as it will be conquered again, Allah willing. We will rule the world, as has been said by the Prophet Muhammad. We will face a battlefront that is broader and stronger. Its beginnings were in Palestine, in Iraq, in Afghanistan, and in Chechnya. What has begun will be completed. It will not stop. The Zionist entity reached completion, and it is beginning to decline, until it will wane and come to its end. Similarly, America has occupied, thundered, and foamed with rage, and proclaimed like Pharaoh, 'I am your supreme god,' but it will come to its end, and they have begun to realize that their end is near. We have begun to read in American and European newspapers that 'our glory is on the wane, and there is nothing to do about it.' This morning on Al-Jazeera TV, I saw American scientists and strategic theoreticians, who said that America would soon come to its end. They said it before about the USSR, and indeed it has come to its end, and we say now that America and the EU will come to an end, and only the rising force of Islam will prevail."

--Sheik Ali Al-Faqir, former Jordanian minister of Religious Endowment, Al- Aqsa TV (Hamas-Gaza) May 2, 2008

In a speech broadcast by Iranian TV in July of 2004, Iranian President Mahmoud Ahmadinejad said:

"The message of the Islamic Revolution is global, and isn't restricted to a specific place or time. Have no doubt. Allah willing, Islam will conquer what? It will conquer all the mountain tops of the world..."[17]

---

17   YouTube, Ahmadinejad: Islam will conquer the world video, Iranian TV, 7/2004

The Methods Employed by Islam in Jihad

Further evidence that the Antichrist will be Islamic is that the martyrs in Revelation are beheaded (20:4), a form of execution prescribed in the Koran for unbelievers: "...Smite ye above their necks and smite all their finger tips off them." (8:12)[18] And again in 5:36: "The punishment of those who wage war against God and His Apostle, and strive with might and main for mischief through the land is execution [clarified by the translator to be beheading], crucifixion or the cutting off of hands and feet from opposite sides or exile from the land."[19] It's often argued that these Koranic verses were meant to be applied only in war; this is small comfort when the last recitations received by Muhammad commanded as a religious obligation *offensive* war against those who aren't Muslims. Surah 9:29 specifically targets Christians and Jews: "Fight those who believe not in Allah nor the Last Day...nor acknowledge the Religion of Truth from the People of the Book, until they pay the Jizyah [penalty tax] and feel themselves subdued [as dhimmis[20]]." Especially interpreted in the context of Muhammad's deathbed injunction, "Let not two religions be left in the Arabian Peninsula," the application of jihad as a doctrine is given wider field, and by extension, the Koranic verses pertaining to it.

In addition to the beheading of unbelievers, Shari'a law specifies that Muslims who commit apostasy are to be executed (decapitated); if an apostate somehow escapes such punishment by authorities, Shari'a law grants that a citizen can perform it with

---

18 Abdullah Yusuf Ali, *The Meaning of the Holy Qur'an*, Aman Publications, Beltsville, MD, 2006
19 Ibid.
20 The dhimmi status under Muhammad consisted of such discriminations as paying a penalty tax, being required to wear identifying clothing, to yield the road to Muslims, live in ghettoes, being barred from certain types of jobs and not being given equal justice under the law. For more details regarding dhimmi status of present day Islamic states, see Samuel Shahid, "rights of Non-Muslims in an Islamic State," http://www.answering-islam.org/NonMuslims/rights.htm

impunity.[21] Today, the only government still using decapitation as a form of execution is Saudi Arabia, with Yemen, Iran and Qatar retaining it on their books as explicitly allowable.[22]

Finally, if Western Europe is to be the source of the Antichrist, why is there no mention of it in the Old Testament prophecies of God's judgment on Israel's enemies? Instead, the nations who help the Antichrist against Jesus and the saints are confined to the Middle East and Islamic Central Asia.[23] In fact Kittim, considered to be the peoples of Cyprus and the coastlands of the Mediterranean (i.e., Rome), are those mentioned in Daniel 11:30 as coming against As-Sufyani.

Modern Signs of the Nagid's People

The process of corruption by the *Nagid*'s people has already begun. In 1967, after taking back Jerusalem, Israeli Defense Minister Moshe Dayan made a decision that would prove to be a curse to the Israeli government even to this day: he agreed to leave guardianship of the Temple Mount in the hands of the Islamic Waqf, as it had been during the British occupation. The Waqf now restricts the Jews' entrance to a single gate and escorts them off of the Mount if they have or wear anything that has Hebrew letters. Christians and Jews are generally restricted to tour groups. They're permitted at very limited times of the day, and not on any religious holidays or other days considered to be sensitive to the Waqf. They're escorted off the Mount if they bring any religious objects or show any sign that they're praying.[24] Islamic control of the Mount has led to many

---

21   "Apostasy or Riddah," Muhammadanism.org, http://www.muhammadanism.com/Government/ Government_apostasy_1.htm
22   Nina Shen Rastogi, "Decapitation and the Muslim World: is there any special significance to beheading in Islam?," Slate, http//www.slate.com/id/2211593
23   Walid Shoebat, "Islam and the Final Beast: a practical way of interpreting prophecy," pp.26-28, http://answering-islam.org/Walid/gog.htm
24   World Net Daily, 2005, "10,000 Jews to Ascend Temple Mount," http://www.

riots and violent attacks from both Jews and Muslims.

Another example of Israel's covenantal corruption comes in the concessions it's made to the Palestinian Arabs. As a result of global terrorist attacks and the political instability in the Middle East, the international community has been putting pressure on Israel to make peace with Syria and the Palestinians, and Israel has found itself caught between the proverbial rock and a hard place. It isn't within the scope of this book to discuss in detail the founding of the state of Israel and its ongoing conflict with the Palestinian Arabs. However, while most Westerners are aware that the Jews and Palestinians have been in conflict over the land of Israel since the day of its inception in 1948, few are familiar with some important facts which might change their opinion over who has legitimate rights to the region.

- Israel was the homeland of the Jewish people continuously for 1500 years. Some Jews have always remained on the land, even after the Diaspora at the hands of the Romans (when "Judea"—the very name from which is derived the term "Jew"—was renamed "Palestine" in an effort to annul their claim to the land). In fact, the cohesiveness of the scattered Jewish people is in large part due to the shared hope that they would one day return to their land. In contrast, the Arabs living in Palestine didn't claim any nationalistic identity as a people until the establishment of the state of Israel. Up until then and even a decade beyond, the word "Palestinian" was used almost exclusively to refer to Jews. Even after the establishment of the state of Israel, Ahmed Shuqeiri, who in 1964 would become the first PLO chairman, stated to the UN Security Council that the Arabs considered Palestine to be nothing more than southern Syria,

---

cephas-library.com/israel/ israel_10.000_plan_to_ascend_temple_mount.html

a sentiment shared by other Arab leaders at that time. In short, there has never been a Palestinian Arab nationality, language, or culture as distinguishable from the Arab states around them. "Palestinian" in its current use, had its origins as a nationalist movement imported from Egypt, Turkey and France for strictly political purposes. In the words of Zuhair Muhsin, late member of the PLO Executive Council, "There are no differences between Jordanians, Palestinians, Syrians and Lebanese. We are all part of one nation. It is only for political reasons that we carefully underline our Palestinian identity…Yes, the existence of a separate Palestinian identity serves only tactical purposes. The founding of a Palestinian state is a new tool in the continuing battle against Israel."[25]

- The aggressor of the 1948 war was the Arab League, consisting of Egypt, Trans-Jordan, Syria, Iraq, Lebanon and reinforcements from other Arab nations. On the very day the Palestinian British Mandate expired, they launched the war with the sole intention of thwarting the establishment of a Jewish state. Over 200,000 Arabs had already left by the time Israel was declared a state, with no indication by Arab leaders or the media that their exodus was forced.[26] Even so, according to various sources (including Arabs), the leaders of the Arab League evacuated many of the Palestinian Arabs on the assumption that it would be a temporary displacement during the fighting; the majority of these evacuees became those given refugee status by the UN.[27]

---

25 "The Peace FAQ: 'Palestinians', the Levant Arabs," http://www.peacefaq.com/palestinians.html, p. 14
26 Palestine Facts, "Israel's Independence Arab Flight: Why did Arabs leave the new State of Israel?" p.3, http://www.palestinefacts.org/pf_independence_refugees_arabs_why.php
27 For quotes and sources, see Rabbi Shraga Simmons, "The Refugee Issue," p.3, http://www.aish.com/ jw/me/48883137.html; Palestine Facts, "Israel's independence, Arab Flight," http://www.palestinefacts.org /pf_independece_

- The approximately 720,000 Palestinian Arabs who were displaced at Israel's inception were not descendants of Arabs who were historically tied to the land. Most were recent immigrants from Syria, Egypt and Iraq, looking to take advantage of the jobs created by those Jews who had immigrated to the land in the 1800's and early 1900's. In fact, by the end of the 1948 war, so few Palestinian Arabs qualified for refugee status under the UN (defined as those forced to leave their "permanent" or "habitual" home country), that it made a specific exception for them, granting refugee status to any Arab who had lived in Israel for as little as two years before the war.[28]
- Even from the start, the refugees' countries of origin have refused to allow them to resettle. In fact, Arab leaders continue to forbid any Arab country from accepting refugees, despite the numerous studies citing benefits to host countries, and millions of international relief dollars given to the Palestinian Authorities for the purpose. The claim by these countries that they had no room for their own refugees can be easily refuted by historical documents. For example, in 1949, an editorial from a Damascus newspaper stated that Syria needed 5 million people to work their land. By 1951, they were so desperate, they officially requested that the Egyptian government permit 500,000 agricultural workers to emigrate to Syria to develop land which would be given to them as their own property; significantly, the request was denied, because Egypt couldn't spare the labor.[29] So,

refugees_arabs_why.php
28   Ibid., p. 4, quoting Joan Peters, *From Time Immemorial: The Origins of the Arab-Jewish Conflict over Palestine,* 1984
29   Joseph E. Katz, Eretz Yisroel.org, "Palestinian Refugees, were denied resettlement opportunities, http://www.eretzyisroel.org/~peters/resettlement.html, p. 3, quoting Musamaret El Geib Newspaper (Cairo), June 3, 1951

instead of being permitted to return to their homelands, Palestinian refugees have been confined to refugee camps for six decades, and even those who have managed to gain entry into Arab nations to build normal lives have been denied citizenship. The only explanation for this behavior lies in the Arab declaration given at a refugee conference in Homs, Syria: "Any discussion aimed at a solution of the Palestine problem which will not be based on ensuring the refugees' right to annihilate Israel will be regarded as desecration of the Arab people and an act of treason."[30] Responsibility for the present Palestinian refugee problem can be laid on the shoulders of Arab leaders, as even King Hussein of Jordan stated in 1960, "Since 1948 Arab leaders have approached the Palestine problem in an irresponsible manner...they have used the Palestine people for selfish political purposes. This is ridiculous and, I could say, even criminal."[31]

- The international community continues to demand that Israel give up part of their one-tenth of one percent of the Middle East for Palestinian Arabs to make their own Islamic state, thereby adding to the 99.9 percent of the Middle East already controlled by Islam.

The reality is that Israel as a Jewish state must exist as a homeland for Jewish refugees from throughout the world, and the West should value it as the sole democracy in a sea of fascist Islamic states. Yet instead of supporting Israel, the global community demands that it give up a large portion of its land to a "Palestinian People" that doesn't exist, and who will never be satisfied until Israel is annihilated. Even many Christians support the "two state solution." Yet any Christian who believes in the Bible as divine

---

30 Ibid., p. 5, quoting Berlut al Massa (Lebanese daily), July 11-12, 1957
31 Ibid., quoting an Associated Press interview of January 1960

revelation must believe that the land was promised to Israel by God through Abraham, and that His promise will never be revoked. There are many Old Testament prophecies regarding the return of the remnant to the land—prophecies that had their partial fulfillment in the establishment of Israel as a state in 1948.

Unfortunately, Israel itself has inadvertently legitimized the Palestinian myth by participating in negotiations with the Palestinian Liberation Organization (PLO) and the Palestinian Authority (PA). In an attempt to bring peace to its citizens and stay on the good side of the international community, Israel has made concessions that may ultimately cause its demise. Even the ultimate compromise has been proposed by Israeli intellectuals and former politicians in the 2003 Geneva Accord, which among other concessions, called on Israel to re-divide Jerusalem and grant sovereignty over the Temple Mount to an independent Palestinian Arab state.[32]

There are many in Israel today who support Israel's attempt at treaties with the Palestinians and Islamic states simply because they're weary of conflict, and don't realize the spiritual implications of such a compromise. However, we must be very wary of those who are pressuring Israel to give up their Promised Land to Syria and the Palestinians in exchange for the illusion of peace. A quick glance at recent history demonstrates that when land is conceded, it only leads to more violence by the Palestinians: in the Oslo Accords of 1993, Israel granted the PLO autonomy over a large portion of Judea, Samaria and the Gaza Strip in return for the promise to recognize Israel's right to exist and to stop the Intifada against it. However, not only did Palestinian violence continue, but in fact, the Palestinian Arabs took advantage of their autonomy to create military and paramilitary armies exceeding what the Accords allowed.[33]

---

32   Palestine Pacts, Current Events Geneva Accor, What was the 2003 Geneva Accord agreement?, http://www.paletinefacts.org/pf_current_geneva_accord.php, page 1
33   Ynet News, "The State of Israel," p. 10, http://www.ynetnews.com/articles/0,7340,L-3284752,00.html

Again, in 2006, the year following Israel's disengagement from the Gaza Strip, the Palestinians launched four times the number of Qassam rockets from their territories into Israel than they had the year before.[34]

The Conspiracy

The Princes and the Prophets

Ezekiel gives us more details as to how the *Nagid*'s people will function:

Ezekiel 22:24-31:
[24]Son of man, say to her, "You are a land that is not cleansed or rained on in the day of indignation. [25]There is a conspiracy of her prophets in her midst, like a roaring lion tearing the prey. They have devoured lives; they have taken treasure and precious things; they have made many widows in the midst of her. [26]Her priests have done violence to My law and have profaned My holy things; they have made no distinction between the holy and the profane, and they have not taught the difference between the unclean and the clean and they hide their eyes from My Sabbaths and I am profaned among them. [27]Her princes within her are like wolves tearing the prey by shedding blood and destroying lives in order to get dishonest gain. [28]And her prophets have smeared whitewash for them, seeing false visions and divining lies for them, saying "Thus says the Lord God," when the Lord has not spoken...[31]Thus I have poured out My indignation on them; I have consumed them with the fire of my wrath; their way I have brought upon their head,"

---
34 Wikipedia, "Israeli-Palestinian conflict," p. 13, http://en.wikipedia.org/wiki/Israeli-palestine, quoting from Shiloah, le-heker ha-Mizrah ha-tikhon ve-afrikah, Mekhon, *Middle East contemporary Survey, Volume 11*

declares the Lord God.

When most Americans hear the word conspiracy, they immediately dismiss it as being an invention by irrational people who are paranoid or delusional; we're taught it's something that can't occur in a democratic government because it would require the consent of too many people. Yet here it is in prophecy: a conspiracy among princes, prophets and priests to "devour lives for dishonest gain."

Revelation also paints a picture of this conspiracy between the religious sector and the state. In the second seal, the red horseman is given the power to take peace from the earth that "they should kill one another." He's given a sword—not a *rhomphaira*, the most common New Testament metaphor for violence and dissension, but rather a *machaira*, which is specifically used to refer to the magistrate's sword (Acts 12:2; Romans 8:35, 13:4; Hebrews 11:37); this is in essence the executioner's sword, since certain magistrates could kill a man on the spot for any reason. Corresponding to the second seal is the second letter to Smyrna, in which the Church is told that they'll be persecuted and cast into prison apparently at the hands of "those who say they are Jews but are not, but are a synagogue [court] of Satan."[35]

In order to understand how a politico-religious conspiracy could ultimately succeed in turning modern democratic Israel into a dictatorship, one must understand that the State of Israel is defined as a Jewish state, so their parliamentary democracy doesn't have the separation of church and state associated with secular democracies. This means that political parties in Israel are defined not only by their political platforms, but also by their views on Jewish law. In addition, some elements of Israel's system are similar to those found in theocracies, specifically the religious courts. While secular courts handle criminal cases, the religious courts—Jewish, Christian

---

35 This will be discussed in more detail in Part Two.

and Islamic—are charged with judgment in civil cases involving marriage, divorce, custody, property and questions regarding conversion; they can have a huge impact on Israel's civic life.

The religious nature of Israeli politics, along with the jurisdiction of the religious courts, could easily lend itself to the type of conspiracy prophesied in Ezekiel, and can already be detected to some degree. For example, in 2006, due to complaints by the left wing Reform movement, Rabbi David Druckman was brought before the Chief Rabbinate for an unprecedented disciplinary hearing because he expressed dissent with the Israeli government regarding the Gaza/West Bank disengagement plan. Druckman said the hearing was retaliation for his "daring to speak God's word against handing over Jewish settlements in the Land of Israel to the worst of our enemies," which according to him, "is an unforgivable betrayal of the Torah of Israel, the people of Israel and the Land of Israel."[36]

In February 2009, Haaretz reported that the High Rabbinical Court, the highest of the official state Jewish religious courts, exposed their bias toward the Ultra-Orthodox camp when they stated in a decision that all Jewish people, including rabbis and religious court judges, are subject to the rulings of Ultra-Orthodox decisors. As the decision phrased it, "...All Jewish people are subject to their decisions, to do what they teach and not to stray from their teachings." The court panel was headed by Rabbi Avraham Sherman, who one year earlier nullified all conversions performed by the state's religious conversion court system, a decision which was being considered by the High Court of Justice at the time of the article.[37] By nullifying conversions, local rabbinical courts can (and do)

---

36   Maariv, Israel Behind the News: Israel Resource Review, "Rabbi Faces Unprecedented Disciplinary Hearing for Expressing Dissent," June 7, 2006, http://israelbehindthenews.com/bin/content.cgi?ID=2505&q=1
37   Yair Ettinger, "Rabbinical Court Proves Subservience to Ultra-Orthodox: Recent ruling relates to the important question of the source of the

force couples to get divorced, deem their children non-Jewish, and place them on the rabbinate's blacklist of those who have restrictions on whom they may marry.[38] The Likud party, which holds only one fewer seat in the Knesset than the majority Kadima party right now, supports the authority of the Orthodox Rabbinate in all matters of personal status and religious practice in Israel.[39]

As more Orthodox parties react against liberal attempts at peace with the Palestinians, an antidemocratic backlash can be detected in the government. In October 2010, the Israeli cabinet passed a watered down amendment spearheaded by Foreign Minister Avigdor Lieberman of the ultranationalist Yisrael Beitenu party, which would have required all new, non-Jewish citizens to take a loyalty oath to a "Jewish and democratic" state. In its original form, it would've required all current citizens to take the oath, stripping citizenship from those who refused. The Association for Civil Rights in Israel lobbied against the oath, stating that it was "but the latest example of antidemocratic laws that ostracize and delegitimize minority views..."[40] The amendment was killed in the Knesset, but Labor Knesset member Issac Herzog said that the strong support for the bill showed that fascism was "devouring the margins of society," and warned that Israel is on a "most dangerous slippery slope."[41] Many in Israel speculated that Prime Minister Netanyahu supported the bill in order to win Lieberman's backing

---

rabbinical courts' authority," Haaretz Daily Newspaper, Haaretz.com, published June 23, 2009, http://www.haaretz.com/print-edition/news/rabbinical-court-proves-subservience-to-ultra-orthodox

38 Ibid., p. 2
39 About.com, Judaism: "Primary Political Parties of Israel," p. 1, http://judaism.about.com/od/politics/a/ potparties.htm
40 Yahoo! News, "Critics: Israel loyalty oath undermines pluralism," Associated Press, Oct. 11, 2010, http://news.yahoo.com/s/ap/20101011/ap_on_re_mi_ea/ml_israel_stifling_dissent, p. 1
41 Haaretz.com, "Livni: Loyalty oath amendment is 'politics at its worst,'" Oct 10, 2010, http://www.haaretz.com/misc/article-print-page/livni-loyalty-oath-amendment-is-politics-at-its-worst, p. 1

of concessions in peace talks with the Palestinians, for example the extension of restrictions on Jewish construction on the West Bank.[42]

It's easy to see Israel's dilemma: on the one hand, the struggle to preserve itself as a *Jewish* state while granting citizenship to those who demand its annihilation, and on the other hand, the challenge of remaining a *democracy* while protecting itself from those citizens. It doesn't take much imagination to see where all of this could end up. Eventually Israel may be forced to decide which is more important to its survival: remaining Jewish or remaining democratic. Even if the government doesn't become downright fascist, the necessity of the Prime Minister to make concessions to extremists within parliament could mean such a diminution in civil liberties that it would be fascist in function, if not in name.

Even the anti-Christian government described in the letter to Smyrna (Rev2:8-11) would not be out of the question if the president and prime minister were in agreement regarding socio-politico-religious programs, and had a majority of radicals in the Knesset to back them. An example of such a party is the Ultra-Orthodox Shas, which has been proposing anti-religious freedom legislation since 1997 in an attempt to ban the distribution or possession of Christian literature, and make illegal both preaching the gospel, and changing one's religion.[43] In the future, the president could even

---

[42] Yahoo! News, "Critics: Israel loyalty oath undermines pluralism," Associated Press, Oct. 11, 2010, http://news.yahoo.com/s/ap/20101011/ap_on_re_mi_ea/ml_israel_stifling_dissent, p. 2

[43] Maoz-israel Ministries, "The intricacies of Passing a Law in Israel," Oct, 1998 http://www.maozisrael.org/site/News2?abbr=nav_&page= NewsArticle&id=5119. According to one bill presented, the distribution or possession of materials relating to the New Testament and Jesus as Messiah would be punishable by three months in jail. Another bill forbids preaching "with intent to change one's religion," would result in three years in prison or a $13,000 fine; it would also make it illegal to change one's religion. According to the article, this second bill "makes assurances that only those who preach 'under the shadow of the cross' would be affected by the law." Similar anti-religious freedom legislation was proposed as recently as 2007. (ASSIST News service, Dan Wooding, "Shas seeks harsher punishment for missionaries," http://www.assistnews.net/Stories/2007/s07030096.htm)

influence public television to push anti-Christian or pro-Islamic propaganda by appointing certain members to the Broadcasting Authority.

From those who now support treaties with the Arabs will ultimately arise the people of the *Nagid* to Come. They'll claim that Israel has entered the Messianic Age; they'll tell the people "'Peace, peace,' but there is no peace" (Jer 6:14), not only because disaster is on the horizon, but because they themselves will be oppressing those who don't support them. These people will not only be citizens, but religious and political leaders, as well as modern day "prophets"—the Sanhedrin, the new historians, economists and politicians.

The Priests

The prophecies of Daniel indicate that the third temple must be rebuilt, and although this seems very far from happening, it's become a very front-burner topic in Israel. Several organizations have been busy making temple robes and utensils according to the exact specifications of the scriptures, and efforts are being made to breed the perfect red heifer necessary to anoint the priests. Models and blueprints of the third temple have been designed,[44] and Jewish groups are even trying to impact public opinion through advertising. In March of 2010 for instance, a group called "Our Land of Israel" sponsored a campaign using posters on 200 buses in Jerusalem calling for the construction of the temple on the Temple Mount.[45]

However, perhaps the most important aspect of the temple system is the 71-man religious court called the Sandhedrin, which

---

44 "Third Temple Plans for Rebuilding in Jerusalem," http://www.squidoo.com/templejerusalem

45 J'lem posters call for 3rd Temple, Abe Selig, Jerusalem Post, 3/29/10, http://www.jpost.com/LandedPages/ PrintArticle.aspx?id=172008

has been reorganized. It's important to note that this entity hasn't been sanctioned by any orthodox religious authority in Israel, nor were the rabbis comprising it appointed by the president. It's not a functioning legal court at this point (although that's its ultimate goal), but rather a group of rabbis who are making moves towards re-establishing the temple worship.[46] In November of 2009, three rabbis from this Sanhedrin (of which at least some members have dubious backgrounds[47]) met with Adnan Oktar (also known as Harun Yahya), an influential Turkish author who's promoting the rebuilding of Solomon's temple on the Temple Mount. According to an interview on Radio Jerusalem, the purpose of their meeting was to discuss common ground in Jewish and Islamic doctrine that would allow a cooperative effort in building a temple to be shared by all religions. In a statement on their website,[48] the Sanhedrin justifies their dialogues with Muslims according to the Noahide tenet that, "All proper religion has a common foundation. At that foundation we are 'co-religionists' in bringing all mankind closer to G-d." This foundation is based on seven laws given to Noah after the flood, which according to the Noahides don't constitute a religion in and of themselves, but rather "set a universal [minimal] standard of proper religion and embody the truths that the peoples

---

46 According to Wikipedia, the group regards itself as a "provisional body awaiting integration into the Israeli government as both a supreme court and an upper house of the Knesset, while the Israeli secular press regards it as an illegitimate fundamentalist organization of rabbis." The group claims to be recognized and supported by the Jewish community, Wikipedia, "2004 Attempt to Revive the Sanhedrin," http://en.wikipedia.org/wiki/ 2004_attempt_to_revive_the_Sanhedrin

47 Rabbi Yosef Dayan is known to have threatened to put a death curse on Prime Minister Ariel Sharon, and Rabbi Yisrael Ariel was sympathetic to an extremist attempt to blow up the Dome of the Rock in the 1980's and wants Christians and Muslims expelled as "idolators." See Richard Bartholomew, "Sanhedrin Makes Link with Turkish Author to Oppose "the Unbelievers," 7/12/09, http://barthsnotes.wordpress.com/2009/07/12/ Sandherin-makes-link-with-turkish-athor-to-oppose-the-unbelievers/

48 "Statement of Jerusalem Court," pp. 3,4,6, http://www.thesanhedrin.org/en/index. php/ Hachrazah_5769_Tamuz_9

of the world must come to recognize and share." Later reiterated in the Torah given to Israel, they consist of: belief in one God, honoring that God, honoring all human life, the sanctity of the family (as laid out in codes of sexual morality), honoring private possessions, honoring God's creation, and maintaining social order through the establishment of Courts of Justice." According to their website, the goal of the Sanhedrin is to "struggle against the denial of Truth, especially against atheism, not against other believers…this will be done by forming an alliance of all conscientious people, namely, the righteous among Christians, and Muslims, along with devout Jews, who will come together and unite in this common cause… We are all the sons of one father, the descendants of Adam, and all humanity is but a single family. Peace among Nations will be achieved through building the House of G-d, where all peoples will serve as foreseen by King Solomon in his prayers at the dedication of the first Holy Temple." Their final call is, "Let us establish a house of prayer in His name in order to worship and serve Him together, for the sake of His great compassion."

Other Jewish groups have also been involved in dialogues with Muslims around the idea of a third temple. The Interfaith Encounter Association's Yoav Frankel says, "This vision of religious shrines in peaceful proximity can transform the Temple Mount from a place of contention to its original sacred role as a place of worship shared by Jews, Muslims and Christians."[49]

Of course such a paradigm shift for Muslims is probably years down the road; as of right now, Jews aren't even allowed to pray on the Mount. Even if through Oktar's influence Muslim public opinion changes, who knows what impact this would have on the religious authorities responsible for making such a project happen. What I find very interesting, however, is that Oktar has endeared himself to

---

49   Joel Richardson, "Muslim leader wants Temple Rebuilt," WorldNetDaily, http://www.wnd.com/ index.php?fa=PAGE.view&pageId=106055

Christians, Jews and Muslims by his very vocal repudiation of evolution. He's travelled all around the world, including many venues in America, to promote his voluminous work *The Atlas of Creation*, and has gained respect by people of all three faiths (despite authoring books under his pseudonym denying the Holocaust[50]). To have such a prominent Muslim, already acknowledged by Muslims, Christians and Jews, promoting the idea of cooperation in the building of this temple is unprecedented. It may be that a leader such as As-Sufyani himself will have to arise in order to achieve such an undertaking, but the fact that the Jewish Sanhedrin is open right now to discussions about sharing a temple with Muslims and other faiths is already an indication of their corruption. By focusing on the superficial commonalities between Muslim and Jewish doctrines, they're whitewashing the irreconcilable fact that the two don't worship the same God. When such a structure is finally built upon the Temple Mount, the *qodesh* will already be corrupt. Of course many revolutions are founded on the premise of peace and unity only to end in tyranny, and the ecumenical appearance of this Noahide covenant may be no different.

History Repeats Itself

The *Nagid* to Come and his people will have far reaching influence in the life of Israel both religiously and politically. The fact that the president plays such an important role in the Knesset and court systems creates a number of opportunities for conspiracy and corruption at many levels of government. Anyone questioning whether such a conspiracy could take place in a democratic government, has only to look at Hitler's rise to power in Germany's parliamentary system to understand how his "people" (some perhaps

---

50 *The Journal of Historical Review*, July-August 1997 (Vol. 16, No. 4), p. 35. http://www.ihr.org/jhr/v16/v16n4p35_Weber.html

unwittingly) contributed to his rise to power in a very short time: the Prime Minister of Bavaria who lifted the ban on the Nazi party, legitimizing it despite Hitler's failed coup against the government; Gregor Strasser, a member of the *Reichstag* (legislative body) who organized the Nazi party in northern Germany when Hitler was banned from public speaking; the interior minister of Brunswick who appointed Hitler administrator for the state's delegation to the *Reichsrat* (the other legislative body) in Berlin, making him a German citizen and so eligible to run for president; the industrialists and international bankers who influenced President Paul von Hindenburg to appoint Hitler chancellor of the coalition government, and who issued the "Reichstag Fire Decree" eliminating many German civil liberties. Von Hindenburg would twice dissolve the *Reichstag* (once at Hitler's prompting), which eventually led to the passage of the "Enabling Act," effectively transforming Hitler's government into a dictatorship. I'm not asserting that this exact thing will happen in Israel. I'm merely pointing out that if it's happened before, it most certainly could happen again, particularly with Satan's help.

Part Two:
The Dragon and the Beast:
Islamic Prophecies in Revelation

The book of Revelation is divided into four major parts: 1) the letters to the Church; 2) the seven seals; 3) the Little Book; 4) Christ's second coming. The letters give us insight into what's happening to the Church during each seal of the seventieth week. The seals describe events affecting the whole beast kingdom, while the Little Book "zooms in" on Israel during the second 3 ½ year period of the seventieth week.

6

Identifying the Seven Churches of Revelation

The Letters as Part of the Prophecy

Revelation 1:1-8

¹The Revelation of Jesus Christ, which God gave Him to show to His bondservants, the things which must shortly take place… ³Blessed is he who reads and those who hear the words of the prophecy, and heed the things which are written in it, for the time is near. ⁴John to the seven churches that are in Asia: Grace to you and peace, from Him who is and who was and who is to come; and from the seven spirits who are before His throne; ⁵and from Jesus Christ, the faithful witness, the first-born of the dead and the ruler of the kings of the earth. To Him who loves us and released us from our sins by His blood, ⁶and He has made us to be a kingdom, priests to His God and Father; to Him be the glory and the dominion forever and ever. Amen. ⁷Behold, He is coming with the clouds, and every eye will see Him, even those who pierced Him and all the tribes of the earth will mourn over Him. Even so, Amen. ⁸I am the "Alpha and the Omega," says the Lord God, "who is and who was and who is to come, the Almighty."

Revelation has long been avoided as sermon material because of its controversial interpretations; some even argue that it shouldn't be in the Bible at all. But although every prophet spoke about the end time, only three received their message directly from Christ Himself: Daniel, Ezekiel and John (compare Dan 10:5-6, Ezek 8:2 and Rev 1:10-18). In fact, Revelation shares a lot in common with Daniel and Ezekiel (not to mention all the other prophets and Christ Himself in Matthew 24), which confirms its authenticity. Maybe more importantly is that it's the only other book in the Bible apart from the Gospels in which Christ speaks directly to the Church; and yet amazingly, many Christians don't even bother to read it!

Revelation is often seen as consisting of two parts: the letters, written to seven historical churches in modern Turkey, and "the prophecy," which tells about the end days. But John includes the letters as part of the prophecy, and promises that anyone who reads Revelation and does what it says will be blessed. This is because prophecy is not just prediction of future events; it's God calling His people to repentance in order to avoid judgment. The letters are part of the prophecy because in them, Christ exhorts the Church to fulfill its mission before the rapture and His second coming. Just like the Old Testament prophets were God's mouthpiece to Israel, John is the prophet to the Church, the mouthpiece of Christ Himself. He says that if we read and do the things that Christ exhorts the Church to do in the letters, we'll be blessed by avoiding the worst of the worst; if we don't, we'll be as guilty as Israel and Judah who ignored their prophets.

Although Revelation was written to seven first century churches during a time of severe persecution, John also says it was written for the Church when the "time is near," and when the things in it must "shortly take place." Clearly this wasn't the case for the historical seven churches of Revelation. So why did He address His letters to them?

Seven Lampstands, One Church

Revelation 1:10-13; 16,20
[10] I was in the Spirit on the Lord's day and I heard behind me a loud voice like the sound of a trumpet,[11] saying "Write in a book what you see, and send it to the seven churches: to Ephesus and to Smyrna and to Pergamum and to Thyatira and to Sardis and to Philadelphia and to Laodicea." [12] And I turned to see the voice that was speaking with me. And having turned, I saw seven golden lampstands: [13] and in the middle of the lampstands, one like a son of man…[16] and in His right hand He held seven stars…[20] the seven stars are the angels of the seven churches and the seven lampstands are the seven churches.

The following evidence tells us that together, the seven churches of Revelation are a type of the end time Church:

- The trumpet was used to call Israel together both for war and worship, and here is Jesus' trumpet voice, gathering the Church of the end days to do battle against the antichrist kingdom.
- Starting with verse 4 John's opening address serves to directly refute the major tenets of Islam: in it, he confirms the doctrine of the Trinity and the sonship of Jesus; he makes it clear that Christ, not Muhammad, is God's faithful witness; he affirms Christ's crucifixion and resurrection for the atonement of sin; he declares that Christ, not Al Mahdi or the Prophet Jesus, is "ruler of the kings of the earth" with dominion forever; and finally, he declares that it is the Lord God (in Hebrew "Yaweh"), not Allah, who is the Almighty and the A-Z of all things.
- The image of Christ among the lampstands is a broad

symbol of His presence in the universal Church, rather than of seven specific churches in Asia. The number seven represents wholeness or completion in scripture. One school of thought says that these represent the universal Church throughout history, each one standing for a different Church era.[1] While correlations can be made, this isn't what they were primarily intended to represent, since the time was clearly not near in every era of the Church's history!

- Jesus exhorts each church to read all of the letters. Taken as letters to the historical churches, this would be especially strange, since the searing criticisms of Laodicea seem to have nothing to do with the praiseworthy churches of Smyrna, Thyatira and Philadelphia. However, this command makes sense if He were writing to the universal Church at the end, for the letters combined would give it a roadmap of what is to come.
- Each letter is addressed to the *angelos* or angel of a church. This word can refer to either a human or angelic messenger, and some think these were bishops or messengers who delivered John's letters. However, all the other New Testament church epistles were addressed to the entire church body, not to its Bishop or messenger; even John, in his portion of the greeting says, "to the seven churches that are in Asia." Others say the angels are heavenly angels that protect or somehow represent each church. But these are the same angels symbolized by the seven stars in Jesus' hand, indicating His favor and protection of them; this isn't His role with angelic beings. More importantly, however, is that the

---

[1] The seven Church eras are considered to be: 1) **Ephesian:** conclusion of apostolic era; 2) **Smyrnian:** Roman Emperors to Constantine (10 Roman persecutions); 3) **Pergamian:** Holy Roman Empire beginning with Constantine; 4) **Thyatirian:** Inquisition; 5) **Sardinian:** Church of the Reformation; 6) **Philadelphian:** missionary age; 7) **Laodicean:** present age.

flow of revelation always comes from a heavenly messenger to the prophet, not the other way around; if these angels to the churches are heavenly beings, how is it that Christ would be telling John to deliver a message to them to give to the churches? John says that Christ's voice sounds like flowing water and that a double-edged sword comes out of His mouth. Since water is used repeatedly as a symbol of cleansing and salvation, and the double-edged sword is symbolic of both judgment (Rev 19:15; Eph 6:17, Heb 4:12) and the division between believers and unbelievers (Matt 10:34), we are to understand that the cleansing salvation of the Lord will come to the Church by the words of exhortation He's about to give to the messengers. In scripture, this type of message was given to the people through the prophets, and that's exactly what these angels are: prophets to the Church of the end time, carrying God's message of exhortation, warning and comfort. They're not necessarily seven specific prophets, but those Christians at each stage of the seventieth week who understand the prophecy and are obedient to Christ; their word will reach many Christians in the Church who are falling away, as well as the many non-Christians who have no understanding of the signs of the age. These are the same stars of Daniel 8:10, those with insight who give understanding to the many in Daniel 11:33 and are said to shine like the stars forever because they lead the many to righteousness.

- Finally, each of the seven letters contains something that connects it to one of the seven corresponding seals.

The Document with the Seven Seals

Revelation 5:1-6
¹And I saw in the right hand of Him who sat on the throne a book written inside and on the back, sealed up with seven seals. ²And I saw a strong angel proclaiming with a loud voice, "Who is worthy to open the book and to break its seals?" ³And no one in heaven or on the earth or under the earth was able to open the book or to look into it. ⁴And I began to weep greatly, because no one was found worthy to open the book or to look into it; ⁵and one of the elders said to me "Stop weeping; behold, the Lion that is from the tribe of Judah, the Root of David, has overcome so as to open the book and its seven seals." ⁶And I saw between the throne and the elders a Lamb standing, as if slain...

According to William Barclay, "the only ordinary document that was sealed with seven seals was a will. Under Roman law the seven witnesses to a will sealed it with their seals and it could only be opened when all seven, or their legal representatives, were present."[2] This scroll is in effect, God's will and testament regarding the earth. In this case, only one person—Jesus Christ—breaks the seals, but He has "seven horns and seven eyes, which are the seven spirits of God." This means that He's the only witness to the terms within the scroll, and yet because He is God's perfect representative, He's worthy to break every seal. This will is our inheritance—it is the title to the earth.

In the time of John, when a person went bankrupt and had to sell his land, a document was drawn up that included the terms by which the *go-el* or "kinsman redeemer" could buy the land, thereby keeping it in the family and tribe. The title to the land, along

---

2   William Barclay, The Daily Study Bible series, *The Revelation of John*, vol 1, (Westminster Press, Philadelphia, 1960), p. 209

with the terms of the redemption, would be rolled up and sealed; only a relative that qualified under the law could break the seals to open the document and fulfill the terms of redemption. We are the debtors who sold our very souls to the devil in the garden, losing the earth in the fall. Satan holds title to the earth now as "prince of the power of the air." John weeps because he believes there's no one qualified to break the seals; he knows that if no one can open the book, the earth can't be redeemed, and everything he's suffered for the gospel's sake has been for nothing. But according to Revelation 5:9, Jesus is our kinsman redeemer, worthy under the law to break the seals because He bought us and the earth with His blood.

The number seven and its multiples seem to be especially tied to time. Consider these God-ordained sevens in the Jewish calendar: there are seven days of the week; the Sabbath is the holy seventh day; there are seven feasts of Israel, the first being Passover, celebrated on the 14th day of the first month (which was originally the seventh month, until God rearranged the calendar at the first Passover). The Feast of Unleavened Bread lasts for seven days; Pentecost is the day after seven Sabbaths are counted from the Feast of First Fruits; the Feast of Trumpets starts on the first day of the seventh month, and the Feast of Tabernacles on the 15th, a festival which lasts seven days. Every seventh year was a Sabbath year, a time of rest for the ground, and after seven Sabbaths of years was the time of Jubilee, when all land reverted to its original owner.

Likewise in Revelation, the "sevens" appear to be linked with time: seven seals corresponding to the seven years of the seventieth week of Daniel (though each seal does not necessarily correspond to one year); seven trumpets in the seventh seal; and seven bowls in the seventh trumpet. So if the scroll is the title to the earth, and Christ is our kinsman redeemer, then each broken seal is one step towards taking back possession of the earth. Since each letter corresponds to one seal, then each one contains a specific message for the Church during that period of the last week.

Remarkably, despite the proximity of all seven Asian cities addressed in the letters, every one of them was a very prominent city of culture, government or commerce in John's time. Each city is a type of Israel or Jerusalem under Islam, while each church is a type of the universal Church in that period; thus with each seal, we get a picture of the escalation of persecution within the beast kingdom, and with each letter, the progression of apostasy within the Church. Evidence points to the beast's capital (Babylon), being Jerusalem itself. If this is true, it could mean that the seven letters are written to the Church at Jerusalem, or at least in Israel. Since Jerusalem was the headquarters of the first century Church, the "mother Church" as it were, these would still go out to the universal Church.

7

The Seven Seals and Matthew 24: Seals 1-3

When the disciples ask Jesus in Matthew 24 what the signs will be of His second coming and of the end of the age, His answer aligns perfectly with the seven seals of Revelation; but instead of difficult to understand imagery, His explanation uses plain language and gives some nice details. Together the seals must represent seven years, with the midpoint coming sometime in the fourth, otherwise they have no real meaning. However, this doesn't necessarily mean that each one corresponds to a year. For example, although most appear to describe some period of time, the sixth seal is a single cosmological event. Similarly, the seven trumpets of the seventh seal can't be assumed to divide a year up evenly, as is demonstrated by the fifth trumpet, which lasts for five months. Secondly, it must be understood that the consequences of a broken seal don't necessarily stop once the next seal is opened; once broken, its effects continue throughout the week. This is evidenced by the Despicable Person of Daniel, who, although being the person that conquers in the first seal, clearly continues his wars and conquests until he comes to his end.

In the seven letters, we learn by Christ's exhortations what the Church is experiencing at each stage of the seventieth week. In the first four letters, He praises the Church for its strengths but warns it to repent of its sins in order to be ready for the rapture of the faithful at the fourth seal; in the fifth letter, those who are left behind are warned to prepare for the final rapture at the seventh trumpet, while in the sixth, Jewish Philadelphia is praised for its courage during Jacob's Trouble. Finally, Laodicea is warned to come back to Christ before He brings the kingdom.

The seven seals describe the big picture of what's going on in the Middle East. The first three are the birth pangs that will culminate in As-Sufyani's fourth seal attack on Israel and the start of Jacob's Trouble. It's a period marked by the persecution and falling away of the Church, particularly during the second and third seals. When the seventh trumpet of the seventh seal is about to be blown, the Little Book is opened. At this point, the narrative becomes topical. It describes the major figures and events of the second half of the week from their beginning at the Abomination of Desolation. This approach appears to confuse the chronology, until we realize that the narratives are placed here because the seventh trumpet marks the culmination of all the events they describe.

In the following chapters, each letter will be matched with its corresponding seal and discussed in relation to the Islamic prophecies. Because the events in the Little Book revisit the fourth, fifth and sixth seals, they'll be discussed after the sixth seal and the church of Philadelphia.

The Time of the First Seal

Islamic prophecy

As-Sufyani will come and establish himself. He'll go to Syria and raise a 30,000 man army there, with which he'll conquer Syria and

Iraq. Next he'll send armies to attack Iran, Afghanistan, Tajikistan, Turkmenistan and Uzbekistan, then go south to Mecca and Medina in Saudi Arabia.

The First seal: White Horse

Revelation 6:1,2
[1]And I saw when the Lamb broke one of the seven seals, and I heard one of the four living creatures saying as with a voice of thunder, "Come." [2]And I looked, and behold, a white horse and he who sat in it had a bow; and a crown (stephanos) was given to him; and he went out conquering and to conquer.

The white horse and laurel crown of the first horseman symbolize As-Sufyani's victory in battle. In John's day, when the Romans made a conquest, they would wear victors' wreaths and enter the city in chariots drawn by white horses; in the Old Testament, the bow is always the symbol of military might. Jesus predicted that many false Christs would arise and there would be wars and rumors of wars (Matt 24:6). Islam also predicts the rise of false Mahdis and prophets. No doubt false Messiahs will arise from within Islam, Judaism and Christianity, each with his own apostles.

The First Letter: Ephesus

Revelation 2:1-7
To the angel of the church in Ephesus write: The One who holds the seven stars in his right hand, the One who walks among the seven golden lampstands says this: [2]"I know your deeds and your toil and perseverance, and that you cannot endure evil men, and you put to the test those who call themselves apostles and they are not and you found them to be false; [3]and you have perseverance and have endured for my name's sake, and have not grown

weary. **⁴But I have this against you, that you have left your first love. ⁵Remember therefore from where you have fallen, and repent and do the deeds you did at first; or else I am coming to you and will remove your lampstand out of its place—unless you repent. ⁶Yet this you do have, that you hate the deeds of the Nicolaitans, which I also hate. ⁷He who has an ear, let him hear what the Spirit says to the churches. To him who overcomes, I will grant to eat of the tree of life, which is in the Paradise of God."**

Ephesus as a type of Jerusalem

Ephesus means "desirable," and Jerusalem certainly is desirable to Muslims. The ultimate goal of Islam is to reclaim this city, and when Al Mahdi conquers it, he'll make it the new capital of the Islamic Empire. Historically, Ephesus claimed the title of "the first and greatest metropolis of Asia," and was said to be Asia. It was such a center of commerce that Strabo referred to it as the "market of Asia."[1] Likewise, as the new capital of Islam, Jerusalem may have all the wealth and commerce of oil-rich Saudi Arabia transferred to it, with all the imports described in Revelation 18:11. In addition, Ephesus was dubbed the "highway of the martyrs" because Christians were taken through it on their way to the arenas of Rome; one day, Jerusalem will produce its own share of martyrs in the beast kingdom.

The Church at Ephesus as a Type of the First Seal Church

Discerning false apostles and hating the deeds of the Nicolaitans: Historically, the apostles were emissaries sent out by Christ to preach Him to those who didn't know Him, and to guide the churches in the true gospel; therefore a false apostle is one who

---

1   Barclay, *The Revelation of John*, vol 1, p. 70

preaches a false Christ or a false gospel about Jesus. Many of the epistles were written to get the churches back on the right track after exposure to such false apostles, in particular the various Gnostic sects. The Nicolaitans were among such heretics. Originally a deacon in the church at Antioch, Nicolaus taught that the "flesh must be abused." Although some believe that Nicolaus himself began the heresy, others say it was his followers who perverted his words to mean that man, by abusing his flesh with sinful indulgence, could keep his soul pure and grow in faith because grace would abound to cover his sins. In short, it was a doctrine of compromise; one could participate in the world and share in the grace of Christ simultaneously with no adverse consequences.

According to Jesus, the church at Ephesus was successful at discerning false apostles and their gospels, including the Nicolaitans. In the time of the first seal, these false Christs and their apostles will come from Muslims, Jews and even from within the Church itself. Sunnis may believe As-Sufyani is Al Mahdi, justifying his violence by the hadith which says that he will "beat [those in error] until they return to the truth." Jews may preach the *Nagid* of the Covenant or the *Nagid* to Come as the Messiah, praising him for re-establishing the temple worship and for bringing peace with Syria and the Palestinians. People within the Church will be promoting a false gospel too; the Nicolaitans of John's time are a type of those to come who will preach a gospel of compromise with the world and with Islam.

Already there are heresies within the mainstream Church that will pave the way to apostasy in the end time. Gnosticism is experiencing a revival today, even if it isn't explicitly identified as such. Some churches are preaching that Christ didn't have a physical resurrection, and others, like the Jesus Seminar, use unscholarly textual criticism to deny the real Jesus. Other heresies that have been attracting followers from mainstream denominations in the last few decades include the denial of the Trinity, espoused by Oneness

Pentecostals and various Church of God splinter groups, and the denial of eternal damnation. The latter may take a variety of forms, including Christian Universalism, Annihilationism and Conditional Immortality.[2] Corresponding more directly to the doctrine of the Nicolaitans is the so called "new evangelism," espoused even by some mainstream evangelicals, which in essence teaches that people of other religions don't need to abandon the religion of their culture in order to be saved; they can merely "add" Christ to their existing belief systems.[3] This has become a prevalent missionary strategy, particularly in Islamic countries where Christians are in danger of persecution and martyrdom.

You have endured for my name's sake, and have not grown weary, but you have left your first love: Most commentaries state that the love Christ mentions here is the church's love for Him, but this doesn't fit the context. A church that "toils, perseveres and endures for the sake of Christ's name" surely does so because it loves Him. Since the church of Ephesus is a type of the first seal church, it's reasonable that Paul's letter to the Ephesians would give us clues as to its shortcomings. In it, Paul reveals that the goal of the Church is to know the fullness of *Christ's love for us*, so that we can love each other. This fullness is achieved by the power of the Holy Spirit which brings about personal change in the believer's life, and builds up the Church in love and unity. Paul summarizes

---

2   Christian Universalism or Universal Reconciliation is the belief that in the end everyone on earth will be redeemed by Christ. This usually involves some sort of purgatory whereby sinners are cleansed by a defined period of punishment. Annihilationism claims that at the time of judgment, God will simply destroy the souls of those who don't have a relationship with him rather than condemn them to eternal punishment. Conditional Immortality revolves around the belief that the human soul is not created immortal, but is rather granted immortality by God upon a person's accepting Christ as Savior; in other words, this is how Christ gives eternal life.

3   Roger Oakland, "The New Look of Christian Missions," excerpt from his book *Faith Undone,* Lighthousetrailsresearch.com, (2007), http://www.lighthousetrailsresearch.com/blog/?p=212

this beautifully in 3:16-21: "[I pray that you may] be strengthened with power through His Spirit in the inner man; so that Christ may dwell in your hearts through faith; and that you, being rooted and grounded in love, may be able to comprehend with all the saints what is the breadth and length and height and depth, and to know the love of Christ which surpasses knowledge, that you may be filled up to all the fullness of God." According to him, it's this fullness of Christ's love—the power of the Holy Spirit working within us to do "exceeding abundantly beyond all that we ask or think" —that brings glory to Him in the Church (3:20-21). It's this love that allows the Church to love each other in all the ways Paul describes in the letter to the Ephesians, so that the world may know they are His disciples (John 13:35).

It's also this love for one another that overflows into love for the community at large. When the body of Christ ministers to each other through the gifts of the Holy Spirit—prophetic words, healing, prayer—that love is palpable by anyone who walks in the room. If the Holy Spirit is being neglected in the first seal church, then His works of power are not being manifested; the result is that it lacks unity and love, and fails to reveal Christ's glory to the world. According to Ephesians 4:13-16, it is also lacking the maturity needed to avoid being deceived by false doctrine, something that Paul feared (Acts 20:29-30), and that is progressively revealed in the seven letters of Revelation.

I will remove your lampstand from its place: Like historical Ephesus, the Church of the first seal will have orthodoxy, but it will have lost the knowledge of the fullness of Christ's love. Here, Christ exhorts it to repent. This is a call to revival—to rediscover the love of Christ through the gifts of the Holy Spirit in order to build up the Church in love and unity. If such a revival doesn't take place, God will remove His spirit altogether, and with it, the church as the lampstand that displays its light and fire.

To him who overcomes, I will grant to eat of the tree of life, which is in the Paradise of God: In Ephesians 3:6, Paul says that the Gentiles are "fellow heirs and fellow members of the body and fellow partakers of the promise in Christ Jesus through the gospel." Likewise, Jesus states that those who regain their love for each other and do the works they did at first (i.e., those who remain fellow members of the body), will be rewarded by eating from the tree of life in Paradise (i.e., will be fellow heirs and partakers of the promise).

Christ's Title to the Church

The One who holds the seven stars and walks among the lampstands: By calling Himself this, Jesus reminds the Church that He's always present among His people. By stating that the stars are in His right hand, He emphasizes that the prophets He has sent are true and speak with His power and authority. Through them, He gives the Church knowledge of Himself (Eph 4:11-15) and knowledge of what He's about to do (Amos 3:7).

The Time of the Second Seal

Islamic prophecy

While As-Sufyani is conquering the Middle East, a Caliph will die and there will be a struggle for the kingdom among three Caliphs, causing a civil war in Muhammad's nation.

Second Seal: Red Horse

<u>Revelation 6:3,4</u>
³And when he broke the second seal, I heard the second living creature saying, "Come." ⁴And another, a red horse went out and to him who sat on it was granted to take peace from the earth, and that men should slay one another; and a great sword was given to him.

This seal is described by Christ in His predictions of both civil war (nation against nation[4]) and international war (kingdom against kingdom) during this period (Matt 24:7). Muhammad also prophesied civil war in his "nation." He mentions Mecca and Medina specifically, but gives no indication whether it goes beyond Saudi Arabia to the countries of the Middle East, many of which now have Arabs as their majority ethnic group; of course the dragon of Revelation 12 includes Rome, giving us a clue that perhaps Muslims could take over Western Europe by civil war (more on that later). Obviously the civil war happening now in Libya, along with the unrest in Egypt, Syria, Afghanistan and Jordan are frighteningly portentous; depending on who ends up in control of these countries, Israel will be in a very dangerous position. This present time can't be the horseman of the second seal, however, which comes after As-Sufyani begins to conquer, although it's possible that the turmoil going on right now is the very catalyst that will bring him to power—the man of the hour who will calm the troubled seas and lead Israel to peace with Palestine and Syria.

As far as Saudi Arabia goes, there are currently three different parties: the terrorists; the regressionists, who desire a theocratic government and Shari'a law; and the progressives, comprised

---
[4] The term "nation" in the Bible is an ethnic, not a political designation. In fact, the Greek word translated here as "nation" is *ethnos*, from which English derives the words ethnic and ethnicity.

mostly of the royal family and intellectuals. This latter group tries to find a moderate ground in combining Islam and more secular aspects of modern society. If something were to happen to the royal family (and even among them there are opposing political philosophies), there very well could be a free-for-all for control of the government.[5] It's out of the violence and chaos of civil war that Al Mahdi is prophesied to come. Already, in the wake of the so-called "Arab spring," the people of Saudi Arabia are calling for reform, and King Abdullah is 87 years old and in poor health.

As mentioned earlier, the sword given to the red horseman is not simply that of violence and dissension, typically symbolized by the *rhomphaira*. Instead, it represents the authority to govern because it's the *machaira* used by the Roman magistrates. In other words, the violence is propagated by the empire's authority against those who are perceived as its enemies. As-Sufyani will ultimately command the fate of many nations, even if at this point it's only through the violence of his followers and proxies. By the second seal he hasn't yet shown his true colors by invading Israel, but if his type in Antiochus IV holds true, he'll control it through his proxy, the *Nagid* to Come, for according to the letter to Smyrna, Christians are being jailed and persecuted by the Jewish courts.

The Second Letter: Smyrna

Revelation 2:8-11
[8]To the angel of the church in Smyrna write: The first and the last, who was dead and has come to life says this: [9]"I know your tribulation and your poverty (but you are rich), and the blasphemy by those who say they are Jews and are not, but are a synagogue of Satan. [10]Do not fear what you are about to suffer. Behold, the devil

---

[5] Newsmax.com, Tawfik Hamid, "Strong Royal Family Vital to Keeping Saudi Arabia Progressive," http://ww.newsmax.com/tawkik_hamid/saudi_islam_muslim/2009/08/28/253591.html

is about to cast some of you into prison, that you may be tested and you will have tribulation ten days. Be faithful until death and I will give you the crown of life. ¹¹He who has an ear, let him hear what the Spirit says to the churches. He who overcomes shall not be hurt by the second death."

Smyrna as a type of Jerusalem

Smyrna was a wealthy city, where every aspect of culture flourished. It was so beautiful that it was called the crown, the ornament and the flower of Asia. Paralleling this, Gabriel refers to Israel as the "Beautiful Land" and the "Jewel of the empire" (Daniel 8:9; 11:20). In an ironic metaphorical parallel to Antichrist's capital, however, the gulf's cool west wind often carried the foul odor of the raw sewage that drained into it from the city.[6] It was a big producer of myrrh, for which it was named. Myrrh was a resin used in embalming and in the temple sacrifices and was therefore associated with suffering, sacrifice and death, which will all be a part of the beast kingdom.

The Church at Smyrna as a Type of the Second Seal Church

...your tribulation and your poverty, the blasphemy by those who say they are Jews but are a synagogue of Satan: Many of the Christians in the ancient world were poor because they were from the slave class, but many also lost their jobs because they refused to participate in the pagan worship and feasts associated with their trade guilds. In addition, according to Barclay, heathen mobs would sometimes attack them, destroying their homes and taking their possessions. However, most of the persecution of the earliest Church was at the hands of the Jewish leadership (Acts 13:50;

---

6   Barclay, *The Revelation of John*, vol. 1, p. 89

14:2,5; 14, 19; 17:5), and historically there was a large population of Jews in Smyrna who had extreme animosity towards the church. Like in many cities, the apostles drew converts from either Jews or "God-fearers," gentile seekers in the synagogues. In Smyrna, this brought down severe persecution on believers. Jewish leaders would alert Roman authorities of Christians' withdrawal from pagan social customs as a threat to the fabric of society, which would result in their arrest for sedition and other crimes against the empire. This was the same method used to get Christ crucified.

The devil is about to cast some of you into prison: Only the government can put people into prison, and in Israel it's the president-appointed religious courts that deal with issues of religious conversion. The term *synagogue* means "assembly" and is usually thought of as being the area where men gathered to discuss the scriptures. However, it's also used various times in the scriptures to refer to the assembly of the Jewish religious courts (e.g., Matt 10:17, Luke 12:11, Acts 9:2; 26:11). In the letter, Christ makes it very clear that Smyrna's poverty and persecution will come at the hand of the corrupt synagogue. If the Shas party of Israel finally gets its legislation passed, this "synagogue of Satan" will be able to imprison Christians for preaching the gospel and arrest its citizens for converting to Christianity.

Be faithful until death and I will give you the crown of life: Not only will many in the Church be imprisoned during this period, but some will die. The promised reward to the overcomers in Smyrna is a *stephanos*, the victor's laurel, along with the promise that they won't be hurt by the second death.

Christ's Title to the Church

The First and the Last, who was dead and has come to life: an apropos title in writing to those who are about to suffer and die.

This is the promise of resurrection unto everlasting life for those in the Church who overcome, those who "shall not be hurt by the second death."

The Time of the Third Seal

Islamic prophecy

There will be severe drought, oppression, violence and immorality during the final days, causing people to seek Al Mahdi.

Third Seal: Black Horse

Revelation 6:5,6
⁵And when He broke the third seal, I heard the third living creature saying, "Come." And I looked and behold, a black horse; and he who sat on it had a pair of scales in his hand. ⁶And I heard as it were a voice in the center of the four living creatures saying "A quart of wheat for a denarius, and three quarts of barley for a denarius; and do not harm the oil and the wine."

In Matthew 24:7, Jesus predicts famine. Here it is in the third seal, and someone is controlling the rations. A denarius was equal to a day's wage, and a quart of wheat makes one loaf of bread. Can we even imagine spending a day's wages on a loaf of bread? As As-Sufyani consolidates his kingdom, he'll control the oil of the Middle East, which will significantly affect the West. If he and his followers can control limited resources, such as oil and water, they'll have a lot of power in the end time. This ability to control the flow of goods is something that will later serve Al Mahdi in his campaign of

the mark; severe hunger and deprivation can lead a person to make choices he wouldn't otherwise make.

According to Barclay, the comment about not harming the oil and the wine is about the wealthy remaining wealthy: the staples that the common man must have in order to survive are unavailable, and yet even in the midst of deprivation, the rich still have their luxuries.[7] According to Daniel, As-Sufyani will distribute plunder among the kings, buying his enemies and rewarding his supporters. I'm sure these will have plenty of bread, wine and oil.

The Third Letter: Pergamum

Revelation 2:12-17
[12]And to the angel of the church in Pergamum write: the One who has the sharp two-edged sword says this: [13]"I know where you dwell, where Satan's throne is; and you hold fast My name and did not deny my faith, even in the days of Antipas, My witness, My faithful one, who was killed among you where Satan dwells. [14]But I have a few things against you, because you have there some who hold the teaching of Balaam who kept teaching Balak to put a stumbling block before the sons of Israel, to eat things sacrificed to idols and to commit acts of immorality. [15]Thus you also have some who in the same way hold the teaching of the Nicolaitans. [16]Repent therefore; or else I am coming to you quickly and I will make war against them with the sword of my mouth. [17]He who has an ear, let him hear what the spirit says to the churches. To him who overcomes, I will give some of the hidden manna and I will give him a white stone, and a new name written on the stone which no one knows but he who receives it."

---

7   Barclay, The Revelation of John, vol 2, pp. 8-9

Pergamum as a type of Jerusalem

The name Pergamum means fortress, and it was in fact a fortress city, built upon a rocky hill. It was the administrative capital of Asia Minor and considered itself to be the "custodian and defender of the Greek way of life and the Greek worship of the gods."[8] As such, it was the center of worship for Zeus, Asclepios, and the cult of Caesar, which was an important unifying element of the Roman Empire. Pergamum can also mean "abundant marriage" (*per + gamos*), typifying Jerusalem as the center of Al Mahdi's "beast" worship, which will unify Sunnis and Shi'as, as well as Jews and Christians throughout the Islamic Empire.

By referring to Antipas, as "My faithful one, My witness who was killed among you where Satan dwells," Christ links the city to Jerusalem, where God's other faithful witnesses—Christ and the two witnesses of Revelation 11—are killed (Rev 11:8). Keep in mind that Jerusalem also has a fortress of its own—the Temple Mount—and when this is taken over by As-Sufyani and later Al Mahdi, it will become Satan's throne.

The Church at Pergamum as a Type of the Third Seal Church

...even in the days of Antipas: Although little is known about Antipas, tradition holds that John appointed him Bishop of Pergamum during the reign of Domitian, who headed up one of the most intense persecutions of the Church. Tradition says he was martyred by being roasted alive in a hollow bronze bull. "The whole world is against you," they reportedly told him and his reply was "Then I am against the whole world." He could be mentioned here as a type of the faithful Christian who's against everything worldly (*anti*, "against;" *pas*, "everything"). The significant thing here is that Christ is holding up Antipas to the Church as an example of a faithful

---

8   Barclay, The Revelation of John, vol. 1, p. 108

witness for Him: a man willing to be roasted alive for His sake. Jesus doesn't accept half-heartedness. He clearly states that if we deny Him before man, He'll deny us before the Father (Matt 10:33). But remember His promise, that He's with us always, even to the end of the age (Matt 28:20). If we keep our eyes on Him, He'll give us the strength we need to stay faithful to Him no matter what comes.

...you have there some who hold the teaching of Balaam and in the same way hold the teaching of the Nicolaitans: It would've been very difficult to maintain the true gospel in such an oppressively idolatrous environment as ancient Pergamum; the same will be true during the third seal. In this letter, Christ sets up a contrast between the first group as a true and faithful witness that holds onto His name and doesn't deny His faith, and the second group, whom He calls to repentance because they participate in false religions by "eating things sacrificed to idols." In every religious system, the sacrificial meal was eaten by the worshipers as a way of communing with the god and each other. One example of this in the first century Roman Empire was the guild feasts, in which sacrifices were made to the guild's patron god. Paul warned the Corinthians about participating in these feasts: "You cannot drink the cup of the Lord and the cup of demons; you cannot partake of the table of the Lord and the table of demons" (I Cor 10:21). Christians who refused to participate were denied membership to their guilds, which made it nearly impossible for them to earn a living.

Worshiping God and the god of a false religion at the same time is called syncretism, and Israel was constantly guilty of it; they worshiped Jehovah in the temple, but set up their priests in the high places to sacrifice to the Baals. Amos 5 discusses the Day of the Lord, and gives syncretism as a reason for His anger:

Amos 5:21-27
21"I hate, I reject your festivals, nor do I delight in your solemn

assemblies. ²²Even though you offer up to Me burnt offerings and your grain offerings I will not accept them...²⁵Did you present Me with sacrifices and grain offerings in the wilderness for forty years, O house of Israel? ²⁶You also carried along Sikkuth your king and Kiyyun, your images, the star of your gods which you made for yourselves. ²⁷Therefore, I will make you go into exile beyond Damascus," says the Lord, whose name is the God of hosts.

Eating food sacrificed to idols may be simply allegorical, but it may very well be literal too. By this time the temple worship in Israel will almost certainly be re-established, either as a joint venture with Muslims or with the Waqf controlling it to some degree.

As far as the Church goes, this syncretism is already identifiable in the "Emerging Church." In America, it's taken the form of more mystical experience, borrowing from eastern religions, the New Age and Catholic mysticism,[9] while in the Middle East, it involves a melding of Muslim practices and Christian belief. In fact, some "Messianic Muslims" who are said to have received Christ, "remain legally and socially within the community of Islam, referring to themselves as Muslims and they are, in fact, regarded by the Muslim community as Muslims."[10]

Right now, this movement might be on the fringe, but it won't be in Pergamum. The fact that Ephesus is commended for hating the deeds of the Nicolaitans, while at Pergamum they are actually a part of the Church, illustrates a progression towards apostasy. These are the ones described by Jude as having "crept

---

9   Roger Oakland, *Faith Undone: The emerging church...a new reformation or an end-time deception* (Silverton: Lightousetrails publishing, 2007)
10 Network for Strategic Missions, KnowledgeBase-#20263.This was an untitled article excerpted from a book slated to be published by Zondervan in 2007. http://www.strategicnetwork.org/index.php?loc=kb&view=v&id=20263

in unnoticed, those who were long beforehand marked out for this condemnation, ungodly persons, who turn the grace of our God into licentiousness and deny our only Master and Lord, Jesus Christ" (Jude 4). Though they once had insight, and would have shone like the stars in heaven forever (Dan 12:3), they are now "wandering stars, for whom the black darkness has been reserved forever" (Jude 13).

Let's look a little closer at this second group that Jesus addresses. According to the letter, both the Balaamites and the Nicolaitans hold to the same heresy—compromise and participation with the false religion of the regime. But why does Jesus present two different types for the same heresy? If we look at the historical figures, the only difference between them appears to be the targets of each group; while the Nicolaitans were Greek gentiles who taught their fellow Christians to participate in the orgies of pagan religious rites, Balaam taught Balak to put a stumbling block before the Jews through intermarriage with the Moabites.

Both *Balaam* and *Nicolaitan* mean "destroyer or victor over the people,"[11] while *Balak*, means "empty man." From this, an interesting typology emerges. We could say that in the Old Testament, Satan used Balaam, "destroyer of the people," to teach Balak, an "empty man," to encourage idolatrous marriage between Baal and the Israelites, thus denying them their inheritance. Accordingly, we see that in Pergamum, heretics within the Church teach syncretism to open-minded evangelists, who bring others into marriage with the false religion.

To him who overcomes, I will give some of the hidden manna and a white stone with a new name on it: The reward to the faithful within the Church of Pergamum during this time of intense famine is the hidden manna—spiritual food worth much more than anything the world could provide. According to Barclay, the Jews

---
11 Barclay, The Revelation of John, vol. 1, p. 81

had a tradition that when the Ark of the Covenant was lost at the destruction of Solomon's temple (early in the 6th century B.C.), Jeremiah hid its pot of manna in the cleft of Mt. Sinai and will come with the Messiah and retrieve the pot. Thus the hidden manna became associated with partaking of the Messianic age.[12]

The white stone offered as a reward to the Church of the third seal could have a couple of meanings: in court, the jury voted using black and white stones, the white being a vote for acquittal. But it could also correspond to the amulet carried by pagans which had a sacred name of their god on it to grant them protection from demons. It's unclear whether the name on the stone is Christ's (see Rev 3:12) or whether the overcomer gets a special name like Abram and Jacob did.

Christ's Title to the Church

From Him who has the sharp two-edged sword: While there are those who will ultimately fall away and leave the Church, there are also those who will fall away and remain to pollute her from within. This title of Christ here is a clear message that He can discern those who are not His own.

Hebrews 4:12 describes the word of God as being "sharper than any two-edged sword, and piercing as far as the division of soul and spirit, of both joints and marrow, and able to judge the thoughts and intentions of the heart." In Matthew 10:35, Christ says He came not to bring peace, but a sword, "For I came to set a man against his father and a daughter against her mother and a daughter-in-law against her mother-in-law; and a man's enemies will be the members of his household." This is what's described as happening during the birth pang period according to Matt 24:10: "...many will fall away and will deliver up one another and hate

---

12   Ibid., p. 117

one another."

There's an alternative interpretation of the two-edged sword in this letter. When Christ says He will make war against Balaam and the Nicolaitans with the sword of His mouth, He may be referring to Armageddon in Revelation 19:21, when the armies are "killed with the sword which came from the mouth of Him who sat upon the white horse."

8

Seals 4-5

The Great Tribulation and the Time of Distress

Daniel 11, Revelation 12 and Matthew 24 all agree that the Abomination of Desolation marks the beginning of a time of distress:

Daniel 11:45-12:1
^{11:45}And he will pitch the tents of his royal pavilion between the seas and the beautiful Holy Mountain; yet he will come to his end and no one will help him.^{12:1}Now at that time Michael the great Prince who stands over the sons of your people, will arise. And there will be a time of distress such as never occurred since there was a nation until that time.

Revelation 12:7,9, 13; 13:7
^{12:7}And there was war in heaven, Michael and his angels waging war with the dragon...⁹And the great dragon was thrown down... ¹³And [the dragon] persecuted the woman who gave birth to the male child...^{13:7}And it was given [to the beast out of the sea] to make war with the saints and overcome them; and authority

over every tribe and people and tongue and nation was given to him...

Matthew 24:15,16, 21-24, 29
¹⁵Therefore, when you see the Abomination of Desolation which was spoken of through Daniel the prophet standing in the holy place...¹⁶Then let those who are in Judea flee to the mountains... ²¹for then there will be a great tribulation such as has not occurred since the beginning of the world until now nor ever shall. ²²And unless those days had been cut short, no life would have been saved; but for the sake of the elect, those days shall be cut short. ²³Then, if anyone says to you, "Behold, here is the Christ," or "There He is," do not believe him. ²⁴For false Christs and false prophets will arise and will show great signs and wonders so as to mislead, if possible, even the elect. ²⁹But immediately after the tribulation of those days, the sun will be darkened and the moon will not give it light and the stars will fall from the sky and the powers of the heavens will be shaken.

Jesus seems to focus on As-Sufyani's attack as the Great Tribulation of Israel and confirms what we know in light of Islamic prophecies: the attack will be cut short by Al Mahdi (a false messiah), and will be immediately followed by the events of the sixth seal—just in time to authenticate him as Allah's chosen one. This passage confirms that seals 4-6 take place in rapid succession and reveals that the seventh seal trumpets could be blown throughout the entire 42 months of Al Mahdi's authority. With this new information, we can add the seals to our timeline:

| Seals 1-3 | 4 | 5 | 6, 7 | Trumpets | Bowls, Armageddon |

Sufyani's rule-----Abom. set up--------→Mahdi's rule-------7ᵗʰ trumpet--------→Christ's rule
(1260 days)   (30 days)   (1260 days)   (+45 days = 1335)
                                          Persecution   Campaign of
                                          and Battles   mark, Harvest rap,
                                                                                       qodesh cleansed

∽∂∾

The Time of the Fourth Seal

Islamic Prophecy

By the time Al Mahdi comes, As-Sufyani will already be established [i.e. in Jerusalem].

Fourth Seal: Ashen Horse

Revelation 6:7,8
⁷And when He broke the fourth seal, I heard the voice of the fourth living creatures saying, "Come." ⁸And I looked, and behold, an ashen horse; and he who sat on it had the name Death; and Hades was following with him. And authority was given to them over a fourth of the earth, to kill with sword and with famine and with pestilence [death] and by the wild beasts of the earth.

The fourth seal is the point when the Abomination is set up, and according to this timeline, the fifth and sixth seals will be broken within 30 days. In this passage, the term "Death" speaks of the physical aspect of death, caused by famine and the governments of the earth as they come under the control of As-Sufyani. Although the NAS translates the word *therion* as "wild beasts," "wild" is not there in the Greek. In fact, this is the same word used in Revelation 13 to describe the beast governments that arise out of the sea and land.

"Hades," on the other hand, speaks of the spiritual aspect of death. The word translated here as "pestilence" is actually the Greek word *thanatos*, which simply means "death." Given the context, this strange semantic construction (being "killed with death") can only mean the "second death," which is the damnation of the soul.[1] In Matthew 24:11-20, Jesus prophesies that the Church will slip into apostasy as false prophets arise, lawlessness increases, and people's love grows cold. We see all of this fulfilled in the letter to the Church of Thyatira, where the false prophetess Jezebel draws some into adultery with her to give birth to children who will be killed with *thanatos*.

The Fourth Letter: Thyatira

Revelation 2:18-29
[18]And to the angel of the church in Thyatira write: The Son of God, who has eyes like a flame of fire, and His feet are like burnished bronze, says this: [19]"I know your deeds, and your love and faith and service and perseverance, and that your deeds of late are greater than at first. [20]But I have this against you, that you tolerate the woman Jezebel, who calls herself a prophetess, and she teaches and leads my bond-servants astray so that they commit acts of immorality and eat things sacrificed to idols. [21]And I gave her time to repent; and she does not want to repent of her immorality. [22]Behold, I will cast her upon a bed of sickness, and those who commit adultery with her into great tribulation, unless they repent of her deeds. [23]And I will kill her children with pestilence

---

1 Although this term isn't used elsewhere in the New Testament, the concept is everywhere. In Revelation, it's used to refer to eternal damnation in 2:11, and specifically defined as the lake of fire in 20:14 and 21:8.

[death]; and all the churches will know that I am He who searches the minds and hearts; and I will give to each one of you according to your deeds. ²⁴But I say to you, the rest who are in Thyatira, who do not hold this teaching, who have not known the deep things of Satan as they call them—I place no other burden on you. ²⁵Nevertheless, what you have, hold fast until I come. ²⁶And he who overcomes, and he who keeps my deeds until the end, 'To him I will give authority over the nations; ²⁷and he shall rule them with a rod of iron, as the vessels of the potter are broken to pieces,' as I also have received authority from My Father; ²⁸and I will give him the morning star. ²⁹He who has an ear, let him hear what the Spirit says to the churches."

Thyatira as a Type of Jerusalem

Thyatira was a great commercial city, a center for dyeing and woolen goods. The city itself was indefensible because of its situation, but was important to Pergamum in that it would delay an invasion, giving the city more time to muster its own defenses.² It's possible that the name Thyatira was derived from a combination of *thura*, "door" and *teros*, "to watch or guard."

As the cloth was dipped in the dyes of Thyatira, so will the beast's capital be baptizing the souls of men into its false religion. Decisions will be made by every person in the empire: to die a martyr or to compromise and be physically saved at the cost of one's soul. Jerusalem itself will eventually become the door of the beast kingdom, guarded and fought for jealously first by As-Sufyani, and then by Al Mahdi and his armies.

---

2   Barclay, The Revelation of John, vol. 1, p. 125

The Church at Thyatira as a Type of the Fourth Seal Church

***I know your deeds, and your love and faith and service and perseverance, and that** that your deeds of late are greater than at first*: This letter marks a wonderful change in at least part of the Church. In previous letters, Christ rebuked the Church for their lack of love and faithlessness, warning them to do the deeds they did at first. Here at Thyatira, He commends them for their love, faith, service, perseverance and deeds *greater* than at first; in fact, Christ says that He places no other burden upon these obedient, faithful believers. They're a blameless bride, who has guarded her door (*Thura+teros*) from unholy elements that would creep in to destroy. Although Christ rebukes Thyatira for their tolerance of Jezebel and the apostates born of her lies, He doesn't appear to count it as a blemish against these faithful ones.

To [the overcomer] I will give authority over the nations; and he shall rule them with a rod of iron: In His millennial kingdom, Christ's throne will be in Jerusalem, thus He will appoint faithful saints to govern in other parts of the world. Among them will be these overcomers, to whom Christ promises to give the same authority that He's been given by the Father. Their rapture is shown symbolically at the midpoint of the week as the male child of Revelation 12 "who is to rule all the nations with a rod of iron." This same group is seen at the sixth seal worshiping God in heaven before His throne.

...you tolerate the woman Jezebel, who calls herself a prophetess, and she teaches and leads my bond-servants astray so that they commit acts of immorality and eat things sacrificed to idols. In Matthew 24:11-13 Jesus speaks of false prophets, and here in the fourth seal, is Jezebel, a self-proclaimed prophetess. There's no mention of the syncretism of Balaam and the Nicolaitans; those who started off as compromising their faith have now abandoned it altogether as they commit adultery with Jezebel.

The question is, who is this prophetess? Her type, the historical Jezebel, was the daughter of the king of Tyre and was so devoted to Baal that as queen of Judah, she set up altars to him and killed hundreds of God's prophets. When King Ahab wanted a vineyard adjacent to the palace, he offered to buy it from Naboth ("sprout"). But Naboth refused, saying that God had forbidden him to sell the inheritance of his fathers. In the end, Jezebel got the vineyard for Ahab by hiring false witnesses to accuse him of blasphemy and treason; for this he was stoned to death. If this type holds true, it could mean that the Jezebel of Thyatira will be powerful enough to rob new converts (sprouts) of their inheritance, either spiritual or physical, by falsely accusing them of blasphemy and treason. This would be confirmed by Ezekiel 13:18, which describes the prophetesses of that day "hunting down the lives of my people."

The incredible thing is that Thyatira "tolerates" her (the Greek word here is *aphiemi*, which has the connotation of pardoning). How is this possible? Jezebel would have to be someone very powerful and have a reputation for being Christian, otherwise the Church wouldn't pardon her apostasy. If this person or entity arises only in the latter days, it could be anyone or anything. But who would she be if she existed right now? What entity could we look at within the Church that calls herself a prophetess, the very mouthpiece of God? Who has clothed herself like a queen, lain with kings and killed Christians and Jews by falsely accusing them? And who, despite teaching unscriptural doctrines and preaching ecumenism with Islam, is still accepted by the rest of the Church as being Christian? I hate to say it, but it adds up to the Catholic Church, a monolith so powerful that in much of the world it's the very face of Christianity. It calls itself a prophet by putting its traditions on equal par with scriptures, even going so far as to claim the infallibility of ex-cathedra decisions of the Pope and Ecumenical Councils. Out of this belief have come such unscriptural doctrines as Mary's role as co-redeemer and co-mediator, as well as the adoration of the Eucharist. During the Catholic Church's rule over the Holy Roman Empire, she lay with every king imaginable, and promulgated the Inquisition, killing protestant Christians and taking over vast holdings. In fact, if Jezebel is the Catholic Church, the Protestant Reformation could be the chance of repentance that Jesus mentions. There are in fact growing signs of Catholicism's compromise with Islam, beginning in 1966 with its statement in the Vatican II *Lumen Gentium:*

"The plan of salvation also includes those who acknowledge the Creator, in the first place amongst whom are the Moslems: these profess to hold the faith of Abraham and together with us they adore the one, merciful God, mankind's judge on the last day."[3]

What the Council says in this statement is that Allah and Jehovah are one and the same. In fact, what they're actually saying is that it's possible to be included in the plan of salvation by worshiping only one aspect of one person of the Trinity—God as creator. What they fail to explain is how the Christian Jehovah, who in scripture reveals Himself as a Trinity and the heavenly father of the faithful, could possibly be the God of Islam, who categorically denies the Trinity, and forbids his followers to call him father.[4] The council goes on to back pedal, saying that although the Catholic Church "rejects nothing of what is true and holy" in other religions, it is "duty bound to

---

3 Timothy R. Furnish, "Is Dealing with Islam the Next Pope's Great Challenge," April 11, 2005, p.2, http://www.hnn.us/articles/11269.html

4 "(Both) the Jews and the Christians say, 'We are sons of Allah and His beloved'. Say: why then doth He punish you for your sins? Nay, you are but men of the men He has created."(Surah 5:18) "Certainly [the Christians] disbelieve who say: Surely Allah is the third of the three; and there is no god but the one God, and if they desist not from what they say, a painful chastisement shall befall those among them who disbelieve." Surah 5:73

proclaim without fail that Christ is the way, the truth and the life."[5]

Such is the doublespeak that has come to characterize the Catholic Church's stance on Islam, expressed by both its authorities and theologians. Pope John Paul II, in his book *Crossing the Threshold of Hope*, states: "As a result of their monotheism, believers in Allah are particularly close to us." Yet two paragraphs later he says that the theology of Islam is "very distant from Christianity," since it doesn't include the concept of redemption. About the Koran he says that "it completely reduces Divine Revelation...in Islam all the richness of God's self-revelation, which constitutes the heritage of the Old and New Testaments, has definitely been set aside."[6] To claim that the Koran *reduces* divine revelation implies that it nevertheless *is* divine revelation. But more to the point, it's not the *richness* of the Christian Bible the Koran sets aside, but its *truth*. Why does the Pope take such a dichotomous stance on Islam?

More recently, Pope Benedict XVI has worked very hard to undo the damage caused by his University of Regensburg speech in 2006, which brought down the wrath of the Islamic community (expressed, among other ways, through church bombings). In one attempt to smooth things over, in 2008, the Vatican hosted an unprecedented three day Catholic-Muslim summit, in which scholars from both religions hoped to heal the wounds of Regensburg and promote deeper understanding. In keeping with that spirit, the Pope made a trip to the Middle East in 2009, praying in Istanbul's Blue Mosque and speaking of his deep respect for the Muslim community. What's the message he hopes to send by praying in a Muslim mosque?

Here's another example, excerpted from Peter Kreeft's "Comparing Islam and Christianity":

---

5   Timothy R. Furnish, "Is Dealing with Islam the Next Pope's Great Challenge."
6   Paul II, *Crossing the Threshold of Hope*, (Alfred A. Knopf, inc., 1994), pp. 91-93

"Allah, of course, is the same God Jews and Christians worship... Islam neither merely simplifies Christianity nor merely adds to it [with the Koran], but reinterprets it—somewhat as Christianity does to Judaism. As the Christian interpretation of the Old Testament is not the same as the Jewish one, the Moslem interpretation of the New Testament is not the same as the Christian one; the Koran authoritatively interprets the New Testament as the New interprets the Old... What's missing is...Christ the Mediator between God and man. Mohammed and the Koran are essentially another Moses (lawgiver) and another law. What's missing is grace, salvation, redemption. What's missing is precisely the essential thing... Can Moslems be saved? They reject Christ as Savior; yet they seek and love God. "Islam" means essentially the "fundamental option" of a whole-hearted "yes" to God. Most Moslems, like most Jews, see Christ only through broken lenses. If God-seeking and God-loving Jews, both before and after Christ's Incarnation, can find God, then surely God-seeking Moslems can too, according to Christ's own promise that "all who seek, find"—whether in this life or the next. [7]

Like the *Lumen Gentium* and Pope John Paul II, Kreeft proceeds to point out that no man can come to the Father except by Jesus. Because of this, he says the Church should continue to preach the gospel to Muslims, in order to reunite its "separated Islamic brothers and sisters" to "our common Father."

So what is Kreeft doing here? He's making Islam acceptable by putting it on the same level as Judaism, proposing that it too is in essence Christianity without Jesus. But Kreeft is wrong to compare the error of Islam to that of Judaism: while Judaism denies that the New Testament fulfills the Old, Islam denies them both. To receive

---

[7] "Comparing Christianity and Islam," http://www.peterkreeft.com/topics-more/religions_islam.htm

Christ is Judaism's fulfillment, but Islam's undoing—why? Because Islam is *anti-Christ* at its very foundation! "Islam" is most decidedly not a whole-hearted "yes" to the God of Judaism and Christianity. Yes, individual Muslims can and will be saved if they receive Christ; but this is true for people of any religion. What exposes the error of Kreeft's position is that many Jews who receive Jesus keep their Jewish traditions which, along with the Old Testament, are confirmed and deepened by the knowledge of His atoning sacrifice. In contrast, a Muslim who receives Christ must either abandon the Islamic traditions and scriptures or deny everything Jesus said about Himself, including the very *possibility* of vicarious atonement (Koran 6:164; 17:15; 53:38-39).

It's impossible to know exactly what kind of relationship the Catholic Church will have with Al Mahdi, but it isn't so difficult to believe that it will be Jezebel. After all, what harm would it do to permit Catholics to say the *Shahada*[8] if Allah is the same god as Jehovah, and Muhammad is considered to be a legitimate prophet?[9]

I will cast her upon a bed of sickness, and those who commit adultery with her into great tribulation, unless they repent of her deeds. And I will kill her children with pestilence [death]: If Jezebel is the Catholic Church and her lovers are those in Thyatira who, like the "Emerging Church" today, want to be reunited, then their children must be those who are "converted" by them; and because Christ says they will be killed with death (of the spiritual variety), they must not truly know the Lord. Yet to those Christians who join themselves with Jezebel, Christ gives another opportunity to repent

---

8   The *Shahada* consists of the confession, "There is no god but Allah, and Muhammad is his prophet." Upon saying it, a person is considered to be converted to Islam.

9   In his article, "Is Dealing with Islam the Next Pope's Great Challenge?" p. 2, Timothy R. Furnish names three Catholic theologians who claim that Muhammad was a legitimate prophet who disclosed the God of the Old Testament to the Arabs: Hans Kung, Giulio Basetti-Sani and Michael Scanlon. http://www.hnn.us/articles/11269.html

before being cast into the Great Tribulation—a chance to turn back to Him in time for the rapture.

...the deep things of Satan as they call them: Obviously these apostates in the Church are not openly calling their rites and beliefs the "deep things of Satan;" there's no way the Church would tolerate that kind of blatancy. Historically, this term refers to the mystery religions of the first century, those which required initiates to undergo special ceremonies and learn the secrets of the religion; in other words, mysticism. In America, the "Emerging Church" that's springing from evangelical Protestantism is already committing adultery with Jezebel in large part through its focus on mystical experiences derived from the Catholic mystics of the third century through modern times. According to Roger Oakland in his book *Faith Undone*, this movement is undoing the Reformation by reinterpreting and placing less emphasis on scripture and reinstituting the trappings of the Roman Catholic Church: incense, candles, icons, the Eucharist (specifically devotion to Christ in the Eucharist[10]) and most importantly, mystical meditation in contemplative prayer—a.k.a. "the deep things of Satan." Oakland explains the similarities between the contemplative prayer of modern Catholic mystics and the transcendental meditation of eastern religions and Wicca, pointing out that they even share the same terminology.[11] He notes that through contemplative prayer, many have seen visions of the Virgin Mary, and come to the conclusion that all religions lead to God. He also quotes Richard Foster, one of the most influential and well-known evangelical Christians in support of contemplative prayer, who admits to its dangers, and suggests that a protective

---

10 Devotion of the Eucharist is the practice of blessing the bread and wine to transform it into the actual body and blood of Christ, then placing them on the altar to have the faithful worship Christ in the Eucharistic elements.

11 *Faith Undone*, "When West Meets East," and "Monks, Mystics and the Ancient Wisdom," pp. 81-121

prayer be said beforehand to chase away "dark and evil spirits."[12] Yet despite the admitted dangers, Foster still believes that "We should all, without shame, enroll in the school of contemplative prayer."[13]

Oakland also quotes Thomas Merton, one of the most revered Catholic monks as saying: "I am deeply impregnated with Sufism," and, "Asia, Zen, Islam, etc., all these things come together in my life. It would be madness for me to attempt to create a monastic life for myself by excluding all these. I would be less a monk."[14]

It must be pointed out that Sufism is the mystical sect of Islam, and in it they have what is called *Marifah* (sometimes referred to as *Gnosis* by Muslims[15]), defined as the "mystical intuitive knowledge of spiritual truth reached through ecstatic experience, rather than revealed or rationally acquired."[16] Sufis use various means to reach this, including meditation, ecstatic trance through music and whirling dance, and other rituals such as repeating the 99 names of Allah (often using Dhikr beads to keep track) and repeating passages from the Hadith and the Koran.

By identifying the dragon as Satan in Revelation 12, a clear association is made between the "deep things of Satan" and the religion of the beast empire: Satan first works through As-Sufyani, then transfers his power and throne to Al Mahdi as the beast out of the sea. With the beast out of the land, an unholy trinity emerges: the beast out of the sea (Al Mahdi), the dragon (Allah), who is worshiped because he gives his authority to the beast, and the false prophet (Prophet Jesus).

---

12 Ibid., p. 99, quoting from *Prayer: Finding the Heart's True Home*
13 Ibid., p. 100, quoting from *Celebration of Discipline*
14 p. 84, quoting from Mike Perschon, "Desert Youth Worker: Disciplines, Mystics and the Contemplative Life"
15 Hena Zuberi, "MM Treasures—Ma'arifah: Being Acquainted with Allah," http://muslimmatters.org/2011/04/10mm-treasures-maarifah-being-aquainted-with-Allah
16 "Marifah," http://www.nethelper.com/article/Marifah, p.l

Christ's Title to the Church

The Son of God, who has eyes like a flame of fire, and His feet are like burnished bronze: Fire is often associated with purging or purifying, especially in the context of tribulation and God's judgment (Isa 5:24, Zech 13:9, I Cor 3:13). The "flame of fire" in the Lamb's eyes are the seven Spirits of God (Rev 4:5). Isaiah 11:2 defines them as the Spirit of the Lord, wisdom, understanding, counsel, strength, knowledge and the fear of the Lord. By these "He will judge the poor, and strike the earth with the rod of His mouth." Because this letter marks the rise of Al Mahdi, it's very significant that Jesus calls Himself the Son of God, with eyes that burn with the Holy Spirit of God, a testimony to both the beast kingdom and the Christian apostates.

The feet are the source of a man's balance, strength and direction. For example, the scepter of Judah is between his feet (Gen 49:10); the priests' big toe was anointed with the blood of the ram (Lev 8:24); God is said to keep the feet of the saints (I Sam 2:9); when someone is victorious in battle, he places his feet on the defeated one's neck (Josh 10:24); God descended to earth with thick darkness under His feet (2 Sam 22:10), and the dragon will be trampled underfoot (Ps 91:13). Conversely, a man's feet may be almost gone (Ps 73:2), or go down to death (Prov 5:5); feet can be caught in a net, put in stocks; Christ's feet were pierced on the cross. Here we see His feet of "pure" bronze, glowing as if they've been in a furnace. He's passed through the purifying fire of His suffering, standing firm in the face of His test, and now stands firm in His power and authority as judge. Christ's expectations of the Church during its darkest hour are to be sons of God in the face of those who would strip away their inheritance; to maintain the fire of the Holy Spirit, which gives insight and discernment into the spiritual realities; and to stand firm in the Lord against all trials.

The Time of the Fifth Seal

Fifth Seal: Martyrs under the Altar

Revelation 6:9-11
⁹And when he broke the fifth seal, I saw underneath the altar the souls of those who had been slain because of the word of God, and because of the testimony which they had maintained; ¹⁰and they cried out with a loud voice, saying, "How long, O Lord, holy and true, will You refrain from judging and avenging our blood on those who dwell on the earth?" ¹¹And there was given to each of them a white robe; and they were told that they should rest for a little while longer until the number of their fellow servants and their brethren who were to be killed even as they had been, should be completed also.

Unlike the previous seals, this one doesn't trigger an action on the earth, but points to As-Sufyani's persecution of the saints both before and at the Abomination of Desolation (depicted in Revelation 12 by the dragon waiting to devour the male child). When it is broken, these Christians express their desire to be avenged. Notice that they're still souls, not yet resurrected. The vengeance they seek will come in the bowl judgments, thus Christ tells them to wait until the number of their brethren to be killed is complete. This is an indication that some of those in the remaining Church (i.e. Sardis, Philadelphia and Laodicea) will join them in martyrdom.

The Fifth Letter: Sardis

Revelation 3:1-6
¹And to the angel of the church in Sardis write: He who has the seven Spirits of God and the seven stars, says this: "I know your deeds that you have a name that you are alive, but you are dead. ²Wake up and strengthen the things that remain, which were about to die; for I have not found your deeds completed in the sight of My God. ³Remember therefore what you have received and heard; and keep it, and repent. If therefore you will not wake up, I will come like a thief and you will not know at what hour I will come upon you. ⁴But you have a few people in Sardis who have not soiled their garments; and they will walk with Me in white, for they are worthy. ⁵He who overcomes shall thus be clothed in white garments and I will not erase his name from the book of life, and I will confess his name before My Father, and before his angels. ⁶He who has an ear, let him hear what the Spirit says to the churches."

Sardis as a type of Jerusalem

At one time, Sardis was the capital of the Lydian empire and an advanced commercial city of incredible wealth, just as Revelation 18 indicates that the beast capital will be. Because of its position on a high plateau, surrounded by mountains with only one entrance across a narrow ridge, the historical city of Sardis was considered to be impregnable. In fact, not once but twice in history, the pride of the Sardinians would be their undoing, for they believed themselves so safe that they didn't even put guards at the entrance of the citadel. Both the Persians under Cyrus and the Greeks under Antiochus III would scale the ridge and conquer the city. So also will Al Mahdi think himself invincible, the ruler of the world, for "who is like the beast, and who can make war against him?" (Rev 13:4)

The name "Sardis" is plural because there were actually two cities, one on the plateau, and one below it on the plain. Israel today is said to have two contrasting capitals: the secular Tel Aviv with its high energy and night life, and the more sober religious center of Jerusalem. The beast's capital will also be a divided kingdom illustrated in the dichotomy of the harlot and the remnant woman. One more note of parallel between Sardis and the beast's capital: in Roman times, the city was destroyed by an earthquake, just as Jerusalem will be (Rev 16:18-19; Zech 14:5).

The Church at Sardis as a Type of the Fifth Seal Church

You have a name that you are alive, but you are dead… strengthen what remains: In the first four letters, Jesus first addresses the faithful in the Church, then gives a warning to those who aren't. To Sardis, however, He indicates that the whole Church is dead, with the exception of only a few who have not soiled their garments. This is because the faithful of Thyatira have been raptured, leaving behind those who have committed adultery with Jezebel.

What's surprising is that Sardis has a reputation of doing works that make it appear to be alive, yet Jesus says those deeds are unacceptable. According to Jesus in Matthew 7:21-23, "Not everyone who says to me 'Lord, Lord' will enter the kingdom of heaven, but *he who does the will of My Father* who is in heaven. Many will say to Me on that day, 'Lord, Lord, did we not prophesy in Your name, and in Your name cast out demons and in Your name perform many miracles?' And then I will declare to them, 'I never knew you; depart from Me, you who practice lawlessness.'" As the remaining unfaithful of Thyatira, these people have involved themselves with whatever "deep things of Satan" Jezebel teaches; thus Christ's exhortation to wake up is a call back to the true gospel.

I will not erase his name from the book of life: The consequence of not obeying Him is being erased from the book of life. This is a very sobering passage because it clearly states that a Christian can lose his salvation. In fact, this is the only church where the reward for repentance is that Jesus will *not* do something punitive. Even so, Jesus tells them that those who repent of committing adultery with Jezebel will have the same opportunity to prove their faithfulness as those who are newly converted at this time; but again it will be through their suffering and martyrdom.

This passage begs a question of any era, not just the seventieth week: what in our lives as Christians would cause Jesus to blot us out of the book of life? In I Corinthians 9:26-27, Paul states that even he isn't exempt from the possibility of such judgment, when he compares living in the faith to training for the Olympic games: "I run in such a way as not without aim; I box in such a way as not beating the air; but I buffet my body and make it my slave, lest possibly, after I have preached to others, I myself should be disqualified."

In this letter, Jesus indicates that we do in fact play a role in our own salvation. This contradicts a common belief held by some that salvation comes from the mere belief that Jesus is Savior, and what we do after that is of no consequence. Yet eternal life (which begins immediately upon receiving Christ) doesn't spring from *belief* in Jesus, but rather from *Jesus Himself*; only by being in Him can we draw life from Him. The same teaching is found in the gospels: "I am the true vine, and My Father is the vinedresser. Every branch in Me that does not bear fruit, He takes away; and every branch that bears fruit he prunes it that it may bear more fruit...Abide in me, and I in you. As the branch cannot bear fruit of itself, unless it abides in the vine, so neither can you unless you abide in Me. I am the vine, you are the branches; he who abides in Me and I in him, he bears much fruit for apart from Me you can do nothing. If anyone does not abide in Me, he is thrown away as a branch and dries up; and they gather them and cast them into the fire and they are burned (John 15:1-6)."

According to Galations 5:21-22, the fruits we are to bear are love, joy, peace, patience, kindness, goodness, faithfulness, gentleness and self-control. Notice that none of these fruits can exist in a vacuum; they are all expressed only through our relationship with other people—in other words, through our works. Works can be accomplished through our own power, yet Paul says that even acts of great sacrifice done without the Holy Spirit (and the love that only He can give us) are empty and dead, and profit us nothing (I Cor 13). In contrast, when we maintain a trusting, ongoing relationship with Jesus, then we are in Him, and His Spirit is in us. This means that technically, our works are not our own, but rather those of the Spirit bearing fruit in us and shining through us. This is essentially what it means to be a Christian (Matt 3:8, 5:14-16; John 13:35; Gal 2:20). This is why James makes the argument that works will spring from true faith: "What use is it, my brethren, if a man says he has faith but he has no works? Can that faith save him? If a brother or sister is without clothing and in need of daily food, and one of you says to them, "Go in peace, be warmed and be filled," and yet you do not give them what is necessary for their body, what use is that? Even so faith, if it has no works, is dead, being by itself. But someone may well say, 'You have faith and I have works;' show me your faith without the works, and I will show you my faith by my works. You believe that God is one. You do well; the demons also believe and shudder. But are you willing to recognize, you foolish fellow, that faith without works is useless (James 2:14-20)?"

In every one of the letters to the Church, Christ alludes to their works, often stating that they fall short before God; this is an indication that the Spirit is not in them. Scripture clearly teaches that we all stand before God at the end of time for our deeds to be judged (Rom 14:10; II Cor 5:10). Notice that when Jesus judges, he links those works done towards others to our relationship with Him: "For I was hungry and you gave me something to eat; I was thirsty and you gave me something to drink; I was a stranger and you invited me in; naked and you clothed Me; sick and you visited Me; in prison and you came to Me" (Matt 25:35-36). And likewise, "I never knew you; depart from Me, you who practice lawlessness" (Matt 7:23).

As His body, the Church is Christ's hands and feet on this earth: the testimony of our lives and the confession of our mouths are the very things that bring Satan down from his place as prince of the power of the air (Luke 10:17-20; Ephesians 3:10; Rev 12:11). In His graciousness, Christ gives the Church more opportunities to fulfill its purpose on this earth, that it may be blessed by His coming, and not ashamed.

If therefore you will not wake up, I will come like a thief: Since Sardis remains on earth during the Mahdi's 3 ½ year reign, Christ's admonition for it to wake up looks forward to the Feast of Trumpets, the Ten Days of Awe culminating in Yom Kippur (the day Christ returns in the clouds, depicted in Revelation 14). At the sounding of the trumpet, the following is read: "Awake you that are sleeping, and ponder your deeds; remember your Creator and go to Him for forgiveness…look well to your souls and consider your deeds; let each one of you forsake his evil ways and thoughts, and return unto the Lord, so that He may have mercy on you." Jesus says to Sardis that He'll come like a thief in the night to those who don't wake up and heed His warnings through the prophets. But those who are awake and waiting will be like the ten virgins who are prepared with their oil to meet the bridegroom.

You have a few people in Sardis who have not soiled their garments…He who overcomes shall thus be clothed in white garments: The white garments here are common clothes (in contrast to the priestly robes given to the martyrs), and symbolize salvation through the righteousness of Christ, given by Him as a free gift to cover our nakedness and shame. The Church has soiled their garments by committing adultery with Jezebel, while the few who haven't soiled their garments are those who come to Christ as a result of the testimony and rapture of Thyatira.

Christ's Title to the Church

He who has the seven Spirits of God and the seven stars: Because Christ possesses the wholeness of God's spirit—all discerning, all seeing, all present, and all powerful—He can assert His authority to judge the Church, even through the prophets which He holds in His hand.

9

The Sixth Seal

The Time of the Sixth Seal

Islamic prophecy

Al Mahdi is chosen and begins to gather an army of supporters in Saudi Arabia. Militias from around the Middle East begin to swear their allegiance to him, including one that defeated As-Sufyani's army in Iraq. From Saudi Arabia, he'll head to the Sea of Galilee where he'll be joined by even more supporters. On his way, As-Sufyani will send troops to attack him, but they'll be swallowed up by an earthquake between Medina and Mecca—a major sign to Muslims that he is truly the chosen one of Allah. He will fight As-Sufyani in Jerusalem and be victorious. Then he'll turn and conquer Turkey. Here, he'll be informed that Al Dajaal is on the move, so he'll return to Jerusalem and prepare to battle him from the Temple Mount. Al Dajaal will remain for 40 days or months.

At some point, faithful Muslims will receive another sign of Al Mahdi: on the first day of the month of Ramadan, the moon will be eclipsed, and in the middle of the month, the sun will be eclipsed. In addition, an earthquake will divide Medina into three parts, and the hypocrites will flee to Al Dajaal.

Sixth Seal: Earthquake, Sun and Moon Darkened, Stars Fall

Revelation 6:12-17
¹²And I looked when He broke the sixth seal and there was a great earthquake and the sun became black as sackcloth made of hair, and the whole moon became like blood; ¹³and the stars of the sky fell to the earth, as a fig tree casts its unripe figs when shaken by a great wind. ¹⁴And the sky was split apart like a scroll when it is rolled up, and every mountain and island were moved out of their places. ¹⁵And the kings of the earth and the great men and the commanders and the rich and the strong and every slave and free man, hid themselves in the caves and among the rocks of the mountains; ¹⁶and they said to the mountains and to the rocks, "Fall on us and hide us from the presence of Him who sits on the throne, and from the wrath of the Lamb; ¹⁷for the great day of their wrath has come; and who is able to stand?"

Revelation 12, which includes the events of the sixth seal, depicts an earthquake that swallows up the dragon's army, just as Islamic prophecy's earthquake swallows up As-Sufyani's army. The fact that a major earthquake is also described in the sixth seal makes it very possible that these are one and the same events. Because of this, I have put the Medina earthquake of Islamic prophecy at this point in the timeline; although its description fits the seventh bowl earthquake that destroys the city of Babylon in Revelation 18, there's no real evidence to support that Medina is Babylon. Another reason is that the prophecy has the people of Medina running to Al Dajaal. This couldn't happen after the seventh trumpet because the witnesses (interpreted by Muslims to be Al Dajaal) will already be gone, whereas here at the sixth seal, they've just arrived (more on this later). Like the scriptural earthquakes, the timing and shared location of the two Islamic earthquakes make it possible that they will be one and the same.

The seals up to this point have been all about mankind at the hands of As-Sufyani: conquest, civil war, famine, persecution. Now, it's God's turn. In Matthew 24:29 Jesus states that the cosmic events of this seal are a manifestation of the powers of heaven being shaken. Both the darkening of the sun and the earthquake are reminiscent of another time the powers of heaven were shaken: at Christ's crucifixion, and His resurrection, respectively. At this seal, the 144,000 Jews are sealed, foreshadowing the final victory of Israel.

The Sixth Letter: Philadelphia

Revelation 3: 7-12
⁷And to the angel of the church in Philadelphia write: He who is holy, who is true, who has the key of David, who opens and no one will shut and who shuts and no one opens, says this: ⁸"I know your deeds. ⁹Behold I will cause those of the synagogue of Satan, who say that they are Jews, and are not, but lie—behold I will make them to come and bow down at your feet, and to know that I have loved you. ¹⁰Because you have kept the word of My perseverance, I also will keep you [in] the hour of testing which is about to come upon the whole world, to test those who dwell upon the earth. ¹¹I am coming quickly; hold fast what you have, in order that no one take your crown. ¹²He who overcomes, I will make him a pillar in the temple of My God, and he will not go out from it anymore; and I will write upon him the name of My God, and the name of the city of My God, the new Jerusalem, which comes down out of heaven from My God and My new name."

Philadelphia as a Type of Jerusalem

According to Barclay, the city of Philadelphia was built with the express intention of being a missionary of Greek culture and language to Lydia and Phrygia, just as the beast's Jerusalem will be for Islam. The same earthquake that destroyed Sardis in A.D. 17, also hit ancient Philadelphia. However, instead of being left in peace to rebuild, as Sardis was, Philadelphia was plagued for years with earthquakes—tremors happened on a daily basis, causing many to abandon the city. Those who stayed would run out of buildings at the slightest tremor to avoid being crushed.[1]

Another connection to the historical city is the fact that Philadelphia was the last city to stand against Turkish invasion, a bastion of Christianity until halfway through the fourteenth century. The name of this city then is significant, since this is the last loyal Church of the seven, the Jewish Church who remains to preach the gospel in Israel throughout the Great Distress: *Philadelphia*, "one who loves his brother."

Philadelphia as a type of the Sixth Seal Church

I will cause those of the synagogue of Satan, who say that they are Jews, and are not, but lie—to bow down at your feet, and to know that I have loved you: This significant promise is evidence that Philadelphia is the Jewish Church, at least in part made up of the 144,000 who turn to Christ at the sixth seal. Imagine the encouragement they'll feel knowing that they'll finally be vindicated before their fellow Jews who spurned and persecuted them for following Jesus. Note the similarities between what Jesus promises to Philadelphia and this passage in Isaiah:

---

1   Barclay, The Revelation of John, vol. 1, p. 159

Isaiah 66:5
"But to this one I will look, to him who is humble and contrite of spirit, and who trembles at My word. Hear the word of the Lord you who tremble at His word: Your brothers who hate you, who exclude you for My name's sake, have said, 'Let the Lord be glorified, that we may see your joy.' But they will be put to shame."

I will keep you from the hour of testing which is about to come upon the whole world: By this, Jesus refers to the trumpet judgments starting in the next seal, during which we see the 144,000 kept safe from the scorpion locusts. At the seventh trumpet, Philadelphia will be taken up in the harvest rapture, thereby missing the bowl judgments on the beast kingdom.

Hold fast what you have, in order that no one take your crown: These courageous believers have already won their crowns and need only hold on to them for a little longer in order to overcome. Like the faithful of Thyatira, Jesus places no burden on the Church of "brotherly love."

He who overcomes, I will make him a pillar in the temple of My God, and he will not go out from it anymore: The vision of men hiding themselves from the great earthquakes and hailstorms of the latter time is very poignant given the history of ancient Philadelphia. This is God's guarantee of rest and safety for those who stay in Jerusalem, appealing to their fellow Jews to turn to Jesus.

I will write upon him the name of My God, and the name of the city of My God, the new Jerusalem, which comes down out of heaven from My God and My new name: The new city and temple spoken of here are those that descend out of heaven in Revelation 21. These are their inheritance.

Christ's Title to the Church

He who is holy, who is true, who has the key of David, who opens and no one will shut and who shuts and no one will open: The fact that Christ chooses this uniquely Jewish epithet to describe Himself to Philadelphia is more evidence that it's the Jewish Church. In fact, the reference is taken from Isaiah 22:22. This open door could refer to Philadelphia's evangelistic mission.

The 144,000

Revelation 7:1-4
[1]After [the breaking of the sixth seal], I saw four angels standing at the four corners of the earth, holding back the four winds of the earth so that no wind should blow on the earth or on the sea or on any tree. [2]And I saw another angel ascending from the rising of the sun, having the seal of the living God; and he cried out with a loud voice to the four angels to whom it was granted to harm the earth and the sea [3]saying, "Do not harm the earth or the sea or the trees until we have sealed the bond-servants of our God on their foreheads." [4]And I heard the number of those who were sealed, 144,000 sealed from every tribe of the sons of Israel [12,000 from each].

This is a very solemn event, almost as if all of creation pauses to watch with John as the 144,000 Jews are "sealed"—12,000 from "every tribe."[2] This sealing process is uncannily close to the one described by Ezekiel just before the Babylonian invasion:

---

2   The list that follows actually excludes the tribe of Dan, naming in its place, Manasseh, one of Joseph's sons. There's disagreement as to why this is the case, but whatever its name, the passage states clearly that no tribe is left out.

Ezekiel 9:1-6
¹Then he cried out in my hearing with a loud voice saying, "Draw near, O executioners of the city [Jerusalem], each with his destroying weapon in his hand." ²And behold, six men came from the direction of the upper gate which faces north, each with his shattering weapon in his hand; and among them was a certain man clothed in linen with a writing case at his loins. And they went in [to the temple] and stood beside the bronze altar. ³...And he called to the man... ⁴and said to him, "Go through the midst of the city, even through the midst of Jerusalem, and put a mark on the foreheads of the men who sigh and groan over all the abominations which are being committed in its midst." ⁵But to the others, He said in my hearing, "Go through the city after him and strike; do not let your eye have pity and do not spare. ⁶Utterly slay old men, young men and maidens, little children and women, but do not touch any man on whom is the mark; and you shall start from My sanctuary."

These 144,000 are Jews who receive Christ, the seal being the "Spirit of promise, given to us as a pledge of our inheritance" (Ephesians 1:13). This group then, comprised of Jewish believers, serves as a literary bridge between the Church in the seals, and Israel in the Little Book. As they do in Ezekiel, these marked people stay in Jerusalem, despite the slaughter going on around them, otherwise Christ wouldn't have to keep them during the distress, as He promises to do. The sealing of the 144,000 as the Church of Philadelphia is the final fulfillment of Joel's prophecy, a clear description of what happens in the sixth seal and the seven trumpets:

Joel 3:28-32
²⁸And...I will pour out my spirit on all mankind; and your sons and daughters will prophesy...³⁰and I will display wonders in the sky

and on the earth, blood, fire and columns of smoke. ³¹The sun will be turned into darkness and the moon into blood before the great and awesome day of the Lord comes. ³²And it will come about that whoever calls on the name of the Lord will be delivered. For on Mount Zion and in Jerusalem there will be those who escape as the Lord has said, even among the survivors whom the Lord calls.

These are the righteous and just of Isaiah 33, who live with the continual testing of the city. These have kept themselves chaste, followed the Lamb wherever He goes, and are blameless, with no lie found in their mouth (Rev 14:4-5). To them God promises that they'll see the Beautiful King and the restoration of Israel with their own eyes:

Isaiah 33:16-22
¹⁶...He will dwell on the heights; his refuge will be the impregnable rock; his bread will be given to him, his water will be sure. ¹⁷Your eyes will see the King in His beauty; they will behold a far distant land. ¹⁸Your heart will meditate on terror: "Where is he who counts? Where is he who weighs? Where is he who counts the towers?" ¹⁹You will no longer see a fierce people, a people of unintelligible speech which no one comprehends, of a stammering tongue which no one understands. ²⁰Look upon Zion, the city of our appointed feasts; Your eyes shall see Jerusalem an undisturbed habitation, a tent which shall not be folded...²²the Lord is our king; He will save us...

This passage is fascinating, in that it recounts some of the characteristics of the Antichrist and his kingdom: the foreign language of those who conquer; the "counting," possibly referring those receiving the number of the beast; the weighing, described in the third seal as one rationing food during the famine (notice how the righteous will be given bread and water); and the counting of towers, which is probably a reference to war, although it's tempting to draw out an interpretation involving minarets!

The Multitude of Gentiles

Chapter 7:9-17
⁹After these things I looked, and behold, a great multitude, which no one could count, from every nation and all tribes and peoples and tongues, standing before the throne and before the Lamb, clothed in white robes, and palm branches were in their hands; ¹⁰and they cried out with a loud voice, saying, "Salvation to our God who sits on the throne and to the Lamb." ¹¹And all the angels were standing around the throne and around the elders and the four living creatures; and they fell on their faces before the throne and worshiped God, ¹²saying, "Amen, blessing and glory and wisdom and thanksgiving and honor and power and might be to our God forever and ever. Amen." ¹³And one of the elders answered, saying to me, "These who are clothed in the white robes, who are they, and from where have they come?" ¹⁴And I said to him, "My lord, you know." And he said to me, "These are the ones who come out of the great tribulation, and they have washed their robes and made them white in the blood of the Lamb. ¹⁵For this reason, they are before the throne of God; and they serve Him day and night in His temple; and He who sits on the throne shall spread His tabernacle over them. ¹⁶They shall hunger no more, neither thirst anymore; neither shall the sun beat down on them, nor any heat; ¹⁷for the Lamb in the center of the throne shall be their shepherd, and shall guide them to springs of the water of life and God shall wipe every tear from their eyes."

There are only two options as to who this group of gentiles is:

the martyred Church, or the raptured Church. It seems unlikely that there would be two separate groups of martyrs, one under the altar, and one before God's throne. In addition, if they were martyrs, John should recognize them as he does the souls of the fifth seal martyrs, and would refer to them as such.

Verse 14 states that this gentile multitude comes "out of the Great Tribulation." According to Vine's Dictionary, the preposition "ek," often means "out of" or "from the midst of," but can also mean "from," in the sense of "away from."[3] While the timing of the rapture is unclear in this passage, the issue is resolved in the Little Book's symbolic image of the gentile Church's rapture: the male child avoids being devoured by the dragon (As-Sufyani's attack at the Abomination of Desolation), and is caught up before the beast rises out of the sea (the trumpet period). In fact, his rapture is the very thing that causes both, for it triggers the shift of heavenly powers spoken of by Christ in Matthew 24.

Although John describes seeing this spectacle at the sixth seal, it doesn't mean that the multitude arrived at this point. In fact, John sees a multitude that's been before the throne serving God "day and night in His temple." For literary purposes, they're placed at the sixth seal in order to explain why the 144,000 are being sealed: with the gentile Church gone, the mantle is passed to the Jewish Church to take over as witnesses to Israel. In fact, in the context of scripture, the multitude in heaven is praising God for the very victory this event represents: "Salvation to our God who sits on the throne and to the Lamb," and "Amen, blessing and glory and wisdom and thanksgiving and honor and power and might be to our God forever and ever, Amen."

One more reference to the multitude in Revelation indicates that they're already in heaven when the beast out of the sea (Al Mahdi) is given authority:

---

3   Vine's Dictionary, p. 831

Revelation 13:5-6
⁵**And there was given to him a mouth speaking arrogant words and blasphemies…**⁶**And he opened his mouth in blasphemies against God, to blaspheme His name and** *those who tabernacle in heaven*. **(italics indicate an alternate translation in the NAS)**

The Islamic Empire will blaspheme Jehovah, but it will also defame "those who tabernacle in heaven." Tabernacles are tents—temporary dwellings. Who in heaven lives in tabernacles? According to Revelation 7:15, God spreads His tabernacle over the multitude of Gentiles. In addition, they're holding palm branches, which are used to build tabernacles for the feast of Sukkos.[4] It only makes sense that Al Mahdi will have to explain to Muslims why so many Christians have simply disappeared; whatever excuse he gives, it will be slanderous.

---

4   Since Sukkos is a fall feast, this is perhaps an indication that Al Mahdi takes over in the fall.

10

The Little Book: Zooming in on Israel Midway through the Week

The Little Book covers the same material as seals 4-6, only this time from the perspective of Israel and the temple.

Revelation 10:1-7
¹And I saw another strong angel coming down out of heaven, clothed with a cloud; and the rainbow was upon his head, and his face was like the sun, and his feet like pillars of fire; ²and he had in his hand a little book which was open. And he placed his right foot on the sea, and his left on the land; ³and he cried out with a loud voice as when a lion roars; and when he had cried out, the seven peals of thunder uttered their voices. ⁴And when the seven peals of thunder had spoken, I was about to write; and I heard a voice from heaven saying, "Seal up the things which the seven peals of thunder have spoken, and do not write them." ⁵And the angel whom I saw standing on the sea and on the land lifted up his right hand to heaven, ⁶and swore by Him who lives forever and ever, who created heaven and the things in it, and the earth and the things in it and the sea and the things in it, that there should be delay no longer, ⁷but in the days of the voice of the seventh angel,

when he is about to sound, then the mystery of God is finished, as he preached to His servants the prophets.

Jesus is shown here having dominion over all creation, as well as victory over Israel (the land) and the gentiles (the sea). This passage bursts with meaning for Israel! Like in the days of Exodus, the Son is clothed with a cloud, and his feet like pillars of fire to once again lead His people out of the city which is "mystically called Sodom and Egypt" (Rev 11:8). In Revelation 18:4 He says, "Come out of her my people that you may not participate in her sins and that you may not receive of her plagues." And so, out of the bondage of Egypt, the Jerusalem of the beast, He will lead Israel to the promised land of the millennial kingdom; and out of Sodom, the city too wicked to save, He will rescue them from the rain of judgment's fire.

He comes from the presence of God, His face shining like the sun, like Moses off of Sinai, and around Him, the rainbow symbolizes His covenant with all nations through Noah. "'For this is like the days of Noah to Me; when I swore that the waters of Noah should not flood the earth again. So I have sworn that I will not be angry with you, nor will I rebuke you. For the mountains may be removed and the hills may shake, but My lovingkindness will not be removed from you, and my covenant of peace will not be shaken,' says the Lord who has compassion on you" (Isaiah 54:9). This Lion of Judah cries out with a lion's roar, and he "thunders with His voice wondrously, doing great things which we cannot comprehend" (Job 37:5).

The Little Book introduces six topical narratives of what happens in Israel beginning with the Abomination of Desolation and culminating at the seventh trumpet. These are : 1) the temple and the two witnesses, 2) the dragon, 3) the woman, 4) the male child, 5) the beast out of the sea, and 6) the beast out of the Land.

The Temple and the Two Witnesses

John as the New Ezekiel

Immediately after Jesus speaks of His prophets in verse 7, we have a description of John being told what to prophesy, and if we look at Ezekiel's visions, it's hard to miss the parallel:

Revelation 10:8-11
[8]"Go, take the book which is open in the hand of the angel who stands on the sea and on the land [Jesus]"...[9]And He said to me, "Take it, and eat it; and it will make your stomach bitter but in your mouth it will be sweet as honey."...[11]And they said to me, "You must prophesy again concerning many peoples and nations and tongues and kings."

Ezekiel 2:10
When He spread [the scroll] out it was written on the front and back; and written on it were lamentations, mourning and woe.

Ezekiel 3:1-3
[1]Then He said to me, "Son of man, eat what you find; eat this scroll and go, speak to the house of Israel."[2] So I opened my mouth and He fed me this scroll. [3]And He said to me, "Son of man, feed your stomach, and fill your body with this scroll which I am giving you." Then I ate it, and it was sweet as honey in my mouth.

Like his counterpart Ezekiel, John is told to eat the Little Book and, like Ezekiel, John finds it sweet in his mouth: there will be victory for Israel in the end. Yet like Ezekiel, lamentations, mourning and woe are written on it, making his stomach bitter.

Revelation 11:1-2
¹And there was given me a measuring rod like a staff, and someone said, "Rise and measure the temple of God, and the altar and those who worship in it. ²And leave out the court which is outside the temple, for it has been given to the nations; and they will tread underfoot the holy city for 42 months."

Ezekiel 40:3
So He brought me there [to the land of Israel] and behold, there was a man whose appearance was like the appearance of bronze, with a line of flax and a measuring rod in his hand; and he was standing in the gateway [and he measured the temple].

Ezekiel 43:9-12
⁹"Now let them put away their harlotry and the corpses of their kings far from Me; and I will dwell among them forever. ¹⁰As for you, son of man, describe the temple to the house of Israel, that they may be ashamed of their iniquities; and let them measure the plan. ¹¹And if they are ashamed of all that they have done, make known to them the design of the house, its structure, its exits, its entrances, all its designs, all its statutes and all its laws. And write it in their sight so that they may observe its whole design and all its statutes, and do them. ¹²This is the law of the house: its entire area on the top of the mountain all around shall be most holy. Behold, this is the law of the house.

The State of the Temple

John is told not to bother with the outer courts of the temple which will be trampled by the nations; instead, he's instructed to measure the inner temple, the altar, and those who worship there because they're all corrupt. The witnesses come for 1260 days to call Israel to repentance during the reign of Al Mahdi. What they find in the temple will be the same thing Ezekiel finds in chapter 8: 1) the "seat of the idol which provokes to jealousy," 2) men prostrating themselves toward the east, 3) wall carvings of unclean things and 4) women performing the mourning ritual for Tammuz.

The Seat of the Idol

No one knows for sure what is meant historically by "the seat" of the idol; perhaps it was a pedestal supporting an idol of Baal. In the future third temple, however there will be no idols, for Muslims are fiercely monotheistic. Instead there will be the Koran, displayed in the prayer sanctuary just as it is now, on a lectern called the *kursi* which means "seat" or "throne."

Prostration towards the East

Ezekiel describes men engaging in sun worship by prostrating themselves towards the east. Likewise, John sees Muslims facing the holy city of Mecca towards the east and performing the *salaat*, prostration in prayer.

Carvings on the Temple Walls

Each mosque has a *qibla*, the Mecca-facing wall where Muslims prostrate themselves in prayer. On the *qibla* is the *mihrab*, a decorative niche marking the focus of prayer. While the walls of the prayer sanctuary are often kept relatively plain, the front doorway and the *mihrab,* are usually highly decorated. While Muslims don't use animals or humans in their mosque artwork, they do use intricate geometric and floral patterns interspersed with calligraphy quoting important verses from the Koran. Ezekiel's description of insect and reptile carvings on the temple walls may not be a literal parallel with Islam's mosque decorations, but these specific creatures were considered by God to be unclean, and therefore match up with the blasphemous quotations of the Koran upon the mosque walls.

Ritual of Mourning

Finally, Ezekiel describes the ritual mourning of Tammuz, who was a Sumerian god in the area of modern day Iraq and was associated with Baal, and Hubal of the Arabs. Tammuz was a pastoral god, responsible for supplying a shepherd with green grass, healthy lambs and plentiful milk. There were two annual festivals around the cult of Tammuz, one celebrating his marriage to the goddess Inanna (in Akadian, Ishtar), and the other lamenting his death at the hands of demons from the netherworld. Shi'a Muslims also have a mourning ritual, called *Ashura*. Every year thousands of pilgrims gather at holy sites in Iraq to mourn the death of Imam Hussein, Muhammad's grandson who, in the 7th century, was beheaded by Sunnis in the battle of Karbala. This historical event is observed by reenactments of the battle by men dressed in medieval military uniforms. In addition, men sob, cut their scalps with blades and flagellate themselves with chains and whips tipped with sharp pieces of metal, while the women look on and wail.

Whitewash

In addition to the desecration of the temple, Ezekiel describes the attitudes and behavior of the people of Israel. He says that they act according to the ordinances of the nations around them (9:12), giving this as the reason for Judah's fall to Babylon. This parallels the defection of Israel to the "ordinances" of those Muslim nations surrounding it when Antichrist comes to power. He mentions that the prophets of Israel will mislead God's people by saying "Peace!" when there is no peace, a reference to Israel's covenant with Syria.

Ezekiel speaks of the "whitewashing" that will be necessary to allow such blasphemy and abominations to occur: "And when anyone builds a wall, behold, they plaster it over with whitewash."

All over the news there are Jewish and Christian organizations holding summits and gatherings to promote unity with Muslims. As I mentioned earlier, the Jewish Sanhedrin has even been discussing the possibility of making the third temple a cooperative effort with them. Yet by focusing on the superficially similar teachings between the religions, the essential incongruities are whitewashed, along with the fundamental Koranic teachings regarding jihad. Nowhere does our media discuss the vitriolic Arabic sermons and news talk discussions regarding Islam's sense of destiny to conquer the world, in which Jews are routinely referred to as "pigs and monkeys" and their historical ties to Israel are denied, along with the holocaust in many cases.

In the gospel, Jesus states that the road to life is narrow and difficult. The letter to Thyatira indicates that those who compromise with Islam are left behind to be purified by the fire of the Great Tribulation, while those who apostatize die the second death. There's no way to reconcile the beliefs of Christianity or Judaism to those of Islam; the closer to the dividing line, the greater the risk of compromise and apostasy later on. The same political correctness that has finally made acceptable many things prohibited by scripture, is paving the way to Israel's ultimate destruction.

There's also a literal parallel to this Ezekiel passage regarding the whitewashing of walls. Historically, when Muslims conquered a city, they converted the churches into mosques, whitewashing the walls to cover up Christian artwork. This could point to how easy it will be for As-Sufyani and Al Mahdi to take over the third temple. Similar to the *mihrab* of the Islamic mosque, Jewish synogogues have what's called the *Aron kodesh*, which means "holy ark," a highly decorated niche that houses the Torah. It's supposed to be on the wall facing Jerusalem, but in practice is often placed on the east wall of the synagogue. When the third temple is taken over, it will be very easy to convert the *Aron kodesh* into the *mihrab*, and to whitewash the walls to hide any trace that the temple was Jewish. Could this act in the temple be the Abomination of Desolation?

The Two Witnesses

Revelation 11:3-10
³And I will grant authority to my two witnesses, and they will prophesy for 1260 days, clothed in sackcloth. ⁴These are the two olive trees and the two lampstands that stand before the Lord of the earth.⁵ And if anyone desires to harm them, fire proceeds out of their mouth, and devours their enemies; and if anyone would desire to harm them, in this manner he must be killed. ⁶These have the power to shut up the sky, in order that rain may not fall during the days of their prophesying; and they have power over the waters to turn them into blood, and to smite the earth with every plague, as often as they desire. ⁷And when they have finished their testimony, the beast that comes up out of the abyss will make war with them, and overcome them and kill them.⁸And their dead bodies will lie in the street of the great city, which mystically is called Sodom and Egypt, where also their Lord was crucified. ⁹And those from the peoples and tribes and tongues and nations will look at their dead bodies for three and a half days, and will not permit their dead bodies to be laid in a tomb. ¹⁰And those who dwell on the earth will rejoice over them and make merry; and they will send gifts to one another, because these two prophets tormented those who dwell on the earth.

The two witnesses are Moses and Elijah, this day being foreshadowed by their presence with Jesus on the Mount of Transfiguration, and prophesied in Malachi 4:4-5. Their first purpose is to prophesy—to call Israel to repentance—wearing sackcloth, the Biblical sign of a grieved and repentant heart. Moses was both the giver of the Law, and the one who called Israel out of Egypt to be a nation under God in the Promised Land. Elijah, meaning "Yahweh is God," was the prophet who condemned Ahab and Jezebel, proving that Baal and his prophets were false (here we see that Jezebel's name in the letter to Thyatira is not arbitrary).

It's possible that these two men are not literally Moses and Elijah, but men fulfilling their roles, just as John the Baptist fulfilled Elijah's role the first time around. Whatever the case, they'll be a sign to Israel because they'll perform the same signs as their historical counterparts: "to shut up the sky in order that rain may not fall during the days of their prophesying; and power over the waters to turn them into blood and to smite the earth with every plague, as often as they desire."

The image of the witnesses as both olive trees and lampstands refers to the vision of Zechariah 4:14, in which the olive trees are the anointed ones that stand by the Lord of the whole earth, and are symbolized by the lampstand with seven lamps. Since the lampstands also symbolize the Church in Revelation, we can take this to mean that the witnesses are both part of, and stand by, His body in the Church that remains at this seal—Philadelphia. As part of their ministry, we would expect Moses and/or Elijah to travel throughout the Middle East, preaching the gospel, and baptizing converts—an act considered by Muslims to be the point of no return.

The description of the two witnesses fits the Islamic prophecy of Al Dajaal, who will go throughout the Middle East deceiving people into believing that he's the Christ by performing miracles, such as bringing rain and bread to those who believe in him. He'll present Muslims with two options: fire and water. One hadith warns them to jump into the fire, because it's really water and vice versa.

This fire could very well be the teaching of hell for believing in the false religion, while the water would refer to Christian baptism.

In Islamic eschatology, it is Al Dajaal who besieges Jerusalem, which is also paralleled in the two witnesses of Revelation. Although we don't tend to think of God's prophets as being warriors, the Greek word for war, *polemeo,* is used several times throughout Revelation 11, 12 and 13, and there's no reason to think it isn't literal war. According to Revelation 11:5, the witnesses kill anyone who would harm them by fire out of their mouths, an obvious allusion to modern weapons. Given these facts, it's completely within reason that in addition to prophesying for the entirety of Al Mahdi's reign, the witnesses will lead "those who know their God" in their siege against the Temple Mount. According to the Hadith, this siege becomes so intense that Al Mahdi's armies are starving when the Prophet Jesus comes to help. It most likely doesn't last the entire 42 months the witnesses preach, but is rather a culmination of a lower level war going on throughout the empire. This would allow for the fulfillment of the Islamic prophecy that Al Mahdi brings peace and prosperity to Israel; likewise, according to Daniel 8:25, he corrupts the many while they're "at ease." Israel's peace would allow for the deception that causes him to succeed.

Both the witnesses and the saints are defeated at the end of Al Mahdi's 1260 days, after which the second beast arises out of the land (Rev 11:7, 13:7,11). This corresponds to the appearance of the Prophet Jesus in Islamic eschatology, as he defeats Al Dajaal and establishes a government with Al Mahdi to rule from Jerusalem. Obviously God could safeguard the lives of the witnesses and saints if He chose to. The only purpose of their failure is to fulfill the Islamic prophecy regarding Al Mahdi's victory, allowing him to continue deceiving the world.

The Dragon

Daniel focused mostly on As-Sufyani, using lots of detail in chapter 11. John, on the other hand, focuses on Al Mahdi and gives only a very abbreviated and symbolic picture of As-Sufyani in the dragon.

Revelation 12:3
And another sign appeared in heaven and behold, a great red dragon having seven heads and ten horns, and on his heads were seven diadems.

In agreement with Daniel's iron beast and the goat's horn out of the horn, Revelation 12 shows us a precursor to the Antichrist. This is As-Sufyani depicted at the midpoint of the week when he persecutes Israel (the woman), who according to verses 6 and 14, flees into the wilderness for three and a half years—the period in which Al Mahdi will rule. Unlike the single-headed iron beast of Daniel's vision, however, the dragon has seven heads wearing diadems. Some insist these represent historical empires, but in fact they must represent modern heads of state since dead kings can't wear crowns. (As we'll see later, among these seven heads are those representing Iraq, Iran and Syria).

Like the fourth beast in Daniel 7:7, the dragon has ten horns, which according to Revelation 17:14, represent ten men who "receive authority as kings with the beast for only one hour. These have one purpose and they give their power and authority to the beast. These will wage war against the Lamb..." This is significant, because in Revelation 12, the diadems sit upon the heads, while in chapter 13, we see a shift has taken place: the beast comes out of the sea with the diadems on the horns. Thus we can interpret the dragon as Satan working through As-Sufyani to set up the Abomination of

Desolation and pursue those of Israel who act wickedly toward the covenant. Yet when As-Sufyani comes to his end, Satan will then stand with Al Mahdi against the witnesses and the saints (the rest of the woman's offspring), whom the Muslims will interpret as Al Dajaal and his army of Christians and Jews.

The Dragon's tail

Revelation 12:3-4
³And another sign appeared in heaven and behold, a great red dragon... ⁴And his tail swept away a third of the stars of heaven and threw them to the earth.

This isn't the first time the Bible uses the tail as a metaphor. Deuteronomy 28 prophesies that, as a result of breaking God's covenant, Israel will be the tail of the alien who oppresses it:

Deuteronomy 28:43,44
⁴³The alien who is among you shall rise above you higher and higher, but you shall go down lower and lower. ⁴⁴...He shall be the head and you shall be the tail.

In another scripture, Isaiah names the false prophets as the tail of Israel:

Isaiah 9:13-15
¹³Yet the people do not turn back to Him who struck them, nor do they seek the Lord of hosts. ¹⁴So the Lord cuts off head and tail from Israel, both palm branch and bulrush in a single day. ¹⁵The head is the elder and honorable man, and the prophet who teaches falsehood is the tail.

Revelation 12:4 isn't the only scriptural reference to thirds, either. Just before Ezekiel describes the abominations of the temple, he says this:

Ezekiel 5:5-12
⁵This is Jerusalem: I have set her at the center of the nations with lands around her. ⁶But she has rebelled against my ordinances more wickedly than the nations and against My statutes more than the lands which surround her; for they have rejected My ordinances and have not walked in My statutes. ⁸...Therefore, I am against you, and I will execute judgments among you in the sight of the nations...¹¹...because you have defiled My sanctuary with all your detestable idols and with all your abominations, therefore I will also withdraw, and My eye shall have no pity and I will not spare. ¹²One third of you will die by plague or be consumed by famine among you, one third will fall by the sword around you, and one third I will scatter to every wind, and I will unsheathe a sword behind them.

It would appear then, that the dragon's tail is Israel —or more specifically, the false prophets of Israel—that sweep away a third of the stars.

The Stars

We recognize this image of stars being cast from the sky in Daniel's vision of the horn out of the horn (Dan 8:9). However, it's possible that Revelation 12:4 isn't describing the same incident. While the horn clearly persecutes (tramples) the stars, no mention is made of trampling by the dragon; his persecution seems to be reserved only for the woman and her unborn child. Keep in mind that stars represent those who are faithful to the covenant and receive the inheritance. Therefore, it's possible that this is a reference to the apostasy of the Church and faithful Jews at the fourth seal, when according to Daniel 11:32, the Despicable Person turns to godlessness those who had been against his covenant.

As far as Christians, these will consist in large part of dead Sardis, the gentiles from Thyatira left behind because of committing adultery with Jezebel. Although they won't be persecuted by As-Sufyani, these apostates will ultimately die because of the false prophets; being convinced to stay under the peace of Al Mahdi, they'll suffer God's judgment on the beast kingdom in Israel.

The rest of the Christians will be the Jews of Philadelphia and any gentiles who receive Christ after the rapture, along with those gentiles of Thyatira who have repented. These are the "other offspring who hold to the commandments of God and the testimony of Christ" (Rev 12:17), and the ones in Daniel "who have insight" and "lead the many to righteousness." Ultimately, they'll be granted the promises and inheritance of Israel—to "shine like the stars forever" (Dan 12:3), but only after they've been refined, purged, and made pure (Dan 11:35).

The Woman

Revelation 12:1-4
¹And a great sign appeared in heaven: a woman clothed with the sun and the moon under her feet, and on her head a crown of twelve stars. ²And she was with child; and she cried out, being in labor and in pain to give birth. ⁴...And the dragon stood before the woman who was about to give birth, so that when she gave birth he might devour her child.

There have been several theories as to the identity of the

woman and her child. Some say she's Mary giving birth to Jesus, which makes no sense—what would it mean that she then runs out into the desert to be nourished for 1260 days? Some say she's Israel and the baby is Christ at His first coming, but it's inconsistent to break with the future timeline of Revelation to describe something that happened 2000 years earlier. If, on the other hand, the child's birth is His second coming, as still others say, why would He be represented as a vulnerable baby *ascending* to God's throne half way through the week?

In Labor and Pain to Give Birth

In interpreting the woman of chapter 12, it's important to know that labor and childbirth are used throughout the Old Testament as a metaphor for the agony and terror of battle, usually in the context of Israel against its undefeatable enemies; the birth is the metaphor for the battle's outcome:

Jeremiah 30:4-7
[4]Now these are the words which the Lord spoke concerning Israel and concerning Judah, [5]"For thus says the Lord, 'I have heard a sound of terror, of dread, and there is no peace. [6]Ask now, and see if a male can give birth. Why do I see every man with his hands on his loins, as a woman in childbirth? And why have all faces turned pale? [7]Alas! For that day is great, there is none like it; and it is the time of Jacob's distress.'"

Isaiah 26:16-18
[16]O Lord, they sought You in distress; they could only whisper a prayer, your chastening was upon them. [17]As the pregnant woman approaches the time to give birth, she writhes and cries out in her labor pains. Thus were we before You, O Lord. [18]We were

pregnant, we writhed in labor, we gave birth as it were only to wind. We could not accomplish deliverance for the earth, nor were inhabitants of the world born [fallen].

The Woman's Description

When Joshua brought the new generation of Israel into the Promised Land, God reiterated the covenant and told them, "Beware, lest you lift up your eyes to heaven and see the sun and the moon and the stars, all the host of heaven, and be drawn away and worship them and serve them..." (Deut 4:19) Since this was the religion of the surrounding Canaanites (in fact, Moses' father-in-law himself was a high priest of the moon cult), God knew this would be a great temptation and ultimate pitfall for them. Israel began worshiping the Baals almost from the moment they set foot in the Promised Land. But when Ahab married Jezebel, it culminated in a wholesale slaughter of God's prophets and a showdown between Elijah and the priests and prophets of Baal. Within 140 years, Assyria would conquer the Northern kingdom and in another 136 years, Babylon would utterly destroy Jerusalem and the temple.

Remember that at the time Muhammad was born (570 A.D.), the moon cult was still very strong in the Middle East; *Allah,* the generic term for "god," was used for each tribe's patron god, who was often a personification of a lunar phase,[1] including the Quraish's patron god Hubal. Modern Islam still carries a vestige of its ancient pagan roots by its own choice of symbols—the crescent moon and star. The woman's relationship to the sun, moon and stars as deity symbols of ancient Babylon and Islam indicates her spiritual triumph over them both. The sun isn't above her to influence or beat down upon her; instead she's clothed with it, shining as Moses did

---

[1] Islam: Truth or Myth?, "Hubal, the moon god of the Kaba", http://www.bible.ca/islam/islam-moon-god-hubal.htm, p. 3, note 14, referencing Carleton S. Coon, Southern Arabia, Washington D.C. Smithsonian, 1944, p. 399

when he had been in the presence of God. She doesn't look up to worship the stars; instead she wears twelve of them in the victory laurel upon her head. Finally, she uses the moon as a footstool beneath her feet, a symbol of her dominion and authority over it. She represents devoted Jews who have not compromised themselves with Islam or As-Sufyani.

Within this remnant are those in Israel who seek the Lord and the coming of His Messiah; they're those in Judea who flee to the mountains, as Christ advised (Matthew 24), and when they fall, they'll be given the wings of a great eagle (perhaps the "little help" of Dan 11:34) to carry them into the wilderness, where they'll "be nourished" with grace (Jer 31:2, "the people who survived the sword found grace in the wilderness").

Through her description, this remnant is also linked to the events of the sixth seal. If you'll remember, the sun turns dark like sackcloth, the moon turns to blood, and the stars fall to earth like the figs from a shaken fig tree. The imagery used to describe these cosmic events is more than poetic; it's prophetic of the 144,000 Jews who become believers during this seal. Sackcloth was worn as a sign of mourning, almost always in connection with repentance; the blood refers to sacrifice, both Christ's and that of the martyrs; and the fig tree symbolizes Israel in the end time prophecies of Jeremiah and Jesus. In this sign, we're shown how the woman will defeat the false religion: the sun (Satan) by her repentance and the moon (the Antichrist) by the blood of the Lamb and the sacrifice of her own life; even the scattered stars (God's people, misled by the teachings of false prophets) will be re-gathered by her evangelism.

The Three Parts of the Remnant

An interesting detail of Revelation 12, is that the woman is mentioned twice, with two different designations given to her time spent in the wilderness: once before the dragon falls, for 1260 days, and once afterward for time, times and half a time. The third time designation of 42 months is used to describe the trampling of the temple and city, and the period of the beast's earthly rule. Why would John use three different designations to refer to the same time period? If we look at how he uses them, an interesting correlation emerges:

<u>42 months</u>
Beast (Rev 13)
Temple and city (Rev 11)

<u>1260 days</u>
Witnesses (Rev 11)
Woman before dragon's fall (Rev 12:6)

<u>Time, times and half a time</u>
Insolent King (Mahdi)/time of great distress when the saints
    are overcome (Dan 12:7)
Woman after dragon's fall (Rev 12:14)

The Remnant that Fights

Although Revelation 13 doesn't specifically mention that the beast controls the temple, we know that he's responsible for the trampling of the outer courts and city in Revelation 11:2, because, like his rule, it lasts for 42 months. Likewise, we can connect the two time periods given in Revelation to two groups within the remnant of Israel. The first are those who stand in battle against As-Sufyani (as if in childbirth), and become the witnesses' army during their 1260 day ministry. Towards the end of that time, they'll go up to the Temple Mount to fight against Al Mahdi. We would surely expect some Jews to fight for their country, just as any countryman would, and who better to lead them than Moses or Elijah? As far as the woman receiving the wings of eagles to take her to a place in the wilderness, consider this passage in Isaiah:

Isaiah 40:29-31
^{29}He gives strength to the weary, and to him who lacks might He increases power. ^{30}Though youths grow weary and tired, and vigorous young men stumble badly, ^{31}yet those who wait for the Lord will gain new strength; they will mount up with wings like eagles, they will run and not get tired, they will walk and not become weary.

Unlike those whom Christ warns to flee from Judea, this passage doesn't speak of women and nursing children, but only of young men who need power and might—in other words, an army. It's impossible to know what the eagle's wings will be—perhaps foreign aid.

The Remnant that Flees

The second group consists of those who, after being persecuted by the dragon, flee to the wilderness, just before Al Mahdi arises. There she'll stay for the whole period of his reign—"a time, times and half a time." The question is whether this is a literal wilderness, and what will these refugees be doing there? There are several Old Testament scriptures indicating that survivors from Israel will go into other nations to be witnesses[2]:

Micah 5:7-8
^{7}Then the remnant of Jacob will be among many peoples like dew for the Lord, like showers on vegetation which do not wait for

---

2   Other scriptures are Isa 43:19-21; Jer 31:2.

man or delay for the sons of men. ⁸And the remnant of Jacob will be among the nations, among many peoples like a lion among the beasts of the forest, like a young lion among flocks of sheep...

Ezekiel 20:34-38

³⁴And I shall bring you out from the peoples and gather you from the lands where you are scattered, with a mighty hand and with an outstretched arm and with wrath poured out, ³⁵and I shall bring you into the wilderness of the peoples, and there I shall enter into judgment with you face to face.³⁶As I entered into judgment with your fathers in the wilderness of the land of Egypt, so I will enter into judgment with you," declares the Lord God. ³⁷"And I shall make you pass under the rod, and I shall bring you into the bond of the covenant; ³⁸and I shall purge from you the rebels and those who transgress against Me..."

Isaiah 66:5,19-20

⁵Hear the word of the Lord, you who tremble at his word: "Your brothers who hate you, who exclude you for My name's sake, have said, 'Let the Lord be glorified, that we may see your joy.' But they will be put to shame. ¹⁸For I know their works and their thoughts... ¹⁹And I will set a sign among them and will send survivors from them to the nations: Tarshish, Put, Lud, Meshech, Rosh, Tubal, and Javan, to the distant coastlands that have neither heard my fame nor seen My glory. And they will declare My glory among the nations. ²⁰Then they shall bring all your brethren from all the nations as a grain offering to the Lord...to My holy mountain Jerusalem."

Isaiah 11:11-12

¹¹Then it will happen on that day that the Lord will again recover the second time with his hand the remnant of His people, who will

remain, from Assyria, Egypt, Pathros, Cush, Elam, Shinar, Hamath[3] and from the islands of the sea. ¹²And He will lift up a standard for the nations and will assemble the banished ones of Israel and will gather the dispersed of Judah from the four corners of the earth.

Isaiah 35:4-10
⁴Say to those with anxious heart, "Take courage, fear not. Behold, your God will come with vengeance; the recompense of God will come, but He will save you." ⁵Then the eyes of the blind will be opened and the ears of the deaf will be unstopped. ⁶Then the lame will leap like a deer, and the tongue of the dumb will shout for joy…⁸and a highway will be there, a roadway, and it will be called the Highway of Holiness. The unclean will not travel on it… ⁹but the redeemed will walk there ¹⁰and the ransomed of the Lord will return and come with joyful shouting to Zion, with everlasting joy upon their heads. They will find gladness and joy, and sorrow and sighing will flee away.

For this group, "the wings of the great eagle" may very well be modern transport into every country of the world "to a place prepared for her to be nourished," spiritually speaking of course; they may even receive help from the repentant Christians of Sardis. As they grow stronger in their knowledge of the Lord, they would then become witnesses to the Jews in those countries, and bring them back on "horses, in chariots, in litters, on mules and on camels to [His] holy mountain Jerusalem" (Isa 66:20). Christ mentions in Matthew 24 that the gospel will be "preached in the whole world as a witness to all the nations;" this may be one of the ways it happens. Perhaps these refugees become the eagle's voice that

---

3   Pathros is Upper Egypt; Cush can be either Abyssinia, or the southern parts of Arabia along the Red Sea, Elam is Iran, especially the southern part of it now called Susiana; Shinar is Iraq, the plain between the Euphrates and the Tigris.

prophesies the three woes to come in the seventh seal.

The Remnant that Stays

There's one more group within the remnant, and that's the one that stays in Jerusalem to witness to their fellow Jews. They're the 144,000 Jews from every tribe sealed with the Holy Spirit at the sixth seal, and as Christians, they're represented by the twelve stars in the woman's victory laurel. This is the church of Philadelphia and they'll be discussed in more detail later.

The Male Child

Revelation 12:5-11
⁵And [the woman] gave birth to a son, a male child who is to rule all the nations with a rod of iron; and her child was caught up to God and to His throne. ⁷And there as a war in heaven, Michael and his angels waging war with the dragon...⁹And the great dragon was thrown down, the serpent of old who is called the devil and Satan...¹¹And they overcame him because of the blood of the Lamb and because of the word of their testimony, and they did not love their life even to death.

Isaiah 26:18 says that Israel gives birth only to wind, an indication of defeat. Yet although the woman is defeated and flees from the dragon, she gives birth to a child, not to wind! How do we explain the contradiction?

Satan falls from heaven as a direct result of the child's rapture, so it can only be interpreted as victory, but not necessarily for Israel—at least not yet. The angels say that Satan is thrown down because "they" overcame him by the blood of the Lamb, by the word of their testimony and by the fact that they didn't love their life even to death. This same image of Satan falling is used by Christ in Luke 10:18 in describing the impact of the seventy's ministry. Obviously the "they" of this passage are Christians whose victory over Satan comes from bearing faithful testimony to Christ—those in Thyatira who have no other burden placed on them. True, Psalm 2:8-9 says that Christ will rule the nations with a rod of iron, but the reward to the faithful Church is to share in His reign (Rev 20:6). In fact, in His letter to Thyatira, Christ makes this promise: "And he who overcomes, and he who keeps My deeds until the end, to him I will give authority over the nations and *he shall rule them with a rod of iron*...as I also have received authority from My Father." (Rev 2:26-27, italics mine)."

Now look at what Isaiah says about Israel:

Isaiah 66:7-8
⁷Before she travailed, she brought forth; before her pain came, she gave birth to a boy. ⁸Who has heard such a thing? Who has seen such things? Can a land be born in one day? Can a nation be brought forth all at once?

Isaiah 55:5
Behold, you will call a nation you do not know, and a nation which knows you not will run to you, because of the Lord your God, even the Holy One of Israel; for he has glorified you.

Isaiah calls the boy a "land" and a "nation," similar to Revelation 5:9-10, when the four living creatures say to the Lord, "You have made [the gentiles] to be a kingdom and priests to our God..." Although the gentiles were never bound together by ethnicity, culture, or land, God nevertheless knit them together to be a kingdom. Isaiah's prophecy also matches that of Revelation 12, in that the boy is raptured *before* the woman travails—that is, before the persecution of Israel at the hands of As-Sufyani. According to Christ in Matthew 24:8, the first three seals were the "birth pangs." Here at the fourth seal, we see the remnant struggling to bring forth the real fruit of Israel's labor: the Church. Its victory in the rapture is also a victory for Israel, who is glorified because her mission to bring salvation to the earth is accomplished through that "nation" that ran to her.

What throws us off is that the baby is male, when in the New Testament the Church is referred to as a bride; but remember, it's also called the body of Christ, which is a male image. Furthermore, historically, Israel did in fact give birth to the Church! Although this is a highly symbolic depiction, the fact that a great multitude of gentiles stands before God's throne in the sixth seal (7:9-17) is final evidence that the child represents the rapture of the gentile Church.

Although the persecution by As-Sufyani and the deception of the Mahdi will seem like defeat, the suffering endured by Israel during the Great Tribulation will ultimately lead to the end of Satan's rule and bring with it her restoration. But to accomplish her final victory, Israel will face more battles. According to Isaiah, the woman will deliver her own children:

Isaiah 66:8
...As soon as Zion travailed, she also brought forth her sons...

Her sons are "the *rest* of her offspring who keep the commandments of God and hold to the testimony of Jesus" (Rev 12:17, italics mine). They are the Jews in Israel who receive Christ after the rapture, the stars in the woman's crown of victory. After her travail, Israel will "deliver" these sons in the harvest rapture of Revelation 14.

As is so characteristic of God's omnipotence, Satan in his greatest rebellion is unwittingly serving to fulfill the will of God; in attempting to wipe out the Church and Israel, Satan is actually cleansing them in preparation for their marriage with the bridegroom. Satan won't be redeemed in the end, yet in a way that only God can pull off, the worst evil Satan can muster is somehow redeemed. This is a very powerful mystery which is in force even now, if we'll only recognize it and claim it in our everyday lives; if we allow God's hand to work in spite of, or even through it, the suffering and evil in this world can be redeemed by his greater purpose. Every victory we win now through faith brings us that much closer to overcoming the dragon.

11

The Little Book Continued: The Beast out of the Sea

Al Mahdi as the Beast out of the Sea

Revelation 13:1-4
¹And [the dragon] stood on the sand of the seashore. And I saw a beast coming up out of the sea, having ten horns and seven heads, and on his horns were ten diadems, and on his heads were blasphemous names. ²And the beast which I saw was like a leopard, and his feet were like those of a bear, and his mouth like the mouth of a lion. And the dragon gave him his power and his throne and great authority. ³And I saw one of his heads as if it had been slain, and his fatal wound was healed. And the whole earth was amazed and followed after the beast; ⁴and they worshiped the dragon, because he gave his authority to the beast; and they worshiped the beast, saying, "Who is like the beast and who is able to wage war with him?"

Just like Daniel's four beasts were gentile nations, John's beast comes up out of the sea of the gentile world. However in the context of Islamic prophecy the reference to the sea could also be the

Sea of Galilee, where the armies of Al Mahdi gather to fight against As-Sufyani. This scenario could easily fit what Daniel tells us about him in 11:45: he will "pitch the tents of his royal pavilion between the seas and the beautiful Holy Mountain; yet he will come to his end with no one to help him." Could John be describing As-Sufyani on the eve of his defeat, watching Al Mahdi's empire being born upon the shores of Galilee, with Satan transferring his power to him?

In reading this passage the question arises whether the beast is Al Mahdi or his empire, especially because of the use of the pronouns "he" and "his." But the beast here must be the empire because the seven heads represent the kingdoms that comprise it (Rev 17:9,10).

Yet if the beast is an empire, how can it be worshiped? Although *proskuneo* is translated as worship here, according to Vine's dictionary, its strict meaning is "to make obeisance, do reverence to." It's used in this sense to describe a slave prostrating himself before his master (Matthew 18:26), and the act of bowing before a king (Matthew 2:2,18:26; Mark 15:19; the Septuagint also uses it in this sense). Based on this meaning, the passage above describes an empire that the people obey and show reverence to because 1) they perceive that its authority comes from God; 2) they believe its king has earned the divine right to rule because of a miraculous recovery from a "deathblow;" 3) they either take pride in its might and feel protected, or they fear it, believing that it's impossible to win against it. So John's vision of people falling before the beast isn't an overt act of worship, as it has been translated into English, but rather a demonstration of their submission to Islam and Al Mahdi, who as king, represents the empire.

That being said, if we consider the great reverence Muslims have for their religion and their ultimate desire to have every aspect of their lives and community governed by Shari'a law, it's easy to see that the line between Al Mahdi and his government will blur, if not disappear altogether. This is especially true in light of the Shi'ite concept of Imam Mahdi, which at the very least borders on worship. In Shi'a Islam, the concept of Al Mahdi is as tantamount to Islam as Christ is to Christianity, not only for Islam as *the religion*, but because his arrival is the fulfillment of Islam as a perfect world *government*. Thus, Al Mahdi is the government and the government is Al Mahdi, and everything is in islam (submission) to Allah. When the earth is said to worship the dragon, it means that the Muslims continue to worship Allah. When they show obeisance and reverence to Al Mahdi, it's not because he's able to win wars, but more precisely because he wins them in the name of Islam against the enemies of Islam. Although Paul depicts him as displaying himself to be God (II Thess 2:4), we see in Daniel 8:25 that this might in fact be "in his heart"—not an overt claim to deity perhaps, but rather a passive one by allowing his followers to cross that fine line into worshiping him as God.

"The Whole Earth"

Revelation 13:3 says that the whole earth marvels at and follows after the beast. The question is, what is meant by the "whole earth"? Daniel 8 uses this term to describe the land conquered by Alexander the Great, so it may not be the whole earth as we know it today. John was also unaware of much of our modern globe; to him the earth was pretty much the Roman Empire. Because of this fact, we really can't say exactly how nations outside of that area will be affected by the beast kingdom, but we can make some educated guesses based on two facts: one, that Al Mahdi's kingdom will control a significant amount of the oil used by the world, and two, the Muslim population of many major countries will be large, especially in Europe, which is already experiencing a huge explosion of

Muslim immigration.

Imagine a life with little or no fuel: food shortages, high rates of unemployment, no electricity. Such conditions would obviously lead to high numbers of deaths, as well as violence in the streets of our cities. Couple that with large populations of Muslims who will see themselves as soldiers of Al Mahdi in foreign lands. If the Muslims in various nations have access to goods because of their connections to the Middle East, they can use these as a way of bribing people to convert, as ultimately the mark of the beast will be required to buy or sell.

The Body of the Beast

It seems significant that each ancient empire is tied to a particular body part of the beast government, a detail that points to something beyond mere geography. If an empire were an animal, we might think of its body as its land and people, thus the leopard represents the Middle East as the heartland of the beast kingdom. However, the feet of an empire would be the ideological foundation on which it stands, and here that is depicted as being Iran, the center of Shi'a Islam. This is a direct indication that Al Mahdi will be Shi'ite. Of course there's also the connection with ancient Persia, when Haman attempted genocide against the Jews. Finally, the mouth of an empire would be the source of its diplomacy and government—treaties and decrees; here, Iraq is depicted as the mouth. Perhaps this reference ties in more closely to ancient Babylon as the seat of the false religion, and Nebuchadnezzar's decree to bow before the golden image. However, once again we see a connection with Shi'a Islam, whose most sacred sites are found in Iraq. Not only places such as Karbala, where Ali was killed, and Najaf, the site of his tomb, but more importantly the Imam Ali Mosque, where the twelfth Imam is prophesied to reveal himself.

One last indication that Al Mahdi will be Shi'ite is Daniel 8:23, which describes the Insolent King as someone "skilled in intrigue" (translated more literally to be "discerning enigmas"). Not only will this man need to understand how to take advantage of each religion's prophecies to maximize the success of his deception, but this characteristic of understanding deep things is a large part of the Shi'ite Mahdi's identity; after all, he is "Lord of the Universe" and the "hidden Imam" waiting in spiritual limbo to usher in utopia.

The Seven Heads of the Beast out of the Sea

Revelation 17:8-11
⁸The beast that you saw was and is not and is about to come up out of the abyss and go to destruction. ⁹Here is the mind which has wisdom. The seven heads are seven mountains [kingdoms]...¹⁰and they are seven kings; five have fallen, one is, the other has not yet come; and when he comes, he must remain a little while. ¹¹And the beast which was and is not, is himself also an eighth and is one of the seven, and he goes to destruction.

The angel is speaking to John during the rule of the Roman Empire. Thus he tells him that the seven heads consist of:

Five that have fallen: five kings/kingdoms that fell before Rome
One that is: Caesar/Roman Empire
Seventh: One that was and is not and will come and remain a little while: Seleucids/Rashiduns
Eighth: Who was and is not and will come again: a revival of the Seleucids/Rashiduns

Five Have Fallen

Now we understand why a connection was made between the historical periods of Islam and their corresponding ancient empires. Many empires came before Rome, but only three are mentioned in Daniel's vision. If we count the heads on his beasts, there's one on the lion, Babylonia; one on the bear, Persia; four on the leopard, Greece: that makes six—too many, since Rome is the sixth according to the angel. Alternatively, counting only one head per empire gives us only three—too few. Some Bible scholars count Assyria, then include Media as one of the heads of Persia; thus they list Assyria, Babylonia, Media, Persia and Greece. Shoebat says the five are Old Babylonia, Assyria, Neo-Babylonia (Nebuchadnezzar), Persia and Greece.[1] The problem with including Assyria and Old Babylonia is that God had Nebuchadnezzar as the first empire, so there's no justification in counting kings before him; if God had intended to include Assyria or Old Babylonia, He would have included them in the prophecies. Likewise, the statue and beasts don't depict Media as a separate kingdom because in fact, Media never controlled Israel as an independent kingdom, and had already been absorbed into the Medo-Persian empire by the time Cyrus defeated Babylonia.

Obviously, Babylonia and Persia are givens. But not all four divisions of the Greek empire can be included, since the kingdoms of Cassander and Lysimachus never had any control over Israel. The next two heads must be the Ptolemaic and Seleucid empires, each of which controlled Israel. One more king is needed to make five.

The only kingdom that came between Greece and Rome was the Hasmonean dynasty, founded by the Maccabees, the rebel Jews who were victorious against Antiochus IV. Granted autonomy by the Seleucid king Demetrius in 142 B.C., and recognized by the Roman

---

[1] Walid Shoebat, "Islam and the Final Beast: a practical way of interpreting prophecy," p. 17, http://answering-islam.org/Walid/gog.htm

Senate in 139, the Hasmoneans ruled over Israel for 103 years. The first three leaders did well, but as time went on, corruption took hold, and divisions arose between the Hellenist Sadducees, and the opposing Pharisees. Israel experienced as much oppression under some of the Hasmonean rulers as they did under foreign powers. For example, under John Hyrcanus, the Iumeans in the south were forced to convert to Judaism (this is where Herod would later come from), and the temple in Samaria was destroyed. His son Aristobulus was the first to take the title of King, which brought a strong reaction from the people, since he was not from the line of David or Judah. When his brother Alexander Jannaeus took over, he expanded his kingdom through massacre and forced conversions. His brutality, particularly against the Pharisees, brought on a six year civil war that resulted in the death of 50,000 people; when the Jews repented of soliciting the Seleucids' help and returned to Jannaeus, he crucified 800 Pharisees, and slit the throats of their wives and children as they watched.

Thus the fifth head of the beast is the *Nagid* to Come, typified by the Hasmonean dynasty. Its absence in Daniel's beasts can be explained by the fact that they dealt only with the gentile empires that conquered Israel, while the Hasmoneans were a native dynasty. The final list then for the five kings who have fallen is: Babylonia (Iraq), Persia (Iran), the Ptolemies (Egypt), the Seleucids (Syria), and the Hasmoneans (Israel).

One Is

The angel says that the sixth king exists in John's present; this can only be Rome. The question is what modern area corresponds to Rome, and who would be its king? The territory of Rome's empire in John's time included the British Isles, Western Europe, Turkey, Syria, Lebanon, Israel, Jordan and northern Africa. Most

Bible scholars think of the Roman Empire as being Western Europe because the seat of its government was Italy. Islam appears to think along the same lines, as expressed by some of its clerics:

"By Allah, we will conquer Italy. By Allah we will conquer Italy and move into the rest of Europe...The nation of Islam will return... The West is bound to be destroyed. Just like Allah destroyed the Byzantine and Persian empires, he will destroy the West at the hands of the Muslims...These countries will convert to Islam..."
--Egyptian cleric Salem Abu Al-Futuh
Al-Nas TV interview, August 18, 2010

In the Koran, the Prophet Muhammad is asked, "Which will fall first, Constantinople or Rome?" and his response was "Constantinople." Clearly, it did fall to the Muslims in 1453. As a result, many Muslims are waiting for the Islamic conquest of Rome, something we must assume happens, since one of the dragon's heads is Rome. If Rome is in fact Western Europe, the most likely "king" would be the European Union. But how likely is it that Islam could conquer Europe?

"Conquest" by Immigration and Birthrate

The media has coined the term "Eurabia" to refer to the on-going Islamization of Europe. The cause of the phenomenon is twofold: pathologically low fertility rates of Europeans, and the high immigration and birthrates of Muslims. It all revolves around what's called the "replacement birthrate," the average 2.1 births per woman necessary for a culture to maintain its population level and replace its aging workforce. With a birthrate of below 1.3, a country's population is cut in half within 45 years, making it nearly impossible to recover culturally or economically.[2] For the first time on record, birthrates in southern and eastern Europe have dropped below 1.3.[3] While in 1963 Europe represented 12.5 percent of the world's population, by 2008 it was 7.2 percent, and if the current trends continue, by 2050 that figure will drop to 5 percent.[4]

One example is Germany, whose population has been steadily decreasing since 1965,[5] their births-to-deaths ratio causing an annual population loss of roughly 100,000 according to 2008 figures. In 2006, this trend caused enough concern in the government that family minister Ursula von der Leyen, declared that if Germany didn't reverse its plummeting birthrate, they would have to "turn out the light."[6]

One way that a country can make up for declining birthrate is through immigration, and right now, Muslims are the fastest growing immigrant population in Europe and Scandinavia. In 2007, the number of Muslims in the European Union was estimated at 53 million,[7] a figure expected to double by 2015 according to Omer Taspinar.[8] England, whose demographic change was representative of Europe in general, saw an increase in its Muslim population from 82,000 in 1961, to 553,000 in 1981, to 2 million in 2000.[9]

---

2   "The Severe Impact of Europe's Declining Birth Rate," http://www.impactlab.com/2008/06/29/the-severe-impact-of-europes-declining-birth-rate/, June 29, 2008, p. 4
3   Ibid.
4   Ibid.
5   www.un.org/esa/population/publications/ReplMigED/Germany.pdf
6   "The Severe Impact of Europe's Declining Birth Rate," p. 5
7   Wikipedia, "Islam in Europe," quoting Associated Press journalist Don Melvin,"Europe works to assimilate Muslims," Atlanta Journal Constitution, 2004-12-17
8   Ibid., quoting Olmar Taspinar, "Europe's Muslim Street," Brookings Institution, March 2003. Olmar Taspinar is considered to be an expert on Muslims in Europe, and political Islam. He is a professor at the National War College and an adjunct professor at Johns Hopkins University's School of Advanced International Studies.
9   Ed West, "Here's an inconvenient truth: the Islamisation of Europe," *Telegraph* Blogs, May 6, 2009, http://blogs.telegraph.co.uk/news/edwest/9666257/heres_an_inconvenient_truth_the_islamisation_of_Europe

Contributing to the increase in Europe's Muslim population is the fact that the average birthrate of Muslims in Europe is 3.5, which nearly doubles its next generation.

Yet another contributing factor in this population exchange is the disturbing fact that Europeans are leaving their countries in unprecedented numbers. The following figures come from Daniel Pipes' article, "Europeans Fleeing Eurabia:"[10]

- *The New York Times*, *The Daily Telegraph* and *Radio Nederlands* pointed to the murders of Pim Fortuyn and Theo van Gogh as marking a surge in the exodus of mostly middle-class Dutch who feared for their safety. In 2005, a record number of 121,000 people emigrated from the Netherlands. In 2006, the figure was 132,470, with 26 percent of the Dutch population seriously considering emigration; in 2007, The "Emigration Monitor" reported that the number had risen to 32 percent.
- In 2005, Canada's National Post reported that "French Jews are leaving France in ever-growing numbers, fleeing a wave of anti-Semitism," marked by anti-Semitic graffiti, fire bombings, shootings and desecrated graves. Immigration from France to Israel more than doubled between 2001 and 2005, and increased by more than 700 percent from France to Canada. In Miami, entirely French-Jewish communities have been established by the influx of immigrants. In 2007, 7,000 French Jews signed a petition requesting U.S. congress to pass legislation granting them refugee status, stating that "members of the French Jewish community are no longer feeling safe. The number of anti-Semitic acts in France has reached a level not seen since World War II."

---

10   Daniel Pipes, "Europeans Fleeing Eurabia," October 10, 2004, http://www.danielpipes.org/blog/ 2004/10/europeans-fleeing-eurabia

- *Der Spiegel* reported that in 2005, for the first time in recent history, more Germans left the country than entered it.
- The BBC reported that the number of British citizens who chose to emigrate doubled from 53,000 in 2001 to 107,000 in 2005. Over the course of 40 years, some 67,500 more Britons have left the UK every year than have returned, a population loss balanced out by increasing immigration. In 2008 the Telegraph reported that 200,000 British citizens a year are emigrating, more than any time since before World War I. By way of explanation, the newspaper states that "unchecked immigration over the past decade is creating a country many Britons no longer feel comfortable in…"

In the Hadith, Muhammad tells a man not to marry a barren woman, saying: "Marry women who are loving and very prolific, for I shall outnumber the peoples by you." Islamic leaders join him in promoting the idea of conquest by population:

"There are signs that Allah will grant victory to Islam in Europe without swords, without guns, without conquest. We don't need terrorists; we don't need homicide bombers. The 50+ million Muslims [in Europe] will turn it into a Muslim continent within a few decades."
--Mu'ammar Al-Gaddafi
Al-Jazeera TV (Qatar)
April 10, 2006

"If the Muslims [in Europe] manage to ignore these provocations, and to channel their anger in support of the prophet Muhammad and of Islam, into becoming walking propaganda machines…Each person should say: 'I am an ambassador for Islam,' and they should all take action throughout Europe—in the companies where they work, in sports clubs, and in any place where they can mingle and fit

in with the Europeans, and where they can show them their moral values and their success. That will abolish the plan [of Europe to drive out the Muslims] and the Muslims will remain in Europe. We really need ten years for the Muslims in Europe to become firmly established and very successful."
--Egyptian Islamic Preacher Amr Khaled
Dream 2 TV (Egypt)
May 10, 2008

The fundamental issue with any immigrant population is whether it admires the lifestyle and ideals of its host country enough to become a part of it and build it up, rather than choosing to undermine it in some way. The issue of assimilation is a big one for many Muslim immigrants. For example, rather than using the secular civil courts of England, many Muslims prefer to submit to Shari'a law, with Islamic tribunals settling the custody and financial affairs of divorcing Muslim couples. The Church of England's Archbishop of Canterbury, Dr. Rowan Williams, made news when he gave lectures in 2008 supporting English Muslims' entitled "freedom to live under Shari'a law" within England. According to Williams, some citizens don't "relate" to the British legal system; his stance is that officially sanctioning Shari'a law would improve community relations.[11] He further indicated his belief that some parts of Shari'a law, such as divorce proceedings, would inevitably become part of the legal code of England itself.

Presently, there are five Shari'a courts operating legally under England's Arbitration Act; however, a Civitas study estimates that there are at least 85 operating behind closed doors.[12] The study

---

11 Jonathan Petre and Andrew Porter, The Telegraph, "Archbishop Williams sparks Sharia law row," Feb 7, 2008, p. 2, http://www.telegraph.co.uk/news/uknews/1577928/Archbishop-Williams-sparks-Sharia-law-row
12 Steve Doughty, Mail Online, "Britain has 85 Sharia courts: the astonishing spread of the Islamic justice behind closed doors," Daily Mail, June 29, 2009, http://

further reported that among the courts' rulings were found "some that advise illegal actions and others that transgress human rights standards as applied by British courts." Civitas director also pointed out that many Muslims don't voluntarily submit to Shari'a courts, but do so only because of intimidation and even threat of death[13] (this is particularly true of women who suffer great discrimination under Shari'a law).

Like any anti-democratic philosophy, Shari'a law threatens the very ideals that allow it to be practiced. The problem is that as Western society attempts to uphold the fundamental principles of tolerance, free speech and freedom of religion for Muslim immigrants, the pendulum seems to swing in the opposite direction for the rest of its citizens. One example is Paris, where Muslims have often closed down certain streets to line up for prayers, angering local residents. In response to the limited number of mosques available for the country's 5.5 million Muslims, in 2004, Nicolas Sarkozy, France's finance minister at the time, argued that public funds should be used to build mosques in order to support more moderate Islam in the country, hopefully controlling more radical Imams who practice in makeshift mosques.[14] Fast forward to 2008, when "every big city is making its grand mosque, costing millions of Euros."[15] Some 150 mosque building projects were launched in France, 30% of which are being financed by city mayors, thanks to the support of the Socialist Party Deputy Mayor Laurent Cathala.[16] It's doubtful that any other religious group in France is getting equal

---

ww.dailymail.co.uk/new/article-1196165/britain-85-saria-courts-The-astonishing-spread-of-the-Islamic-justice-behind-closed-doors

13   Ibid.
14   Expatica France, "Call for mosque funding revives old debate," 10/31/05, http://www.expatica.com/fr/news/local_news/call-for-mosque-funding-revives-old-debate-...
15   Islam in Europe, "France: Government participates in mosque funding," 12/26/2008, http://islamineurope.blogspot.com/2008/12/france-government-participates-in.html
16   Ibid.

funding for their houses of worship. In fact, many Jewish synagogues are on the verge of closing down because of the mass exodus of Jews from Paris suburbs due to anti-Semitic crime.[17]

Unlike other immigrant groups in Europe, Muslims have high unemployment rates and low incomes and the fact that these immigrants tend to be uneducated and economically disadvantaged not only leads to huge increases in violent crimes,[18] but also puts a strain on the welfare systems of their host countries. Just as an example, in 2002, Swedish taxpayers shelled out $27 billion to immigration-group members, 74 percent of whom live off the dole. Even before the global economic crisis, European governments were scrambling to ease the economic burden of their Muslim immigrant populations; many have had to cut public services in order to keep up with the welfare payments, including closing clinics and emergency rooms, reducing staff in hospitals, and cutting spending for police and the military.[19] Compounding the problem is the fact that Muslims often double dip benefits for multiple wives and their children, despite polygamy being illegal in Europe.[20] One report estimated that immigration reduces France's economic growth by two-thirds. Of course it only contributes to the problem that fundamentalist Muslims view bankrupting the West as a contribution to jihad.[21]

---

17   Devorah Lauter, "Jews fleeing Paris suburbs for 'ghettos' where life is safer," Jewish Review, January 1, 2011
18   Fjordman, "What does Muslim Immigration Cost Europe?" Jihad Watch, http://www.jihadwatch.org/2006/06/fjordman-what-does-muslim-immigration-cost-europe.html
19   Ed West, Telegraph blogs, "Here's an inconvenient truth: the Islamisation of Europe," 2009, http://blogs.telegraph.co.uk/news/edwest/9666257/heres_an_inconvenient_truth_the_islam...
20   London Evening Standard, "Muslim husbands with more than one wife to get extra benefits as ministers recognize polygamy," 5-2-08, http://www.thisislondon.co.uk/news/article-23435519-muslim-husbands-with-more-than-...
21   Ed West, Telegraph blogs, "Here's an inconvenient truth: the Islamisation of Europe," 2009, http://blogs.telegraph.co.uk/news/edwest/9666257/heres_an_inconvenient_truth_the_islam..., quoting David Goodhart's article in *Prospect*

Many modern prophets are telling us that doom will come if we don't accept Muslims as part of a "pluralistic" Western society. This argument would make sense except that Islam itself rejects the idea of pluralism, absorbing each country it conquers into the *ummah,* or nation, of Islam. The fundamental question facing the West is how to deal with an ideology that's both political and religious in nature—and one that reacts with violence every time someone publicly criticizes it. A political ideology in the guise of religion is the perfect vehicle to undermine a democracy, since it can hide behind the protections of religious freedom and free speech. In fact, many governments are either in denial or simply paralyzed by the unavoidable conundrum of how to fend off an oppressive ideology while upholding its democratic values, leaving them with no other option but to whitewash the truth about Islam's ultimate goal of world domination. In the meantime, the Muslim voting block continues to increase.

Conquest by Civil War

All this discussion assumes an ideological victory over the West, but is there any way it could lead to a physical conquest? The West seems determined to live in denial rather than face the possibility that the world's 1.4 billion Muslims could strike out against it in unity. These are the people who assure us that the majority of Muslims today are moderate and peaceful, and therefore don't pose this type of threat. However, when push comes to shove will these moderates side with the Western world or with their prophesied Mahdi and their fellow Muslims?

The scripture speaks repeatedly of the "sorceries," "intrigue," and "deceit" committed by the beast kingdom, which fits the deceptive and coercive tactics that Islam has employed in putting the

---

magazine, 2006, p. 4

West under its spell. In addition to the Palestinian myth and the denial of Israel's tie to the land, it has convinced the West that a minority of extremists have high jacked an otherwise peaceful religion, when in fact mainstream Islam teaches that "Jihad in Allah's Cause (with full force of numbers and weaponry) is...one of its pillars (on which it stands)."[22] What people fail to recognize is that the issue separating fundamentalist and moderate Muslims is not *whether* to fight jihad, only who has the authority to declare it and when.[23] For example, if the majority of Palestinian Muslims are moderate as is asserted, then why don't they ban its terrorist leadership from their own parliament?

If the current population exchange continues, it's clear that Europe will eventually be a Muslim majority. The question is how soon will it happen? Based solely on current demographic trends, historian Bernard Lewis predicted it would be at the end of the century. But British author Paul Weston points out that the Muslim community may opt to take Europe by force rather than waiting for a majority at the voting booth. Given this scenario, he argues that winning a civil war wouldn't depend on an overall majority Muslim population, but rather on the ratio of fighting age men. Counting today's Muslim children who will be 18-40, and taking into account Europe's low birthrate, UN estimates of annual immigration, and a conservative annual emigration rate for males 20-40, Weston predicts that the ratio of European to Muslim fighting age men will be approximately 4:1 by 2025. But as he states, "In the event of civil war erupting, does anyone seriously think that Turkey would remain on the sidelines? By 2025 there will be some 12 million Turkish males of fighting age. They will probably be part of the European Union well before then,

---

[22] Ed Hotaling, *Islam without Illusions: its Past, its Present and its Challenge for the Future* (Syracuse: Syracuse University Press, 2003), p.9, quoting Hitti, *The Arabs*, pp. 75-76, quoting Al-Hilali and Khan in their translators' notes of the *Noble Qur'an*

[23] Ed Hotaling, *Islam without Illusions: its Past, its Present and its Challenge for the Future*

but if not, it is unlikely that the necessity of a visa will stop them from crossing the border in aid of their fellow Muslims." Should this be the case, he says the ratio would drop to 2:1.[24]

By his own admission, Weston isn't a mathematician or a statistician, and thus his estimates may or may not be accurate. However, even if his later suppositions are wrong, he says that counting only those Muslims currently living in Europe who will be 18-40 years old in 2025, the European to Muslim ratio would be 9:1, which doesn't sound very promising for Europe, particularly given the nature of jihad warfare and the martyrdom mentality of fundamentalist Muslims.

Even more important than statistics is the fact that end time prophecy does in fact speak of civil wars (see Isaiah 19:2; Zech 14:13; Ezra 5:9, 6:24). In Matthew 24:7 Jesus said that "nation will rise against nation and kingdom against kingdom." While the term "kingdom" is a political designation, the term "nation" refers to ethnic groups, including those within shared political boundaries, i.e., civil war. If you'll recall, the feet and toes of Nebuchadnezzar's statue was iron mixed with clay, "combining in the seeds of men but not adhering to one another." It's possible that this enigmatic description refers to Western Europe as a kingdom conquered. This is further supported by Jeremiah's prophecy that Ararat and Minni (Armenia), and Ashkenaz (generally agreed to be Germany, Scandinavia and Saxons)[25] will be the countries to come against the end time Babylon (51:27).

One is Yet to Come

In Revelation 17:11, the angel gives John four pieces of information about the beast out of the sea:

---

24   Paul Weston, Gates of Vienna, "Is European Civil War Inevitable by 2025?" http://gatesofvienna.blogspot.com/2007/03/is-european-civil-war-inevitable-by.html
25   Saxons were Germanic tribes that migrated to the western coast of Europe, Scandinavia and England, and ultimately America.

- it existed as an empire before Rome
- it didn't exist as an empire at the time of Rome
- it came as the seventh empire after Rome and "remained a little while"
- it will return as the eighth empire that comes from the abyss and will be destroyed

Alexander's Empire existed before Rome but not at the time of Rome (and not even as part of Rome, since Babylonia and Persia were never taken). It was this whole area that was conquered by the Islamic Empire, but it certainly didn't remain a little while, lasting from 632 until 1922. However, if we count only the Seleucid and Ptolemaic divisions of Alexander's empire (which are the focus of Daniel), we can say that these were revived in the short 30 years of the Rashidun Caliphate. It's this seventh empire—the "Muhammadan dynasty," that will return in our future to be the core of the eighth and final beast kingdom.

The Wounded Head

Revelation 13:3
And I saw one of his heads as if it had been slain [received the deathblow], and his fatal wound was healed.

In the Hadith, Muhammad says, "As Allah opened with us [my family] so he will close, and with us they [Christians] will be saved from polytheism." According to Shaykh Abdullah ben Sadek, "This means that as Allah opened this Religion with the Holy Prophet, so he will close it with Al Mahdi. Therefore, Mahdi is the sealer of the appearance of the Religion..."[26] As the blood descendant of

---

26   The Grand Muhaddith of Morocco, Shaykh Abdullah ben Sadek, Ph.D. in the questions and answer portion of "Al Mahdi, Jesus and the Anti-

Muhammad, Al Mahdi is the resurrection of his dynasty, as well as the modern successor to the dead king of a war-devastated Saudi Arabia, rising from the ashes of the religion's birthplace to become emperor of the world. According to Revelation 17:8, when this happens, those who are not Christians will "wonder" at it. This word "wonder" is *thaumazo,* which means "to marvel at, admire, be astonished at." Now, if this passage referred to the literal resurrection of a man, as some Bible scholars teach, it would astonish everyone, not just non-Christians (assuming one could prove it). But the non-Christians in that part of the world are Muslims, and as 13:3-4 indicates, Al Mahdi's victory over As-Sufyani will be the sign that he's the rightly guided Imam who will rule the world under Islam. As if all this weren't convincing enough, the Shi'as even call the establishment of Al Mahdi's kingdom the *"minor resurrection,"* asserting that he "represents in name, nature and attributes, the last Prophet, Muhammad," and constitutes "the rule of the perfect man over the world."[27]

In the sixth letter of Revelation, Christ quotes directly from Isaiah 22:15-24, identifying Himself with His type in Eliakim ("God will establish"), of whom God says, "Then I will set the key of the house of David on his shoulder, when he opens no one will shut, when he shuts, no one will open." The man that Eliakim is said to replace in this passage is a type of Al Mahdi himself, a man named Shebna, which means "God has returned me." The fact that the sixth letter is linked to the sixth seal, which is the sign of Al Mahdi's establishment in Islamic prophecy, supports the idea that he is the metaphorical resurrection of the prophet Muhammad and a re-establishment of his dynasty.

Christ," The Muhammadan Reality, http://www.muhammadanreality.com / ImamMahdiSignsforthesavoir.htm

27   "Twelfth Imam/Hidden Imam/Imam Mahdi," p. 3, GlobalSecurity.org, http://www.globalsecurity.org /military/intro/Imam-mahdi.htm

Ten Horns, Ten Kings

Revelation 13:1
...And I saw a beast coming up out of the sea, having ten horns... and on his horns were ten diadems.

Revelation 17:12-14
¹²And the ten horns which you saw are ten kings, who have not yet received a kingdom, but they receive authority as kings with the beast for one hour. ¹³These have one purpose and they give their power and authority to the beast. ¹⁴These will wage war against the Lamb...

Remember, these horns start off as generals in As-Sufyani's armies, but three are defeated by or defect to Al Mahdi, leaving As-Sufyani to come under seven banners. In fact, the Hadith specifically names and describes in detail some of these men. It would be common for such trusted men to receive leadership positions over areas in the empire. The prophecies state that at least some of the men in As-Sufyani's armies are coerced into joining him; if the remainder of his generals defect to Al Mahdi, it would explain why the Despicable Person has no one to help him, and why all ten are wearing diadems.

12

The Seventh Seal: Trumpets 1-6

The Time of the Seventh Seal

Islamic prophecy

The Islamic Antichrist, Al Dajaal, will pit himself and his magic against Al Mahdi and the Prophet Jesus. He'll show signs and wonders, but will ultimately be slain, along with his army of Christians and Jews. Together, Al Mahdi and the Prophet Jesus will establish the Islamic world kingdom from Jerusalem, righting all the wrongs of Judaism and Christianity. Those who aren't beheaded will be held hostage, sold into slavery or treated as Dhimmis, "insulted ones."

Seventh Seal: Lightning, Earthquake, Trumpets, Bowls

Revelation 8:1-5
¹And when He broke the seventh seal, there was silence in heaven for about half an hour. ²And I saw the seven angels who stand before God; and seven trumpets were given to them. ³And another angel came and stood at the altar, holding a golden censer;

and much incense was given to him, that he might add it to the prayers of all the saints upon the golden altar which was before the throne. ⁴And the smoke from the incense, with the prayers of the saints, went up before God out of the angel's hand. ⁵And the angel took the censer; and he filled it with the fire of the altar and threw it to the earth; and there followed peals of thunder and sounds and flashes of lightning and an earthquake.

The seventh seal is extremely significant, for it marks the final stage of Christ's taking possession of the earth. Remember that the martyrs were under the altar, asking God to avenge them, and from this same altar, fire is taken and added to the incense and the prayers of the saints, then thrown to the earth. This imagery shows us the connection between the prayers and suffering of the saints and the final redemption of the earth.

The Seventh Letter: Laodicea

Revelation 3:14-22
¹⁴And to the angel of the church in Laodicea write: the Amen, the faithful and true Witness, the Beginning of the creation of God says this: ¹⁵I know your deeds that you are neither cold nor hot; I would that you were cold or hot. ¹⁶So because you are lukewarm, and neither hot nor cold, I will spit you out of My mouth. ¹⁷Because you say, "I am rich, and have become wealthy, and have need of nothing," and you do not know that you are wretched and miserable and poor and blind and naked, ¹⁸I advise you to buy from me gold refined by fire, that you may become rich and white garments, that you may clothe yourself, and that the shame of your nakedness may not be revealed; and eye salve to anoint your eyes, that you may see. ¹⁹Those whom I love, I reprove and

discipline; be zealous therefore and repent. ²⁰Behold, I stand at the door and knock; if anyone hears My voice and opens the door, I will come into him and will dine with him and he with Me. ²¹He who overcomes, I will grant to him to sit down with Me on My throne as I also overcame and sat down with My Father on his throne. ²²He who has an ear, let him hear what the Spirit says to the churches.

Laodicea as a Type of Jerusalem

The name *Laodicea* can be broken down into *laos*, "people," and *dike*, "judgment, punishment." This city was named after the wife of Antiochus I, and its meaning is fitting, given that it's the only church about which Jesus has nothing good to say. Once again, Christ addresses this letter to a city that was a great commercial center of the ancient world, strategically positioned upon the most important road in Asia. Leading from Ephesus on its way to Syria, the road climbed 8500 feet, until it reached a gorge too treacherous to pass. Thus it detoured through the Lycus valley and Laodicea. This makes Laodicea an interesting metaphor for the beast's Jerusalem: the only way to pass the narrow road is to pass through the fire, and this is the message Jesus gives to the Church at the seventh seal.

Laodicea was a center of banking and finance, one of the wealthiest cities in the world. Like Sardis and Philadelphia, Laodicea was destroyed by an earthquake, but was so wealthy that it refused any aid from Rome. The city was a maker of garments and also produced eye salve, so that Christ's allusions to its spiritual poverty, nakedness and blindness were cleverly tied into to the economy of the city.

The Church of Laodicea as a Type of the Seventh Seal Church

You are lukewarm, and neither hot nor cold, I will spit you out of My mouth: Hot is medicinal, and cold is refreshing, but lukewarm is repulsive. If hot describes a church passionate for Him, then cold is a heart-hardened people who actively reject Him. Perhaps Jesus is saying here that those who are most adamantly against him have more of a chance of turning to Him than those who, thinking themselves saved, sit in complacency refusing to respond to the words of the prophecy. It raises an interesting question regarding how God sees us. Jesus said to the Pharisees, "...I did not come to call the righteous, but sinners" (Matt 9:13b). Remember that Christ teaches us we must hear the word *and* do it in order to enter the kingdom. These are those of Sardis who don't respond to His call to repent; they will miss the seventh trumpet harvest rapture and suffer the bowl judgments.

You say, "I am rich, and have become wealthy, and have need of nothing," and you do not know that you are wretched and miserable and poor and blind and naked. I advise you to buy from me gold refined by fire: Such is Laodicea's attitude toward God! Perhaps the Church at the seventh seal has become rich through Jezebel's intrigues, but clearly God sees them as wretched, miserable, poor, blind and naked. It's shocking to see such a wide chasm between how the Church sees itself and what God's reality is; yet still He calls them the Church and advises them to buy from Him gold refined by fire. This image of purification by the fire of tribulation at the hand of God is used repeatedly in scripture: "...for He is like a refiner's fire... (Mal 3:2). Paul, speaking to those teachers and apostles who would build upon the foundation of Christ, says that "...the fire will test the quality of each man's work" (I Cor 3:13b). According to verse 19, the trials Laodicea must suffer are His discipline, executed in love.

Buy white garments, that you may clothe yourself, and that the shame of your nakedness may not be revealed: By advising the Church to *buy* the gold and garments, Jesus emphasizes their focus on material wealth. True wealth comes from what He offers freely, yet even in the gospel, Christ makes it clear that relationship with Him comes at the cost of our very lives: he who hates his life will gain it, but he who loves his life will lose it (John 12:25). Just before the seventh bowl destruction of Jerusalem, Christ echoes His letter to Laodicea "Behold I am coming like a thief. Blessed is the one who stays and *keeps his garments, lest he walk about naked and men see his shame*" (16:15, italics mine). He no longer advises them to *buy* the garments, but rather to *keep* them, indicating that there are those in the Church of Laodicea who do repent, perhaps as a result of missing the seventh trumpet harvest.

Behold, I stand at the door and knock; if anyone hears My voice and opens the door, I will come into him and will dine with him and he with Me: His standing at the door is a metaphor for the nearness of His millennial kingdom. Compare this to what He says in Matthew 24:33 after describing the harvest rapture at the seventh trumpet: "Even so you too, when you see all these things, recognize that He is near, *right at the door*"! The reference to His dining with the Church is also significant, as the marriage supper of the Lamb is imminent.

He who overcomes, I will grant to him to sit down with Me on My throne as I also overcame and sat down with My Father on his throne: Even Laodicea will receive an overcomer's reward: to sit on the throne with Christ! These Christians who were lukewarm, and spit out of God's mouth, will receive the same reward as the martyrs in every seal, from Ephesus to Philadelphia; and by the grace (and discipline) of God, they will be worthy of it!

The Title of Christ to the Church

The Amen, the faithful and true Witness, the Beginning of the creation of God: The way Christ identifies himself to the church at Laodicea is significant. Amen is a term that means "so let it be," a word of fulfillment, of consummation. How fitting for a letter written to the Church of the 7th trumpet, when the "mystery of God is finished." He also calls Himself the faithful and true witness, claiming His authority to judge those who are not faithful and true witnesses, namely Laodicea.

It boggles the mind how Laodicea could even be called "the Church" at all, and in fact this raises many questions as to what constitutes "the Church" in the mind of God. Clearly He sees these people as set apart, but in what way? Christ makes it very plain in the letter to Sardis that it's possible to be erased from the book of life. If these Christians are not taken at Thyatira, and are left behind at the harvest rapture, do they still have salvation? As discussed earlier, Christ preaches a preparation for heaven that involves more than mere belief in Him as Savior. The idea of bearing fruit certainly refers to our personal growth in the Lord, but such growth is intimately linked with our witness to the world through our works and gifts (Matt 5:16, 25:14-30; John 4:36-38). Clearly, the goal of our witness is to bring as many people as possible into the kingdom; this is the mission of the Church.

Trumpets 1-6

The Great Tribulation marks the beginning of Jacob's Trouble, God's chastening of Israel, and like in the Old Testament, He hasn't forgotten to send His prophets to warn them about the coming judgment. Not only will the Jews have the testimony of the Church throughout the first three and a half years, but at their rapture, the two witnesses and the 144,000 will be left to continue their work, their message being intensified by the trumpet plagues.

During the 1260 day rule of Al Mahdi, the witnesses travel around the Middle East, preaching the gospel of Christ, performing wonders, and using fire to kill anyone who would harm them. According to Revelation 11:6, their wonders consist of shutting up the sky, turning water to blood, and plagues of various kinds. A quick scan of the trumpets include all of these: fire and blood from heaven burn the earth; a mountain of fire from heaven turns the sea to blood; a burning star from heaven turns fresh waters bitter; the sun and moon are darkened; a plague of locusts come sting men for five months; plagues of fire and brimstone from the mouths of horses.

Is there any reason to believe that these trumpet plagues are not brought upon the earth by the two witnesses themselves? Even the army of the sixth trumpet that kills a third of mankind appears to be comprised of the saints and the witnesses, who are defeated by the beast at the seventh trumpet (Revelation 11:7). This same army can only be interpreted as Islam's Al Dajaal, leading his Jewish and Christian followers to besiege Jerusalem, only to be defeated by the Prophet Jesus. After all, when the witnesses are killed, the whole earth rejoices and gives gifts to each other "because these two prophets tormented those who dwell on the earth" (Rev 11:10). Is this torment perpetrated through the trumpet plagues and the siege? If God's judgment is upon Israel and the earth in the trumpets, who better to administer them than Moses and Elijah?

In the Song of Moses (Deut 32), God says "I will heap misfortunes on [Israel]...they shall be wasted by famine and consumed by plague and bitter destruction; and the teeth of beasts I will send upon them, with the venom of crawling things of the dust. Outside the sword shall bereave, and inside terror...I would have said, 'I will cut them to pieces, I will remove the memory of them from men,' had I not feared the provocation by the enemy, lest their adversaries should misjudge, lest they should say 'Our hand is triumphant, and the Lord has not done all this.'" Why else would Al Mahdi and Prophet Jesus gloat, unless they had defeated God's own army?

If the witnesses' 1260 days of prophesying involves miraculously calling down the trumpet plagues, then our timeline is correct in putting the seventh seal midway through the week; this would mean it's possible that the trumpets occur throughout Al Mahdi's 3 ½ year reign. On the other hand, it's possible that trumpets 1-5 happen in the first few months; if through his shrewdness and influence Al Mahdi is able to solve the many problems arising from such catastrophic events, he would be seen as a true messiah figure, creating order out of chaos. He could then corrupt the many while they're "at ease."

The plagues are a combination of natural disasters and human warfare; the problem is that it's not always easy to tell which is which. If the witnesses are to be blamed for everything that goes on, their prophecies must be very public, and the connection between what they say and its results must be unmistakable. Notice that these judgments come in thirds, reminiscent of God's prophecy in Ezekiel 5.

Trumpet 1

Revelation 8:6-7
⁶And the seven angels who had the seven trumpets prepared themselves to sound them. ⁷And the first sounded and there came hail and fire, mixed with blood and they were thrown to the earth; and a third of the earth was burned up, and a third of the trees were burned up and all the green grass was burned up.

Notice that in each of the first six trumpets, both witnesses are represented: fire for Elijah, and blood or a plague of some kind for Moses. In this case, it's both blood and hail. It's possible that the sixth seal itself is an event brought on by the witnesses, and if this is the case, there may be a causal relationship between it and the first trumpet. Leaving out the descriptions of the 144,000 sealed Jews and the raptured gentile multitude, it appears that the seventh seal is broken immediately after the sixth seal, with a pause of about 30 minutes before the events of the first trumpet begin. If the sixth seal is caused by large asteroids or meteors entering the earth's atmosphere, the red glow of burning silicate in the atmosphere could give the appearance of blood. Such huge bodies could break up into pieces large and fast enough to survive the earth's atmosphere and, upon impacting the surface, create a shower of meteorites, which John might interpret as hail; this phenomenon was reported at the impact of the 2007 Carancas meteorite that hit near Lake Titicaca in Peru.[1] Alternatively, the dust in the atmosphere from the sixth seal could produce actual hail discolored by the contaminates in the air. A fourth possibility is that the rain of fire and blood are the result of a volcanic eruption, such as from the Jabal at-tair on the Gulf of Aqaba, raining down fire and lava to the earth; the earthquake in the sixth and seventh seals could cause such an eruption.

Trumpet 2

Revelation 8:8-9
⁸And the second angel sounded, and something like a great mountain burning with fire was thrown into the sea; and a third of the sea became blood; ⁹and a third of the creatures, which were in the sea and had life, died; and a third of the ships were destroyed.

---

1   USA Today, Monte Hayes,"Meteorite likely caused crater in Peru,"9/20/07, http://www.usatoday.com/tech/ science/2007-09-20-4026226677_x.htm

Some think this trumpet is the unleashing of an atomic bomb. Yet John knows what he sees; there's a big size difference between a bomb and a mountain. A meteorite two football fields in diameter hitting the Mediterranean would cause a tsunami large enough to inflict catastrophic destruction of coastal cities,[2] destroying ships at sea and in many harbors and choking out life for many miles around ground zero.

Trumpet 3

Revelation 8:10,11
[10]And the third angel sounded and a great star fell from heaven, burning like a torch, and it fell on a third of the rivers and on the springs of waters; [11]and the name of the star is called Wormwood, and a third of the waters became wormwood; and many men died from the waters because they were made bitter.

The star must be symbolic of an event, since neither a single meterorite nor a single bomb could fall on multiple rivers and springs. If the star represents bombs, they would have to be chemical or biological. The question then would be who drops them. If Al Mahdi is deceiving people with peace, and the Islamic world is united in recognizing his authority, it would have to be the witnesses themselves, or an entity that comes against the Islamic Empire.

On the other hand, the star could be metaphorical of a plague of meterorites. The Jordan River alone supplies 75% of the water filling the Sea of Galilee, which is the source of one third of Israel's fresh water. If a number of large meteorites land in the river then, like the meteorite at Carancas, their heated sulfur content could

---

[2] Mark Prado, "Earth Impact by an Asteroid: Prospects and Effects," http://www.permanent.com/a-impact.htm

combine with the water to create sulfurous acid, temporarily poisoning it.[3] In addition, the impact could cause ground water (i.e., springs) contaminated with arsenic or other toxins to leach into the river.

Trumpet 4

Revelation 8:12-13
[12]And the fourth angel sounded and a third of the sun and a third of the moon and a third of the stars were smitten so that a third of them might be darkened and the day might not shine for a third of it, and the night in the same way.[13]And I looked, and I heard an eagle flying in midheaven, saying with a loud voice, "Woe, woe, woe, to those who dwell on the earth, because of the remaining blasts of the trumpet of the three angels who are about to sound!"

This can't be an eclipse, since the stars are also darkened. This plague is reminiscent of Moses' plague of darkness, and also of the darkness that fell at Christ's crucifixion. If the third trumpet is caused by war or natural disaster, the eight hours of darkness could be produced by smoke or dust.

The source of the voice in this passage is worth noting; while all the other prophetic voices in Revelation come from heaven, this one comes from "midheaven," which is the sky—the earthly realm. The only other mention of an eagle in Revelation is the woman in Chapter 12, who's given the "two wings of the great eagle" to go to the place prepared for her by God. Maybe she's the voice of prophecy concerning the woes to come, possibly through various forms of media.

---

3   Piper R.W. Hollier, "Meteorites and sulfurous odors," http://www.mail-archive.com/meteorite-list@meteoritecentral.com/msg59812.html

Trumpet 5

Revelation 9:1-11
¹And the fifth angel sounded, and I saw a star from heaven which had fallen to the earth; and the key of the bottomless pit was given to him. ²And he opened the bottomless pit; and smoke went up out of the pit, like the smoke of a great furnace; and the sun and the air were darkened by the smoke of the pit. ³And out of the smoke came forth locusts upon the earth; and power was given them, as scorpions of the earth have power. ⁴And they were told that they should not hurt the grass of the earth, nor any green thing, nor any tree, but only the men who do not have the seal of God on their foreheads. ⁵And they were not permitted to kill anyone, but to torment for five months; and their torment was like the torment of a scorpion when it stings a man. ⁶And in those days, men will seek death and will not find it; and they will long to die and death flees from them. ⁷And the appearance of the locusts was like horses prepared for battle; and on their heads, as it were, crowns like gold and their faces were like the faces of men. ⁸And they had hair like the hair of women, and their teeth were like the teeth of lions. ⁹And they had breastplates like breastplates of iron; and the sound of their wings was like the sound of chariots, of many horses rushing to battle. ¹⁰And they have tails like scorpions, and stings; and in their tails is the power to hurt men for five months. ¹¹They have as king over them, the angel of the abyss; his name in Hebrew is Abaddon and in the Greek he has the name Apollyon.

Some have interpreted this as being demons because a fallen star (i.e., Lucifer) opens the door of the bottomless pit and releases a plague that's controlled by the Destroyer. But even demons must cause suffering through some kind of earthly action. The description here appears to combine a literal event (the smoke coming up in a column, as described in Joel 2:30), with a locust plague reminiscent of the plagues of Moses and Joel; yet they're clearly metaphorical, for they are no ordinary locusts.

First of all, although they have the teeth of a lion, they're restrained by God from eating anything green, which is after all, what locusts do. Secondly, they have the ability to inflict upon men the same symptoms as those caused by a scorpion sting. These can include muscle cramps, increased heart rate, sweating and tearing of the eyes, as well as difficulty breathing. Note whom the plague affects: only Muslims and other unbelievers, despite the fact that it comes from the pit (which would make us expect the primary target to be God's people). Ironically, although "the Destroyer" is king over them, the locusts don't destroy anything—at least not physically. John describes these locusts as the very Babylonians who destroyed Jerusalem: horses prepared for battle; the faces of men; gold crowns (turbans); long hair;[4] teeth like a lion (symbol of Babylon); breastplates like iron (red like the vermilion worn by the Chaldeans[5]); wings rushing like chariots. Yet this can't be warfare—in what kind of war do soldiers hurt but not kill the enemy?

The question is what modern phenomenon fits John's description? 1) It's something released by burning; 2) it's transported through the air in smoke; 3) it results in respiratory and neurological symptoms that last for five months; 4) it's somehow connected to Babylonia. One thing that matches these details is chemical weaponry. If the Wormwood of the third trumpet represents bombs, then it's possible that trumpets three, four and five are connected: the bombs fall, poison the water and cause smoke thick enough to obscure the sun. Then, from some of the bombs, very low levels of nerve gas are released, causing the neurological and respiratory

---

4   According to Herodotus from *The History of the Persian Wars*, I.195, c. 430 BCE
5   Ezek 23:14

symptoms of scorpions. The connection with Babylonia could merely be spiritual or historical—that it's an attack against Jerusalem as God's judgment. If so, the ones delivering the bombs would have to do so with the explicit goal of not killing anyone; the attacks could continue for five months.

On the other hand, it's an established fact that Iraq has produced chemical weapons in the past.[6] If the third trumpet consists of meteorites, could it be that some fall on chemical weapons plants or storage sites in Iraq, setting them on fire and disseminating small quantities of nerve gas? This would better explain the smoke rising in columns. As for the five month duration, at least one study shows that several types of nerve gas persist in the environment for about that time.[7]

Whatever the mechanism for this plague, the metaphor is too similar to Job to be missed: with God's permission, Satan tries to destroy Job's soul by making him suffer physically—to make him "curse God and die." Just as all of Moses' plagues caused Pharaoh's heart to be hardened towards God, so will these plagues cause the Muslims to curse Jehovah (Rev 16:21). The fact that those with God's seal are protected from this poison brings to mind several passages which describe such protection from venomous creatures: Luke 10:19, Mark 16:18, and Acts 28:3-6.

Trumpet 6

Revelation 9:13-21

¹³And the sixth angel sounded, and I heard a voice from the four horns of the golden altar which is before God, ¹⁴one saying to the

---

[6] Iraq Watch, Wisconsin Project on Nuclear Arms Control, "Iraq's Chemical Weapon Program," http://www.iraqwatch.org/profiles/chemical.html

[7] Wendy J. Davis-Hoover et.al, "Persistence of Sarin, Soman, VX and Lewisite, and Destruction of Tabun and Mustard Gas in Municipal Solid Waste Landfill Leachates," extended abstract #379

sixth angel who had the trumpet, "Release the four angels who are bound at the great river Euphrates." ¹⁵And the four angels, who had been prepared for the hour and day and month and year; were released, so that they might kill a third of mankind. ¹⁶And the number of the armies of the horsemen was two hundred million, I heard the number of them. ¹⁷And this is how I saw in the vision the horses and those who sat on them: the riders had breastplates the color of fire and of hyacinth and of brimstone; and the heads of the horses are like the heads of lions and out of their mouths proceed fire and smoke and brimstone. ¹⁸A third of mankind was killed by these three plagues, by the fire and the smoke and the brimstone, which proceeded out of their mouths. ¹⁹For the power of the horses is in their mouths and in their tails; for their tails are like serpents and have heads; and with them they do harm. ²⁰And the rest of mankind, who were not killed by these plagues, did not repent of the works of their hands, so as not to worship demons, and the idols of silver and of brass and of stone and of wood, which can neither see nor hear nor walk; ²¹and they did not repent of their murders nor of their sorceries nor of their immorality nor of their thefts.

Some theorize that this is a demonic army unleashed upon the earth to plague mankind (or as some would have it, specifically to kill Christians). However, there is no indication that the four angels are demons, and the fire and brimstone coming from the tails and mouths of horses is clearly a metaphor for modern weaponry. The fact is, this isn't the first time in scripture that a military attack is depicted as judgment at the hand of angels. In Ezekiel 9 there are six angels appointed to go through Jerusalem and kill by sword all but a third of the people, who are left as a remnant. These six angels corresponded to the armies of Babylonia which killed the inhabitants of the city with swords.

Because war is fought against a specific enemy for a specific purpose, we must look to the text for clues as to the army's target and reason for fighting. The voice giving the command comes from the horns of the golden altar of incense, which symbolized the prayers of the people going up to God, thus we can assume that this army comes in answer to the prayers of the saints. Verse 20 tells us that John expected the survivors of this army's attack to stop worshiping demons and idols, and to repent of murders, sorceries, immorality and thefts. The only reason to have such an expectation is if God sent the army as a judgment upon people in an attempt to have them repent. This points to the "third of mankind" as being non-Christians.

Instead of the six angels of Ezekiel, this plague is unleashed by four, a number which makes us think of the four points of the compass, as the four angels who hold back the winds of the earth in Revelation 7:1. In Daniel 10:13 and 12:1 we're told that specific angels represent or protect nations in the spiritual realm. Assuming these are heavenly angels (not demons), their position at the Euphrates could be interpreted as their role in protecting the earth by holding back the expansion of the Islamic Empire like an invisible wall (see Isaiah 8:7-8, where the Euphrates is used as a metaphor for Assyria, the type of As-Sufyani). Their release aligns with the purpose of the seven trumpets as the manifestation of Christ taking back the kingdom.

Some believe that China will be the origin of this army because of its large population and their past boasts of being able to raise an army of this size. Alternatively, some argue that the term "twice myriads of myriads" isn't intended to be literal, but is merely a term to describe an army so large that it's too many to count. Notice, however, that John makes a special point of telling us that he heard the number of the horseman—almost in anticipation of our incredulity at such a large figure; this isn't something he would say if he were using idiomatic or figurative language. The problem is that the size of such an army is unprecedented and, quite frankly unfeasible (roughly two thirds of the U.S. population). The logistics and cost of moving and maintaining an army of this size would make it inconceivable, not to mention unnecessary; wars are fought and won with far fewer troops than this. For example, the estimated total number of soldiers in all branches of the U.S. military, including the coast guard and reserves, is 2.5 million.

Imagine a sea of 200 million soldiers stretching out as far as the eye could see. Could John have been seeing people of every nation rising up in their own countries to fight against Muslim occupation?[8] He says their breastplates are red (fire), blue (hyacinth), and yellow (brimstone), possibly an emblem or flag that a resistance movement would organize under. Yet perhaps the most significant information this gives us, is that there's no green, which is the color of Islam.

There are several prophecies that tell us who ally themselves with Al Mahdi, but it's unclear who may arise against him. Jeremiah 51:27-28 lists those nations that God brought against ancient Babylonia: Ararat, Minni, Ashkenaz and the Medes. Ararat and Minni are modern Armenia. According to Rabbinic literature, Ashkenaz was the ancestor of the Saxons, and is the Medieval Hebrew name for Germany. The Saxons migrated into Scandinavia, the European west coast and England (and ultimately to America); they were also invited by the Hungarian kings to settle in parts of modern day Romania during the Middle Ages. According to Walid Shoebat, Russia was settled by Scandinavian tribes, and thus he includes them with Europe in the term Ashkenaz.[9]

---

8   As mentioned earlier, the Hadith mentions that Al Mahdi makes a seven year treaty with the West, which the West breaks; this could be the fulfillment of that prophecy.
9   Walid Shoebat, "Islam and the Final Beast," p. 4, http://answering-islam.org/Walid/gog.htm

While this theory may account for the 200 million men that John sees, however, it doesn't explain the fulfillment of the Islamic prophecy that 70,000[10] Jews and Christians march on Jerusalem from Isfahan, a province in west central Iran. This may be where the Medes come in. The Medes (earlier Iranians) expanded their empire to include all of Iran, which today has an estimated Jewish population of between 25,000 and 40,000 mostly in Tehran, Shiraz and Isfahan (of course this would be a geographical, not an ethnic designation).[11] In addition, if the lions' heads of the horses symbolize Babylonia, members of the Chaldean Christian Church may help to fulfill this part of the prophecy. This subgroup of the Roman Catholic Church is made up of the descendents of ancient Mesopotamia who identify themselves as Assyrians. Its headquarters is in Iraq, having significant populations in Iraq, Syria, Iran, and Turkey. Perhaps most interesting of all, is that the colors of their flag are yellow, blue and red. This could explain why, despite all the prophecies regarding God's vengeful destruction of Assyria (as the type of As-Sufyani), Isaiah 19:25 blesses Assyria as His people.

Scripture indicates that although the 200 million man army kills one third of mankind, ultimately they lose against Al Mahdi, for he overcomes both the witnesses (Rev 11:7) and the saints (Rev 13:7). This is the most obvious timeframe for the Islamic prophecy regarding the slaughter of the unbelievers in Jerusalem (when the rocks cry out to betray the Christians and Jews hiding behind them). As a result, the people say, "Who can wage war against [Al Mahdi]?" This hopelessness is depicted in Isaiah's prophecy about Christ's return:

---

10   Some Muslim scholars say that this number is not necessarily literal, but could be intended to denote a very large number.

11   Another possibility for this number comes from the Pashtans or Pathans, Muslims with large populations in Afghanistan, Pakistan and Iran who claim their origins to be from various Israeli tribes, including the sons of Joseph. It could be that they convert to Christianity and join the witnesses (could this be why Manasseh instead of Dan is named among the 144,000 who are sealed in Rev 7:6?)

Isaiah 63:1-6
¹Who is this who comes from Edom [Jordan], with garments of glowing colors from Bozrah, this One who is majestic in His apparel, marching in the greatness of His strength? ²Why is Your apparel red, and Your garments like the one who treads in the wine press? ³I have trodden the wine trough alone, and from the peoples there was no man with Me. I also trod them in My anger, and trampled them in My wrath; and their lifeblood is sprinkled on My garments, and I stained all My raiment. ⁴For the day of vengeance was in My heart, and My year of redemption has come. ⁵And I looked and there was no one to help. And I was astonished and there was no one to uphold; so My own arm brought salvation to Me and My wrath upheld Me. ⁶And I trod down the peoples in My anger, and made them drunk in My wrath, and I poured out their lifeblood on the earth.

With no armies for Him to help or uphold, Christ comes with His heavenly armies because there's no other hope for the earth.

The Fifth and Sixth Trumpets in Old Testament Prophecy

If the fifth and sixth trumpets depict human warfare, they find precedent in an end time prophecy given by Joel, which appears to go back and forth between literal locusts and metaphors for warfare:

Joel 1:4-7, 2:1-4, 10-11
⁴What the gnawing locust has left, the swarming locust has eaten; and what the swarming locust has left, the creeping locust has eaten; and what the creeping locust has left, the stripping locust has eaten...⁶For a nation has invaded my land, mighty and without number; its teeth are the teeth of a lion and it has the fangs of a

lioness. ⁷It has made my vine a waste, and my fig tree splinters. It has stripped them bare and cast them away...²:¹Blow a trumpet in Zion and sound an alarm on My holy mountain! Let all the inhabitants of the land tremble, for the day of the Lord is coming; Surely it is near, ²a day of darkness and gloom, a day of clouds and thick darkness as the dawn is spread over the mountains, so there is a great and mighty people; there has never been anything like it, nor will there be again after it. To the years of many generations, ³a fire consumes before them, and behind them a flame burns. The land is like the garden of Eden before them, but a desolate wilderness behind them and nothing at all escapes them. ⁴Their appearance is like the appearance of horses and like war horses so they run...¹⁰Before them the earth quakes, the heavens tremble the sun and the moon grow dark and the stars lose their brightness. ¹¹And the Lord utters His voice before His army; surely His camp is very great, for strong is he who carries out His word. The day of the Lord is indeed great, and very awesome. And who can endure it?

Joel appears to describe the fifth and sixth trumpet events by describing a literal locust plague in terms of war. John uses the same images, describing a metaphorical locust plague first, then literal warfare.

13

The Seventh Seal Continued: Trumpet 7

The Seventh Trumpet

Revelation 11:15-19

¹⁵And the seventh angel sounded; and there arose loud voices in heaven, saying "The kingdom of the world has become the kingdom our Lord, and of His Christ and He will reign forever and ever. ¹⁶And the twenty-four elders who sit on their thrones before God, fell on their faces and worshiped God ¹⁷saying, "We give You thanks, O Lord God, the almighty, who is and who was because You have taken Your great power and have begun to reign. ¹⁸And the nations were enraged and Your wrath came, and the time came for the dead to be judged, and the time to give their reward to Your bond-servants the prophets and to the saints and to those who fear Your name, the small and the great, and to destroy those who destroy the earth."¹⁹And the temple of God which is in heaven was opened: and the ark of His covenant appeared in His temple and there were flashes of lightning and sounds and peals of thunder and an earthquake and a great hailstorm.

"In the days of the voice of the seventh angel, when he is about to sound, then the mystery of God is finished as He preached to His servants the prophets" (10:7). Indeed, here is the voice of the seventh angel and in verse 18, the elders prophesy about the final events of the age's consummation. For this reason, the Little Book is opened at the seventh trumpet—not because its events begin at this time, but because they're finished. The chronology of the seventh trumpet events is as follows: 1) the resurrection and ascension of the two witnesses; 2) the appearance of the Ark of the Covenant; 3) the rapture of the 144,000; 4) the beast out of the land and its campaign of the mark; 5) the harvest rapture; 6) the seven bowl judgment.

1) The Resurrection and Ascension of the Two Witnesses (11:8-10)

Revelation 11:8-12
⁸And their dead bodies will lie in the street of the great city which mystically is called Sodom and Egypt, where also their Lord was crucified. ⁹And those from the peoples and tribes and tongues and nations will look at their dead bodies for three and a half days, and will not permit their dead bodies to be laid in a tomb. ¹¹And after the three and a half days the breath of life from God came into them and they stood on their feet; and great fear fell upon those who were beholding them. ¹²And they heard a loud voice from heaven saying to them "Come up here." And they went up into heaven in the cloud and their enemies beheld them.

Having been killed by the Prophet Jesus in their battle against Al Mahdi, the witnesses lie dead in "the great city," Jerusalem, where "also their Lord was crucified." It's not difficult to understand the reference to Sodom—in fact, Jerusalem is compared to it or called this in several prophecies (Isa 1:10, 3:9; Jer 23:14; Ezek 16:51);

this name is for those who participate in the unholy marriage between Israel and the beast. The name Egypt is given to Jerusalem because, just like Egypt oppressed the children of Israel, the beast will oppress the faithful Jewish Church; and just as God rescued the Hebrews with an outstretched hand, He will do so once again by harvesting them off the earth (Rev 14:16). Here we have the second rapture, which is a sign to all of Israel that these two were truly God's prophets; it also serves as a type of the harvest rapture to come: the witnesses are dead for three and a half days, one day for each year that Israel is in distress under Al Mahdi. Their ascension marks the end of the 1260 days and the beginning of the 45 day period before the establishment of Christ's millennial reign.

2) Appearance of the Ark (11:19)

Revelation 11:15, 19
¹⁵And the seventh angel sounded, and there arose loud voices in heaven saying, "The kingdom of the world has become the kingdom of our Lord and of His Christ…" ¹⁹And the temple of God which is in heaven was opened; and the ark of His covenant appeared in His temple, and there were flashes of lightning and sounds and peals of thunder and an earthquake and a great hailstorm.

At the sounding of the seventh trumpet, the kingdom of the world is transferred to Christ, the direct result of which is that the veil is pulled aside to reveal the Ark of the Covenant within the holy of holies in the heavenly temple. The only time this ever happened during the temple years was on the Day of Atonement. The book of Hebrews tells us that the temple on earth is a copy of this heavenly temple; when Christ died, He entered it as priest and sacrifice (Heb 9:24), the consequence being that in the earthly temple, the veil between the outer sanctuary and the holy of holies was torn in half (Matt 27:51). It seems reasonable to suppose, then, that any action taking place in the heavenly temple will have a corresponding action in the earthly temple. The Ark's revelation certainly brings about effects on the earth (earthquake, hailstorm), leading us to believe it could literally appear in the earthly temple; after all, this event does figure into both Jewish and Muslim eschatology. Many Jews believe the Ark was hidden somewhere in Israel at the time of the Babylonian conquest, and will accompany the Messiah's appearance. Muslims believe it's hidden around the Sea of Galilee or in Turkey; Al Mahdi will recover it as further proof of his dominion.

The presence of the Ark of the Covenant in the temple would mark the beginning of its vindication. This is spoken of in Daniel 8:14 as happening at the end of the 2300 evenings and mornings (i.e., the end of Al Mahdi's 3 ½ years).

3) The Rapture of the 144,000 (14:1-3)

Revelation 14:1-4
¹And I looked, and behold, the Lamb was standing on Mount Zion, and with Him 144,000, having His name and the name of His father written on their foreheads. ²And I heard a voice from heaven, like the sound of many waters and like the sound of loud thunder, and the voice which I heard was like the sound of harpists playing on their harps. ³And they sang a new song before the throne and before the four living creatures and the elders; and no one could learn the song except the 144,000 who had been purchased from the earth. ⁴These are the ones who have not been defiled with women, for they have kept themselves chaste. These are the ones who follow the Lamb wherever He goes. These have been purchased from among men as first fruits to God and to the Lamb.

We know Christ couldn't be standing on Mount Zion in Israel because according to Matthew 24:24-31, His first appearance on the earth is in the clouds at the harvest rapture. Setting aside the narratives of the woman and the beasts, the context immediately prior to this passage is the heavenly temple, which sits in a heavenly Jerusalem. This is supported by the fact that the 144,000 are singing before God's throne in heaven; this explains their designation as the "first fruits" of the coming harvest rapture of verse 16.

4) The Beast out of the Land and its Campaign of the Mark (13:11-14)

Revelation 13:11-14
¹¹And I saw another beast coming up out of the earth [land]; and he had two horns like a lamb, and he spoke as a dragon. ¹²And he exercises all the authority of the first beast in his presence. And he makes the earth and those who dwell in it to worship the first beast whose fatal wound was healed. ¹³And he performs great signs, so that he even makes fire come down out of heaven to the earth in the presence of men. ¹⁴And he deceives those who dwell on the earth because of the signs which it was given him to perform in the presence of the beast, telling those who dwell on the earth to make an image to the beast who had the wound of the sword and has come to life.

The Biblical timing of this new Israeli government ("out of the land") fits Islamic prophecy, arising after Al Dajaal (the saints and witnesses) is overcome by Al Mahdi and the Prophet Jesus. This is the judgment described by the angel in Revelation 17: Jerusalem riding on the back of the beast. Although they are said to be equal to each other (i.e., "princes over each other"), Prophet Jesus will defer to Al Mahdi as the Supreme Leader. John describes this government as being like a lamb in that it has two kings. This can only mean that its government is a counterfeit of the true Lamb—Jesus as king and Elijah as His prophet (Malachi 4:5-6, Matt 11:13,14). Verse 13 tells us that the false prophet produces the same supernatural signs that Elijah did, and verse 14 states that he does so in order to deceive the world regarding the authority of the first beast. Paralleling the command to build images to the beast, the Hadith states that the Prophet Jesus will "break all the crosses," turning every church into a mosque and forcing all to obey Imam Mahdi.

How much more perfectly could Satan have planned this? The Muslims will have their prophecies confirmed by having a sign-performing Prophet Jesus authenticating Al Mahdi, while the Jews, who've been awaiting Elijah's return to herald and anoint the Messiah will have a Jewish prophet performing the same signs and wonders as Elijah. Even Christians could be confused, especially if they believe that As-Sufyani was the Antichrist and that Al Mahdi and Prophet Jesus have triumphed over him. Jesus says in Matthew 24:24,26 that "...false Christs and false prophets will arise and will show great signs and wonders, so as to mislead, if possible, even the elect." The Prophet Jesus could be a previously unknown Jew who shows up on the scene from out of nowhere, for the Hadith says that he descends from heaven with dew in his hair. But if Jason as a type holds true (after all, his given name was Jeshu, Hebrew for "Jesus"), this man could very well be the original *Nagid* of the Covenant who was flooded away earlier to make room for the *Nagid* to Come. He returns in rebellion, prompting As-Sufyani to turn on Israel. He flees to the wilderness, only to return with an army to fight on behalf of Al Mahdi, and by triumphing over Al Dajaal, is perceived by Muslims as the Prophet Jesus.

If this is the case, many Jews could interpret these events as the fulfillment of rabbinical eschatology as well. The *Nagid* of the Covenant could be interpreted as Messiah ben Joseph ("the anointed son of Joseph"), especially if he fulfills their prophecies by re-establishing the temple worship before being replaced. As-Sufyani would then be interpreted as Armilus, rabbinical tradition's antichrist figure. He persecutes Israel and kills Messiah ben Joseph, who is later resurrected and returns with Messiah ben David (the anointed son of David) to defeat Armilus. Finally, the two anointed figures rule together in peace over Israel. If Al Mahdi has the physical characteristics of a Jew as the Hadith predicts, and if he fulfills the Shi'ite prophecies of speaking Hebrew, having Jewish followers and ruling "according to the law of David and Solomon," [1] he could make a very convincing Messiah ben David.

The Nagid of Tyre as a type of the Prophet Jesus

The following passage in Ezekiel is one of only two exceptions in the scripture when *nagid* is used to refer to a gentile leader:

Ezekiel 28:2-10, 12-16
[2]Son of man, say to the prince (*nagid*) of Tyre, "Thus says the Lord God, 'Because your heart is lifted up and you have said, 'I am a god, I sit in the seat of gods, in the heart of the seas' yet you are a man and not God, although you make your heart like the heart of God...[7]Therefore behold, I will bring strangers upon you, the most ruthless of the nations, and they will draw their swords against the beauty of your wisdom...[10]You will die the death of the uncircumcised by the hand of strangers."

[12]Son of man, take up a lamentation over the king of Tyre and say to him, "Thus says the Lord God, 'You had the seal of perfection, full of wisdom and perfect in beauty. [13]You were in Eden, the

---

1   "Imam Mahdi the Shi'a Version—Messiah Dajjal Al Mashih???" Theunjustmedia.com http://theunjustmedia.com/Islamic%20Perspectives/Feb10/Imam%20mahdi%20The%20S...

garden of God...¹⁴You were the anointed cherub who covers, and I placed you there. You were on the holy mountain of God, you walked in the midst of the stones of fire. ¹⁵You were blameless in your ways from the day you were created until unrighteousness was found in you...¹⁶by the abundance of your trade you were internally filled with violence and you sinned; therefore I have cast you as profane from the mountain of God. And I have destroyed you, O covering [guardian] cherub...'"

The historical king of Tyre was obviously not a Jew, but this passage is clearly not meant only for him; it's directed to him as if he were Satan himself. The use of *nagid* in this passage as well as the reference to dying the death of the uncircumcised point to the king of Tyre as a type of the Islamic Prophet Jesus, the Jewish *nagid* of Israel under Al Mahdi. This isn't the only scripture to use Tyre as a type of the final beast kingdom (see Isaiah 23, in light of chapter 24; Joel 3; Ezek 26-27, especially in light of chapter 28 and Rev 18:9; Hosea 9:13; Amos 1:9-10). Yet another connection made between the beast kingdom and the king of Tyre is Christ's use of his daughter Jezebel as the type of the false prophetess in His letter to Thyatira. Certainly the Prophet Jesus deserves such a searing rebuke, for by claiming to actually be Jesus of Nazareth he truly is pretending to be God Himself.

The Campaign of the Mark

Revelation 14:6-10
⁶And I saw another angel flying in midheaven having an eternal gospel to preach to those who live on the earth and to every nation and tribe and tongue and people; ⁷and he said with a loud voice, "Fear God, and give Him glory, because the hour of His judgment has come; and worship Him who made the heaven and the earth and sea and springs of waters." ⁸And another angel, a

second one, followed saying, "Fallen, fallen is Babylon the great, she who has made all the nations drink of the wine of the passion of her immorality." [9]And another angel a third one, followed them saying with a loud voice, "If anyone worships the beast and his image, and receives a mark on his forehead or upon his hand, [10]he also will drink of the wine of the wrath of God which is mixed in full strength in the cup of His anger; and he will be tormented with fire and brimstone in the presence of the holy angels and in the presence of the Lamb.

The angel in midheaven is an earthly messenger—perhaps Philadelphia or repentant Sardis– prophesying about what's to come, maybe even preaching it over the airwaves: "repent, because Babylon is about to be destroyed," and "don't get the mark of the beast." Some believe that the Antichrist will demand this mark throughout his entire 3 ½ year reign, but it must begin at the seventh trumpet; otherwise the angel's warning is much too late to make a difference. The campaign isn't a sign of his power and dominion, but rather of its slipping away. At the seventh trumpet, the kingdom becomes Christ's (Rev 11:15) and the temple is vindicated (Rev 11:19, 15:8). This campaign is Satan's last ditch effort to corrupt as many as possible before Christ sets up His millennial reign.

The Image of the Beast

As we've already discussed, neither the Sunnis nor the Shi'as claim that Al Mahdi is an incarnation of Allah, and it would be considered idolatry and polytheism to worship him. Satan has spent centuries building up his false religion, and is already receiving worship in the guise of Allah. To do a complete turnaround at the end of the world and undo everything he's so deeply ingrained in the hearts of Muslims everywhere seems very risky and highly unlikely.

If you'll remember from chapter one, it's the Islamic Satan who's supposed to get the world to worship idols, so it would be counterproductive to have Al Mahdi arrive on the scene demanding worship and idols made in his image, as is described in Revelation 13. How then can we explain this apparent contradiction?

The image John speaks of is the Greek word *eikon*, from which we get the word "icon." It's not a likeness, but rather an image that stands for something else, as for example a flag represents a country. This is an image not of the beast's king, but rather the symbol of the kingdom itself, for the government of Islam can't be separated from its religion. When the Prophet Jesus comes, he'll destroy the images of Judaism (the star of David) and Christianity (the cross), turning synagogues and churches into mosques; and on those mosques will be instead the image of Islam— the crescent moon and star atop minarets of wood, stone and metal.

We must remember that John was attempting to describe modern things with ancient concepts and terms, so when he sees the false prophet "giving breath" to the images, he's actually hearing the voice of the muezzin through the loudspeakers of the minarets, calling the faithful to prayer five times a day. Upon hearing it, the faithful prostrate themselves towards the direction of Mecca to worship Allah, an action that to John indicates reverence and obeisance to the beast.

The Mark of the Beast

Revelation 13:16-18
¹⁶And [the beast out of the land] causes all the small and the great and the rich and the poor and the free men and the slaves to be given a mark on their right hand or on their forehead ¹⁷and he provides that no one should be able to buy or to sell, except the one who has the mark, either the name of the beast or the number of

his name. ⁱ⁸**Here is wisdom. Let him who has understanding calculate the number of the beast, for the number is that of a man; and his number is six hundred and sixty-six.**

Much speculation has been made concerning the mark. Is it a tattoo? A computer chip? Is it literally the number 666, or do the letters of his name add up to it using the system of Gematria? Despite what Hollywood likes to portray, it can't be the literal number 666, or it wouldn't require much understanding to interpret. Yet the numerological system of Gematria is too imprecise to hold the answer: not only is each system language dependent, but even within a system, there may be various methods for calculating values. Furthermore, a person can have first, middle and last names, not to mention nicknames and titles, making it impossible to know exactly what to calculate. Even if it were obvious, it's not a foolproof method of identifying someone like a fingerprint is; for example, both Nero and Caligula had name forms in Greek that added up to 666. This raises an important question: does the number correspond to the Antichrist himself, or to the beast kingdom? If to the Antichrist, it would be a personal name; however, if to the kingdom, then it would point to his false religion, making its identification much more unique. Just like the image of the beast represents the Empire and not Al Mahdi, it seems likely that the number represents Islam in some way.

The most fascinating theory I've heard so far is from Walid Shoebat, who in his book Why I Left Jihad, says that the Greek numerals 666 correspond to the Bismillah, an Arabic phrase foundational to Islam meaning "in the name of Allah." The Koine Greek of the New Testament employed letters to represent numbers in their writing. At the time that Revelation was written, three Greek letters were used for 666: *chi—600, xi—60* and *stigma—6*.[2] According to

---

2   Edward Pothier, "Six Hundred Sixty-Six but not 666," pp. 6,7, Answering Islam,

Shoebat, the *chi* could correspond to the familiar crossed swords of Islam found in many modern seals and logos. As for the *xi*, although the orientation is different, anyone can see the uncanny similarity between it and the Arabic script for "Allah." In the case of the *stigma* the correspondence is less straightforward and unfortunately, Shoebat doesn't address this in his book.

However, one Arabic speaker told me that if it were turned 90 degrees to the left, especially in the context of the *xi*, it could be interpreted as the *bs* of the Arabic root *bsm*, meaning "in the name of." Given the common usage of these symbols in the Muslim world already, it seems very likely that the Islamic Empire would include the crossed swords and the Bismillah on its flag or seal, serving very well as the mark of the beast.

Shoebat's theory is that John actually saw the Arabic script and wrote the symbols down correctly, but a scribe subsequently assumed they were errors and corrected them to match the Greek numeral. The problem with this theory is that the oldest extant manuscripts don't have the numeral 666, but rather spell the words "six hundred sixty-six." Nevertheless, the scripture uses the term "calculate," which implies using the Greek numerals to somehow determine the identity of the beast kingdom. What is perhaps most intriguing is that the Arabic alphabet isn't related to the Greek, having arisen from a different language family. Thus it's truly remarkable that there could be any resemblance between this number and an Arabic phrase that's so significant to Islam specifically. Just as remarkable is that although Greek is read from left to right, the 666 would still make sense in Arabic, which is read from right to left:

---

http://www.answering-islam.org/Religious/Numerics/six.html. The Ionic numeric system, started as early as the 6th century B.C., required 27 letters. Because the alphabet consisted of only 24, the shortage was resolved by reintroducing three obsolete letters into the system, digamma or stigma being 6; the *digamma* fell out of use by 403 B.C., thus *stigma* was used in New Testament times.

600	60	6		
chi	xi	stigma	"Allah"	"in the name of"

The similarity is remarkable, despite the different orientation of the *xi*.

On the left, the stigma, on the right, the Arabic script for "in the name of."

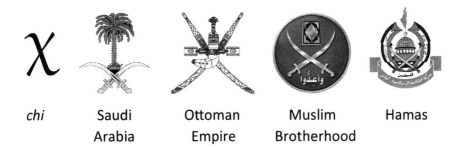

| chi | Saudi Arabia | Ottoman Empire | Muslim Brotherhood | Hamas |

Shoebat argues that the term "number of the beast" in verse 18 could be translated as "the multitude of the beast," making verse 18 read: "Here is wisdom. Let him who has understanding count the multitude of the beast, for the multitude is that of a man [Muhammad]; and his multitude is "in the name of Allah." Unfortunately, there are two problems with this translation. First of all, the Greek has no article before "man," making the more accurate translation be "his number is that of man." In addition, the word for "number" is *arithmos,* and is never used in the New

Testament to mean "multitude," only its calculated number, for example, "the number of them was 4,000." Because of this, there's no reason to think that God is using the word "number" to refer to anything but an actual number

But these facts still support Shoebat's theory, because verse 17 tells us that the number corresponds directly to the name of the beast, so closely tied that they are both used as the distinguishing mark of the Empire. If the name of the Empire is Islam ("submission"), then the numeral tells us who the Empire is in submission to: the name of Allah. The correlation is made between the Arabic and Greek only because Greek was the language of the gentile Church at that time. As for the number belonging to man, John is clearly telling us that the beast religion doesn't belong to God; in other words, it's a manmade invention, one that didn't even exist at the time he wrote the book of Revelation.

A Closer Look at the Bismillah

The Bismillah is an abbreviated form of the longer phrase *B-ismi-llahi r-rahmani r-rahim*, meaning "In the name of God, Most Gracious, Most Merciful." It's said as part of Muslim daily prayers and spoken before each daily task. It's recited before almost every sura of the Koran and is usually the first phrase in the preamble of the constitutions of Islamic countries. In Arabic art, the Bismillah is written in calligraphy and put into all kinds of beautiful shapes and images. To us such a phrase may seem like a shallow idiomatic expression, perhaps like our "amen" has become. But consider that Jesus commanded the apostles to baptize men *in the name* of the Father, Son and Holy Spirit; the blessing of the Messiah is "Blessed is He who comes *in the name of the Lord;*" and the apostles performed miracles *in the name of Jesus*. In short, there is power associated with the name of the Lord because He is the banner under which we live and serve Him. This is also true for those who function under the banner of Allah. The deeper significance of this phrase is that those submitting to Allah are under his guidance, as his instruments, doing everything for his glory. Even more significant to the context of Revelation 13:16-18 is the meaning of the word "bismillah" broken down into its component parts:

"*bi*: by, for, with the aid of, through or by means of

ism: the means by which something is distinguished, as an identifying mark, or by being raised up high so that it may be distinguished, including a name, reputation, light or vibration, and points toward the very essence of something...the underlying reality of something

illah: Allah, the name of the One"[3]

Thus the Bismillah can be more fully translated as "by the distinguishing mark of Allah." Since "Islam" means submission to Allah, one can see how the Bismillah could be used to represent the Islamic Empire. So how will this mark be put on the forehead and hand? The Greek word for "mark" is *charagma*, which means "a stamp or impression," sometimes translated as "graven." It's not the word used for the tattoo a master would give his slave for example, which is a *stigma*. Shoebat points out that many men wear the Bismillah on their helmets during Jihad, and statesmen display it on armbands; he theorizes that this could possibly correspond with the mark of the beast being put on the forehead or hand. The bottom line is that there's no way of knowing. I must point out, however, that the concept of wearing an identifying mark is not at all new in the religion and reign of Islam. In fact, Muhammad himself began it in 628 A.D. when he conquered the Jews at Khaybar. Those

---

3   "The meaning of Bismillah," http://wahiduddin.net/words/bismillah.htm

Jews who were not massacred were forced to accept a *dhimma* which is an agreement to submit to the designation of a *dhimmi*, an "insulted one." According to the *dhimma*, the conquered group agreed to have restricted legal rights in Islamic society. They had to wear clothing or badges that identified them, yield the road to Muslims, live in separate neighborhoods and pay the jizya, a penalty tax for not being Muslim. The doctrine of the *dhimma* came to include all "people of the book," meaning Jews and Christians, and expanded into a formal system of religious apartheid under Shari'a law which, in some form, continues to exist in most modern Islamic countries.[4]

The significant difference between dhimmihood and the mark of the end time, is that instead of singling out the minority groups for persecution, its goal is to coerce them to abandon their faith and join the majority in order to receive certain privileges. In order to receive the mark of Islam, a person will have to say the *shahada*, the Muslim profession of faith: There is no god but Allah and Muhammad is his prophet. Many Jews and Christians will compromise in this way, thinking that externals don't matter to God; yet regardless of what they may believe in their hearts, to receive the mark will be a denial of Jehovah or Christ, which will have dire consequences for their souls.

5) The Harvest by Christ in the Clouds (14:14-16)

Revelation 14:14-16
[14]And I looked, and behold, a white cloud, and sitting on the cloud, was one like a son of man, having a golden crown on His head, and a sharp sickle in His hand. [15]And another angel came out of the temple crying out with a loud voice to Him who sat on the cloud,

---

[4] DHIMMI: Coalition for the Defense of Human Rights, "The Dhimmi: an Overview," http://www.dhimmi.com/ dhimmi_overview.htm. See also Samuel Shahid, "Rights of Non-Muslims in an Islamic State," http://www.answering-Islam.org/NonMuslims/righs.htm

"Put in your sickle and reap, because the hour to reap has come, because the harvest of the earth is ripe." ¹⁶And He who sat on the cloud swung His sickle over the earth; and the earth was reaped.

Notice that Jesus is wearing His golden diadem, since He's been given the worldly kingdom. Many scholars believe this is the only rapture in Revelation, and that it involves the entire Church. Yet the evidence points to this Church as being predominantly Jewish:

- Jesus described this event as being a sign of His coming for those in Judea (Matt 24:30-31). According to Him, Zechariah 12:10-14 will be fulfilled when the house of David and all the inhabitants of Jerusalem see Him in the clouds and mourn Him.
- Jesus uses this same image of the ripe harvest regarding His ministry to Israel (i.e. before the invitation of the gospel is opened to the gentiles).
- The 144,000 are identified as the first fruits of this ripe harvest. In the feasts of Israel, the first fruits were brought in to thank God in advance for the harvest to come: barley around Passover for the spring barley harvest, and loaves of wheat bread at Sukkos for the fall wheat harvest. Since the 144,000 are Jews, the harvest must consist primarily of Jews.
- In Chapter 15 they're described as singing the Song of Moses and the Lamb, meaning that they're Jewish believers. The song of Moses is found in Deuteronomy 32, and prophesies God's vengeance on Israel's enemies in the last days.
- As the harvest group prophesies and worships God and the Lamb, they hold harps, which were used in the official Levitical worship of the Temple (II Ch 5:12, 29:25); harps were also associated with prophesying (I Sam 10:5, I Ch 25:3).

6) The Seven Bowl Judgment

[18] And another angel, the one who has power over fire, came out from the altar and he called with a loud voice to [another angel] who had the sharp sickle saying, "Put in your sharp sickle, and gather the clusters from the vine of the earth, because her grapes are ripe." [19] And the angel swung his sickle to the earth, and gathered the clusters from the vine of the earth and threw them into the great wine press of the wrath of God. [20] And the wine press was trodden outside the city, and blood came out from the wine press up to the horses' brides for a distance of two hundred miles.

The winepress consists of the bowl judgments and Armageddon. The two harvests here represent the fates of the two parts of Jerusalem: the faithful woman is the harvested wheat, and the beast's harlot are the grapes thrown into the winepress of the wrath of God (see discussion of *the harlot* under the seventh bowl).

14

The Second Coming of Christ: The Seven Bowls

Revelation 15:1-7
¹And I saw another sign in heaven, great and marvelous, seven angels who had seven plagues, which are the last, because in them the wrath of God is finished...⁵After these things I looked and the temple of the tabernacle of testimony in heaven was opened, ⁶and the seven angels who had the seven plagues came out of the temple clothed in linen, clean and bright, and girded around their breasts with golden girdles. ⁷And one of the four living creatures gave to the seven angels seven golden bowls full of the wrath of God, who lives forever and ever.

Unlike the other angels that act in the book of Revelation, John describes these angels as being a sign. The only other time he speaks of a sign is when he refers to the woman and the dragon, which were symbolic of literal earthly entities. The number seven symbolizes the fullness and completion of God's judgment on Israel, but the angels themselves must represent human messengers; no heavenly angel in scripture is ever said to be wearing priestly garments, a fact that points to their role as intercessors.[1] It's impossible to tell whether the bowls are caused by supernatural phenomena or human warfare. If by supernatural means, then they must be summoned through the intercession of the saints; this is how the earth knows that Jehovah is responsible for them (Rev 16:21). If by human warfare, however, then these angels represent the 144,000 who return to earth as Christ's heavenly armies. If so, then we would expect to see evidence that Christ is with them, since they follow Him wherever He goes; and in fact this is exactly what we see.

After the angels are given the bowls, we're told that the heavenly temple is filled with smoke from the glory of God and from His power "and no one was able to enter the temple until the seven plagues of the seven angels were finished." Although this is speaking of the heavenly temple, we again expect that something corresponds to it on earth. Ezekiel describes the glory of the Lord as returning to the earthly temple, and indicates that it's Christ Himself, based on the previous vision of Him at the Babylonian destruction of Jerusalem (compare Ezek 1:27-28 and Rev 10:1):

Ezekiel 43:2-7
²And behold, the glory of the God of Israel was coming from the way of the east. And His voice was like the sound of many waters: and the earth shone with His glory...³And it was like the appearance of the vision which I saw, like the vision which I saw when He came to destroy the city...⁴And the glory of the Lord came into the house by the way of the gate facing toward the east...⁵and the glory of the Lord filled the house. ⁷And He said to me, "son

---

[1] Angels are also never said to be dressed in linen, also a priestly garment. But in fact, the best texts we have of this passage say the angels are dressed in stone. Because they come from the tabernacle of testimony which was carried in the wilderness, it's possible that the stone represents the law, written on the stone tablets at Sinai.

of man, this is the place of My throne and the place of the soles of My feet, where I will dwell among the sons of Israel forever..."

In addition, there's a prophecy in Malachi indicating Christ's earthly presence in pouring out judgment upon the city:

Malachi 3:1-3
¹Behold, I am going to send My messenger, and he will clear the way before Me. And the Lord, whom you seek, will suddenly come to His temple; and the messenger [angel] of the covenant, in whom you delight, behold, He is coming," says the Lord of hosts. ²But who can endure the day of His coming? And who can stand when He appears? For He is like a refiner's fire and like a fuller's soap. ³And He will sit as a smelter and purifier of silver, and He will purify the sons of Levi and refine them like gold and silver so that they may present to the Lord offerings in righteousness.

These prophecies establish the temple as His throne, the place from which He's prophesied to command judgment: "A voice of uproar from the city, a voice from the temple, the voice of the Lord who is rendering recompense to His enemies," (Isaiah 66:6). This appears to have its fulfillment in Revelation 16:1: "And I heard a loud voice from the temple saying to the seven angels, 'Go and pour out the seven bowls of the wrath of God into the earth.'"

Christ's physical presence in the earthly temple completes the vindication of the *qodesh* spoken of by Daniel—a natural consequence of His dominion over the earth. Every indication is that Christ and the 144,000 are responsible for carrying out the seven bowl judgments on the earth: 1) by the time Christ comes to Armageddon, He's already been in battle. He rides the white horse of victory and wears all the diadems of the kingdom, His robe having been dipped in the blood of the winepress of God's wrath (the seven bowls); 2) The "righteous acts" that clothe the armies are the very same "righteous acts" that God reveals in the seven bowl judgments (Rev 15:4-16:1). These acts of judgment could only be attributable to the saints because they participate in the execution of the bowls; 3) finally, just before Christ and the armies arrive at Armageddon, Jerusalem herself has been dressed in these same "righteous acts" of the saints, meaning that it has been purged clean by the seven bowls (Rev 19:7-8; see 21:2 where the bride is identified as Jerusalem).

Bowls 1-5

The first five bowls consist of 1) malignant sores; 2) the sea turning to blood; 3) the rivers and springs turning to blood; 4) the sun scorching the earth; 5) the beast kingdom becoming dark. While it's tempting to assume the oceans and rivers merely look like blood, the angel states that this is a punishment for the spilled blood of the prophets and saints, leading us to believe that it could truly be blood. These bowls could represent literal warfare between the armies of Christ and the beast. On the other hand, they could be supernatural plagues brought by Christ Himself or by the power of the Holy Spirit through the intercession of the saints.

Sixth Bowl: Euphrates Dries up,
Armies Called to Armageddon

Revelation 16:12-16
¹²And the sixth angel poured out his bowl upon the great river the Euphrates; and its water was dried up, that the way might be prepared for the kings from the east. ¹³And I saw coming out of the mouth of the dragon and out of the mouth of the beast and out of the mouth of the false prophet, three unclean spirits like

frogs; ¹⁴for they are the spirits of demons, performing signs, which go out to the kings of the whole world, to gather them together for the war of the great day of God the Almighty. ¹⁵(Behold, I am coming like a thief. Blessed is the one who stays awake and keeps his garments, lest he walk about naked and men see his shame.") ¹⁶And they gathered them together to the place which in Hebrew is called Har-Magedon.

Har-Magedon (*Armageddon* in Greek), which simply means "Mount Megiddo," is located in the northwest of Israel, just southeast of Mt. Carmel. An ancient trade route connecting Egypt and Assyria went through a pass that was guarded here. The wide plain below it, called Jezreel, was where Joshua fought against the Midianites; significantly, it was also the place where Jezebel met her end. However, Joel also speaks of the valley of Jehoshaphat as being the site of the final battle. Since this means the "Valley of Judgment" in Hebrew, it could be figurative of Armageddon, but other scriptures indicate that Christ will judge the nations on the Mount of Olives or Zion (Zech 14:3-8, Joel 3:9-17), thus its location is unclear. There is the possibility that there will be more than one battle, during the period of the seven bowls, because Ezekiel 39:4 says that the nations will fight against the "mountains of Israel," and Revelation 14:20 speaks of bloodshed occurring for a distance of 200 miles outside the city.

Ezekiel 38-39 describes the many nations that come against Israel, apparently at Armageddon as well as after the millennial kingdom (see Rev 20:7-9). These include the Islamic countries of Central Asia as well as Iran, Libya, Sudan, Ethiopia, Algeria, Tunisia, Turkey, Syria, Lebanon, Jordan, Yemen, Saudi Arabia, and the other Persian Gulf states. In contrast with Walid Shoebat, Joel Rosenberg includes all the former Soviet Republics and possibly Germany with the kings that support the Antichrist.[2] The kings of the east could be those among the lands of Gog who would need to cross the Euphrates in order to support Al Mahdi, such as Kazakhstan, Uzbekistan and Turkmenistan. By controlling Turkey, Al Mahdi would have access to all of the dams on the Euphrates, possibly allowing him to shut off its flow for their crossing.

Seventh Bowl: Destruction of The Great City

Revelation 16:17-21
[17]And the seventh angel poured out his bowl upon the air; and a loud voice came out of the temple from the throne, saying "It is done." [18]And there were flashes of lightning and sounds and peals of thunder; and there was a great earthquake, such as there had not been since man came to be upon the earth, so great an earthquake was it, and so mighty. [19]And the great city was split into three parts, and the cities of the nations fell. And Babylon the great was remembered before God, to give her the cup of the wine of His fierce wrath. [20]And every island fled away, and the mountains were not found. [21]And huge hailstones, about one hundred pounds each, came down from heaven upon men; and men blasphemed God because of the plague of the hail because its plague was extremely severe.

Revelation 17:1-18
[1]And one of the seven angels who had the seven bowls came and spoke with me, saying, "Come here, I shall show you the judgment of the great harlot who sits on many waters, [2]with whom the kings of the earth committed acts of immorality." [3]And he carried me away in the Spirit into a wilderness; and I saw a woman sitting on

---

2   Joel Rosenberg, *Epicenter: Why the Current Rumblings in the Middle East will Change Your Future*, p. 134, Tyndale House Publishers, Inc., 2006

a scarlet beast, full of blasphemous names, having seven heads and ten horns. ⁴And the woman was clothed in purple and scarlet, and adorned with gold and precious stones and pearls, having in her hand a gold cup full of abominations and of the unclean things of her immorality, ⁵and upon her forehead a name was written, a mystery, "Babylon the great, the mother of harlots and of the abominations of the earth." ⁶And I saw the woman drunk with the blood of the saints, and with the blood of the witnesses of Jesus. And when I saw her, I wondered greatly. ⁷And the angel said to me, "Why do you wonder? I shall tell you the mystery of the woman..." ¹⁵And he said to me, "the waters which you saw where the harlot sits are the peoples and multitudes and nations and tongues. ¹⁶And the ten horns which you saw, and the beast, these will hate the harlot and will make her desolate and naked and will eat her flesh and will burn her up with fire. ¹⁷For God has put it in their hearts to execute His purpose by having a common purpose, and by giving their kingdom to the beast, until the words of God should be fulfilled.¹⁸ And the woman whom you saw is the great city, which reigns over the kings of the earth."

Some want to identify the capital of the beast kingdom as Rome, believing that the seven "mountains" refer to the seven hills upon which it sits. Others believe it will be a literal rebuilt Babylon, and look for this to happen in order for Biblical prophecy to be fulfilled. Those who recognize Islam as the beast kingdom might look to modern Baghdad as "the great city," since it was upon this site that Seleucus moved the deteriorating capital of Babylon. Still others claim that we can't identify the city at all since according to the angel in Revelation 17:5-6, it's a mystery. But the word "mystery" in Greek doesn't mean the same thing as our English word. Vine's dictionary explains it best:

"The *musterion* is primarily that which is known to the *mustes*, the initiated, from *mueo*, to initiate into the mysteries...In the New Testament, it denotes not the mysterious (as with the English word), but that which, being outside the range of unassisted natural apprehension, can be made known only by Divine revelation, and is made known in a manner and at a time appointed by God, and to those only who are illumined by His Spirit. In the ordinary sense, a mystery implies *knowledge withheld*; its Scriptural significance is *truth revealed.*"[3] (italics mine).

Vine's goes on to say that in the ancient Greek world, "the mysteries" were religious rites practiced by secret societies into which one had to be initiated before being allowed to possess certain knowledge (i.e.,"the deep things of Satan" referred to in the letter to Thyatira).

Hence, the designation of "Mystery Babylon" is not an indication that the city's identity is being withheld from John; on the contrary, the angel is *making known* to him the identity of the city and the *reason* and *manner* of its judgment: "Come here, I shall show you the judgment of the great harlot..." John wonders—is amazed, stunned—at this state of affairs. If the city had been Rome or Babylon itself, John wouldn't have wondered at its spiritual filth; after all, Rome had crucified the son of God and, just 37 years later, destroyed Jerusalem and the temple; likewise, Babylon is obviously filthy, being synonymous with idolatry in the scriptures. The angel is surprised that John wonders, and proceeds to explain to him what the beast is, satisfied that this will make it clear to John why the city is being represented by a harlot and is spiritually called Babylon.

---

3   Vine's Dictionary, p. 779

The Harlot

The harlot, we're told, is a city under God's judgment. She is identifiable as the beast's capital because she rides upon its back, is called "the great city who reigns over the kings of the earth," and sits on many people, multitudes, nations and tongues. She's also the capital of the beast's false religion, because she's responsible for the martyrdom of the saints and the witnesses of Jesus (whether this refers specifically to the two witnesses is unclear); in fact, God holds her responsible for the murders of the "saints, apostles and prophets" (Rev 18:20) and "all who have been slain on the earth" (18:24), as well as the sins of all the nations (17:5).

While there's no consistent city referred to throughout scripture as "the great city," we've already seen that Jerusalem is called this in Revelation 11:7-8. We've already discussed the scriptures that refer to Jerusalem as Sodom and drawn parallels between Egypt and the beast kingdom; but is there any evidence that the great city of Babylon spoken of in Revelation 17 is the same great city that's named as Jerusalem in chapter 14?

1) Both Jerusalem and "Babylon" are called harlots, and are judged for being so: Of the metaphorical allusions to prostitutes in the Old Testament, all but two[4] refer to Israel, in particular in the end time prophecies of Isaiah and Ezekiel (Isa 1:21; Ezek 23). This harlotry is repeatedly given as the reason for its judgment: "How the faithful city has become a harlot...I will turn my hand against you, and will smelt away your dross as with lye, and will remove

---

4   The two are Ninevah and Tyre. Ninevah, which had repented 100 years earlier under Jonah's preaching, could be considered a harlot for its return to idolatry as well as for enticing other nations (including the Jews) to do the same (Nahum 3). Like Ninevah, Tyre is likened to a harlot in Isaiah 23:15-17 for its enticement of other nations. In this passage, it could also be acting as a type of Jerusalem (it goes back to its harlot's wages after 70 years of Babylonian oppression), especially under the Mahdi (as a bestower of crowns, v. 8; see Rev 13:1; 17:12).

all your alloy." The term is generally used as a metaphor for idolatry, which desecrates the marriage covenant with God; He has only one wife, and one people, and that's Israel (and by grafting, the Church). The harlotry of Israel in the end time is the adulterous marriage made with the Islamic Empire.

2) *Both Jerusalem and the "Babylon" of chapter 17 are made desolate*: in Daniel 9:27, prophesying about the holy city, the angel tells Daniel that one will come who "makes desolate" the city of Jerusalem. Likewise, "Babylon" will be made desolate by Al Mahdi and his ten kings (Rev 17:16). In a prophecy sandwiched between two Messianic chapters, Isaiah says of Jerusalem, "And you will be called by a new name, which the mouth of the Lord will designate... It will no longer be said of you 'Forsaken,' nor to your land will it any longer be said 'Desolate' but you will be called, 'My delight is in her,' and your land, 'Married'" (62:2,4).

3) *The ten kings and the beast hate the harlot:* Why would the ten kings and the beast hate their own capital enough to eat her flesh and burn her up (Rev 17:16)? The only explanation is that the harlot is Jerusalem, God's capital. Since Satan can't have it, He'll do his utmost to destroy it in his war against Christ and the saints.

4) *Both Jerusalem and "Babylon" drink from the cup of God's wrath*: In Isaiah 51, the Messiah speaks to Jerusalem, saying, "... Arise, O Jerusalem, you who have drunk from the Lord's hand the cup of His anger; the chalice of reeling you have drained to the dregs...Behold, I have taken out of your hand the cup of reeling; the chalice of My anger, you will never drink it again. And I will put it into the hand of your tormentors, who have said to you, 'Lie down that we may walk over you.'" In Revelation 17:2, the angel explains to John that riding on the beast's back is the harlot's judgment, just like the harlot sisters of Ezek 23 are given "into the hand of her lovers," who "executed judgment on her."

With the seventh trumpet, however, His people are told to leave the city, and the cup of His wrath is transferred to the beast kingdom: "And the great city was split into three parts and the cities of the nations fell. And Babylon the great was remembered before God, to give her the cup of the wine of His fierce wrath" (Rev 16:19).

5) Both Jerusalem and "Babylon" killed the saints and the prophets: Jesus refers to Jerusalem as a killer of prophets in Matthew 23:37, and in Luke 11:49-50 Jesus says that God sent Israel prophets and apostles knowing that they would be killed and persecuted "in order that the blood of all the prophets shed since the foundation of the world may be charged against this generation." Accordingly, the angels say at the destruction of Babylon in Revelation 18:20 "Rejoice over her...you saints and apostles and prophets, because God has pronounced judgment for you against her." And again in verse 24, "...In her was found the blood of prophets and of saints and of all who have been slain on the earth." In addition, the two witnesses are killed in Jerusalem, and "Babylon" is said to be drunk with the blood of the saints and the witnesses of Jesus.

The golden cup of the harlot reminds us of Belshazzar drinking from the gold and silver cups pillaged from the temple (Dan 5:2). Here is Jerusalem, then, desecrating her own sacred temple vessels with all kinds of "abominations and unclean things of her immorality," namely the blood of the saints from which she has made herself drunk. This is but one more way Jerusalem gets its mystical name of "Babylon."

6) Both Jerusalem and "Babylon" experience a devastating earthquake at Christ's return: At the pouring out of the seventh bowl, "the great city" experiences an earthquake and splits into three parts. (Remember that the Hadith's Medina earthquake, mentioned in the discussion of the sixth seal, is described in exactly the same way. But the Islamic prophecy also says that as a result of the quake, the people of the city flee to Al Dajaal, something that couldn't happen at this point because the two witnesses have already ascended). There are two Old Testament references to a literal earthquake occurring at Christ's return, both of which happen in Jerusalem, during the commission of God's judgment on both Israel and her enemies at once:

Isaiah 29:5-7
⁵But the multitude of your enemies shall become like fine dust, and the multitude of the ruthless ones like the chaff which blows away; and it shall happen instantly, suddenly, ⁶from the Lord of Hosts you will be punished with thunder and earthquake and loud noise, with whirlwind and tempest and the flame of a consuming fire. ⁷And the multitude of all the nations who wage war against Ariel [Jerusalem], even all who wage war against her and her stronghold and who distress her, shall be like a dream, a vision of the night...

Zechariah 14:2-5
²For I will gather all the nations against Jerusalem to battle...⁴And in that day His feet will stand on the Mount of Olives, which is in front of Jerusalem on the east; and the Mount of Olives will be split in its middle from east to west by a very large valley, so that half of the mountain will move toward the north and the other half toward the south. ⁵And you will flee by the valley of My mountains, for the valley of the mountains will reach to Azel; yes, you will flee just as you fled before the earthquake in the days of Uzziah king of Judah. Then the Lord, my God, will come and all the holy ones with Him!

7) *Both Jerusalem and "Babylon" receive judgment by fire*: As mentioned earlier, Jerusalem is referred to as Sodom in both Old Testament prophecies as well as in Revelation 11:8. Sodom was a city so reprehensible for its spiritual immorality that God rained down fire on it in judgment. God also prophesied that Judah would be judged for its spiritual adultery In Isaiah:

Isaiah 66:3-6, 15
³As they have chosen their own ways, and their soul delights in their abominations, ⁴so I will choose their punishments and I will bring on them what they dread. ⁶...a voice from the temple, the voice of the Lord who is rendering recompense to His enemies... ¹⁵For behold the Lord will come in fire and His chariots like the whirlwind, to render His anger with fury and His rebuke with flames of fire, for the Lord will execute judgment by fire..."

In direct parallel, "Babylon" will be destroyed by fire instigated by a loud voice coming from the temple (16:1), and according to 18:7, for the same reasons.

8) *God's people in both Jerusalem and "Babylon" are told to evacuate*: In Revelation 18:4, God calls His people out of "Babylon," just as He calls them out of Jerusalem in the end time prophecies of Isaiah and Jeremiah (see also Zech 14:5 above):

Revelation 18:4,8
⁴And I heard, "Come out of her, my people, that you may not participate in her sins and that you may not receive of her plagues, for her sins have piled up as high as heaven and God has remembered her iniquities. ⁸For this reason in one day her plagues will come, pestilence and mourning and famine and she will be burned up with fire, for the Lord God who judges her is strong.

Isaiah 48:20
[20]Go forth from Babylon, Flee from the Chaldeans! Declare with the sound of joyful shouting, proclaim this, send it out to the end of the earth; say, "The Lord has redeemed His servant Jacob."

Jeremiah 51:6
[6]Flee from the midst of Babylon and each of you save his life! Do not be destroyed in her punishment, for this is the Lord's time of vengeance; He is going to render recompense to her.

9) *The great harlot and the remnant woman together represent the two sides of Israel:* Although they're not placed side by side in the book of Revelation, these two figures are intended to be types of the two sides of Israel, each being understood in light of the other: the harlot is the adulterous element that supports Al Mahdi, while the remnant woman represents the faithful who will stand with Christ at the end of time. In a prophecy to Judah, God brings both of these images together:

Jeremiah 4:30-31
[30]And you, O desolate one, what will you do? Although you dress in scarlet, although you decorate yourself with ornaments of gold, although you enlarge your eyes with paint, in vain you make yourself beautiful; your lovers despise you, they seek your life. [31]For I heard a cry as of a woman in labor, the anguish as of one giving birth to her first child, the cry of the daughter of Zion gasping for breath, stretching out her hands saying "Ah, woe is me, for I faint before murderers."

In Isaiah, we see this same connection, in that through the judgment of the beast, the sins of Israel are forgiven:

Isaiah 26:20-27:1,9
20 Come, my people, enter into your rooms, and close your doors behinds you; hide for a little while until the indignation runs its course. **21**For behold, the Lord is about to come out from His place to punish the inhabitants of the earth for their iniquity… **27:1** In that day the Lord will punish Leviathan the fleeing serpent, with His fierce and great and mighty sword. Even Leviathan the twisted serpent; and He will kill the dragon who lives in the sea. **9**Therefore through this Jacob's iniquity will be forgiven…

The People's Reaction to the Destruction of the Great City

Revelation 18:8-11
8For this reason in one day her plagues will come, pestilence and mourning and famine and she will be burned up with fire, for the Lord God who judges her is strong. **9**And the kings of the earth, who committed acts of immorality and lived sensuously with her, will weep and lament over her when they see the smoke of her burning, **10**standing at a distance because of the fear of her torment, saying 'Woe, woe, the great city, Babylon, the strong city! For in one hour your judgment has come.' **11**And the merchants of the earth weep and mourn over her, because no one buys their cargoes any more…**19**for in one hour she has been laid waste.

The final destruction of the great city at the seventh bowl takes place quickly, and those who mourn her demise are Muslims and merchants who benefit from Islam's empire. According to Walid Shoebat, Saudi Arabia presently imports all of the items listed in 18:12-14. Because of this, and the fact that the merchants can actually see the city burning from the port, He interprets the great "city" to be Saudi Arabia. However, if the capital of the empire is moved to Jerusalem, as the Islamic prophecies suggest, then the Muslims living there could be involved in the same opulence presently found in Saudi Arabia. In addition, the port of Ashdod is one of the largest ports of Israel, handling 60% of the goods that are imported there. It's a mere 33 miles from the city of Jerusalem, with the land rising from sea level up to Jerusalem's height of about 2700 feet. Remember that the seventh bowl earthquake turns the whole country into a plain, leveling any topographical or manmade obstacles that would obscure the view of smoke rising from the distant mount upon which Jerusalem sits. Also keep in mind that in this electronic age, merchants from all over the world will see the spoke burning from a distance on their televisions, cell phones and laptops.

Armageddon

Revelation 19:11-20
[11]And I saw heaven opened; and behold, a white horse, and He who sat upon it is called Faithful and True; and in righteousness He judges and wages war... [13]And He is clothed with a robe dipped in blood; and His name is called The Word of God. [14]And the armies which are in heaven, clothed in fine linen, white and clean, were following Him on white horses. [15]And from His mouth comes a sharp sword, so that with it He may smite the nations; and He will rule them with a rod of iron; and He treads the wine press of the fierce wrath of God, the Almighty. [17]And I saw an angel standing in the sun; and he cried out with a loud voice, saying to all the birds which fly in midheaven, "Come, assemble for the great supper of God; [18]in order that you may eat the flesh of kings and the flesh of commanders... [19]and I saw the beast and the kings of the earth and their armies, assembled to make war against Him who sat upon the horse and against His army. [20]And the beast was seized, and with him the false prophet who performed the signs in his presence...these two were thrown alive into the lake of fire which burns with brimstone.

There's a hadith that says the Prophet Jesus takes a group of worshipers to Mt. Sinai[5] and upon returning, finds that Gog and Magog have descended upon the Sea of Galilee and devoured all of its water. Its armies lie dead as far as the eye can see, with the corpses so close together that no one can walk between them. It gives no indication of how Gog and Magog are killed, but like the Biblical prophecy, birds of prey are sent to eat the corpses.

Magog is mentioned only once in Revelation, as the nations that attack Jerusalem after Christ's millennial reign (Rev 20:7-9). However, Ezekiel 38-39 indicates that these same nations are among those who support Al Mahdi against Christ and the saints at Armageddon as well. According to the Hadith, Magog is the enemy of Islam, while in the Bible it is its ally. However, there may be a way to reconcile the two prophecies, and it comes in the identity of Magog. Most Muslim scholars identify Gog and Magog as the Khazars, the Turkish, nonethnic Jews of Russia who were historical enemies of Islam.[6] It's possible that, responding to Europe's failure against Islam during the sixth trumpet, Jews from Russia and Hungary will rise up against Al Mahdi, only to lose on the battlefield before Armageddon begins. This would fulfill the Islamic prophecy about Magog, while still allowing for the Islamic nations of scriptural Magog to come against Israel as allies of the beast at Armageddon. When they are defeated, their bodies could be interpreted as belonging to those righteous Muslims whose souls are raptured by Allah. This timing would set up the next Islamic prophecy—the appearance of Satan and his demons to establish an earthly kingdom. According to the Hadith, he will claim to be Allah and will reward

---

5   Muslims claim this to be the traditional site of Mt. Sinai located in the Sinai Peninsula.
6   www.islamicawareness.net/Yaju/gog.html. In contrast, the Amahdis identify Gog and Magog as the West (Capitalism) and Russia (Communism), lending support for Shoebat's theory that Russia helps the West fight against the beast. In this case, Russia would be part of the sixth trumpet's 200 million man army whose defeat would fulfill the Islamic prophecy regarding Magog.

with comfortable lives all those left on the earth who obey him.

This aligns with Zechariah's prophecy about Christ, who after Armageddon, sets up a kingdom with the saints. Together they rule over the earth with a rod of iron, requiring that any who are left of all the nations that went against Jerusalem "go up from year to year to worship the King, the Lord of hosts, and to celebrate the Feast of Booths [Sukkos]. And it will be that whichever of the families of the earth does not go up to Jerusalem to worship the King, the Lord of hosts, there will be no rain on them" (14:16,17).

It seems incredible, but Satan has planned the Islamic religion out so masterfully, that despite Christ's perfect, just and righteous rule, the Muslims will actually believe He is Satan! Even more diabolical is that, because their prophecies state that only the wicked are left behind at this point, the remaining Muslims will assume that they have fallen short, and become even more devoted to Islam. This explains why Satan is able to deceive the nations to rise up against Christ and Jerusalem after he's released from his thousand year prison.

The Resurrection of the Saints

First Resurrection (Before the Thousand Years)

Revelation 20:4-6
⁴And I saw thrones, and they sat upon them and judgment was given to them. And I saw the souls of those who had been beheaded because of the testimony of Jesus and because of the word of God and those who had not worshiped the beast or his image and had not received the mark on their forehead and upon their hand; and they came to life and reigned with Christ for a thousand years. ⁵The rest of the dead did not come to life until the thousand years

were completed. This is the first resurrection. ⁶Blessed and holy is the one who has a part in the first resurrection: over these the second death has no power, but they will be priests of God and of Christ and will reign with Him for a thousand years.

John doesn't state who's seated on the thrones, but by the letters, we know that all the saints who overcome will rule with Christ. Although not specifically described by John, Paul tells us that the dead in Christ will be resurrected and caught up with the living at the seventh trumpet harvest:

I Thessalonians 4:15-17
¹⁵**For this we say to you by the word of the Lord, that we who are alive, and remain until the coming of the Lord, shall not precede those who have fallen asleep. ¹⁶For the Lord Himself will descend from heaven with a shout, with the voice of the archangel, and with the trumpet of God; and the dead in Christ shall rise first. ¹⁷Then we who are alive and remain shall be caught up together with them in the clouds to meet the Lord in the air, and thus we shall always be with the Lord."**

Because John describes the resurrection of the Tribulation martyrs as happening after Armageddon, we must assume that God waits to raise them until the last one is killed; this is evidence that the campaign of the mark continues until Al Mahdi's defeat. There must be many who come to Christ during the seven bowl period, both Jews and gentiles (even those of Laodicea who repent), for God tells them to evacuate Jerusalem before the final bowl (Rev 18:4).

Second Resurrection (After the Thousand Years)

Revelation 20:12-15
[12]And I saw the dead, the great and the small, standing before the throne...[13]And the sea gave up the dead which were in it, and death and Hades gave up the dead which were in them...[15]And if anyone's name was not found written in the book of life, he was thrown into the lake of fire.

The question must be asked whether Christians are present at the Great White Throne judgment. There are several scriptures that teach that even Christians will be judged by God according to their deeds. Two such passages are Romans 14:10, and 2 Corinthians 5:10, which indicate that Christians will stand before the "judgment seat" or *bema* of God. Some people emphasize that the *bema* is different than the *thronos* of the Great White Throne. Be that as it may, it seems reasonable that the second resurrection could include Christians who received Christ during the Millennium. The point is that we'll all be judged by God for our deeds, "whether good or bad." Even knowing that we'll enter heaven by Christ's righteousness, this is a sobering thought.

Here I must make mention of the nature of Hell. For some decades now, segments of the Church have sought to avoid the doctrine of eternal damnation. Some say it's only a temporary punishment for sins for the purpose of correction, allowing people to later enter into eternal life. Others deny hell completely, claiming that those who don't know Christ are not given an immortal soul, and therefore cease to exist when they die. Both of these plain and simply contradict the teaching of Christ throughout the gospels and here again in the book of Revelation, which was revealed to the Church by His very own mouth. How can anyone suggest that Hell is merely a temporary punishment when Revelation 20:14 calls it "the second death," and is in fact the same fire into which Satan is cast? And if only Christians have an immortal soul, then who are all those dead lining up at the Great White Throne, some of whom are not written in the Book of Life?

Just because the idea of eternal damnation is very hard to stomach doesn't negate the reality of it. It's hard to reconcile this concept with that of a loving, merciful God. But the truth is that God is far, far above us; He alone is holy. He's the very definition of justice, righteousness, mercy and grace. Who are we to pretend that we understand fairness better than He, or that we can judge a human heart more accurately and mercifully? Some point to Phillipians 2:10-11 which says that "every knee shall bow and every tongue confess that Jesus Christ is Lord" as proof that all are saved in the end. This isn't what Revelation reveals, however. Just as the demons believe in God and tremble, but aren't redeemed, all the earth will be forced to bow the knee simply because God's presence demands that response; it doesn't speak to the state of their hearts. Revelation shows us that even after Christ's perfect millennial reign, the people of the earth reject Him. What more evidence is needed that God knows the heart and judges rightly? Through the prophecy of Revelation, we're given confidence that for those whom God judges, a thousand lifetimes wouldn't be sufficient to turn their hearts towards Him.

In the scriptures, God repeatedly anguishes over this unavoidable economy of heaven, no more so than when he came to suffer in order to give us a way out. Make no mistake: God is invested in us big time. The real question is do we have His heart? Do we really take seriously the fact that our friends and loved ones will be spending eternity in Hell if we don't pray for them and reach out to them for Christ?

The End of the Story

Throughout the Old Testament, Israel is called God's wife, and in the New Testament, the Church is called Christ's bride. However, in Revelation 21:2, we are told that Jerusalem herself is "the wife of the Lamb," "adorned for her husband" (21:10). This the harlot Jerusalem, once dressed in opulent purple and red, cleansed by God's fiery seven bowl judgment and now dressed in the pure white linen of the righteous acts of the saints. The wedding feast takes place after this presentation of the bride, after the creation of a new heaven and a new earth; thus it must be that the feast is heaven itself, the New Jerusalem holding all the saints who will live with Him forever. It would seem from scripture then, that the saints are both the bride and the guests to the marriage feast.

We now come to the end of the book of Revelation—the happy ending where the Church gets to live forever with Jesus in the New Jerusalem. This part of the prophecy speaks for itself, so I'll close with a few parting thoughts for the present Church. Let's look at ourselves in the mirror of Revelation. Are we Ephesus? Sardis? Laodicea? Do we really want to wait until the seals start breaking before we become Smyrna, Thyatira and Philadelphia? Eternity doesn't begin at the Millennium, it begins now, for that's the gift Christ bestows on each one of us the moment we choose to follow Him. How will we spend that gift in our lifetime? Will we bide our time until we make our escape, or will we allow the Holy Spirit to transform us by the renewing of our minds (Rom 12:2)? Will we bear fruit or be cut off and cast into the fire? Will we bury our talents or will we invest them and profit the kingdom?

While I was writing this book, I read *When Heaven Invades Earth*, by Bill Johnson, and it shook me to the foundations of my faith. In it, he challenges the Church to bring God's kingdom to earth by being conduits of God's power through the Holy Spirit. He calls us to revival—to demonstrate the power and love of God in such a way that the world is irresistibly drawn to Him. As a result of reading this book, I fell under conviction to seek out a church that could disciple me in the gifts of the Holy Spirit, and challenge and guide me in using them to bring people to the Lord. Anyone who's interested in bringing about change in the world must read Bill Johnson's book.

In short, the Church was given a mission by Jesus that will never be completely fulfilled until He comes. What Jesus said so long ago is still true today: the harvest is ripe, but the laborers are few. Let's have the mindset to work tirelessly to bring in the harvest until Christ comes, that we may hear those blessed words, "enter in, my good and faithful servant."

APPENDIX 1

The following are the calculations done by Sir Robert Anderson in his book *The Coming Prince*, (Grand Rapids: Kregel, 1967), pp. 122-128, quoted from the book *Satan in the Sanctuary* by Thomas S. McCall and Zola Levitt, 1983, pp. 86-88:

1. Daniel prophesied that the Messiah would come 173,880 days after Artaxerxes' decree [to rebuild the temple] 69 "weeks"= 483 years (69 x 7) x 360 days (Jewish year in prophecy) = 173,880 days.

2. The actual day of the decree was March 14, 445 B.C. We know from Neh. 2:1-6 that the decree was issued "in the month of Nisan, in the 20th year" of Artaxerxes' reign (465-425 B.C.) We can assume that the decree was dated on the first of Nisan because "The first of Nisan is a new year for the computation of the reign of kings and for festivals." (MISHNA, treatise "Rosh Hashanah.") The first of Nisan, 445 C.C. fell on March 14 (Royal Observatory, Greenwich , Eng.)

3. The actual day of the coming of the Messiah was April 6, A.D. 32. The "coming of the Messiah" was the day on which Jesus made His triumphal entry into Jerusalem and was proclaimed King by the Jews. This is given in Zech. 9:9.

John the Baptist and Jesus began their ministries during the 15th year of the reign of Tiberius Caesar (Luke 3:1, 3, 21) who we know began his reign in A.D. 14. Thus, our Lord started His ministry A.D. 29 and continued as we know, for 3 years before His triumphal entry: thus A.D. 32 was the year. We have it from

John 12:1 that the Lord went to Bethany, on the outskirts of Jerusalem, "six days before the Passover," and from John 12:12 that the Triumphal entry was the "next day." Passover is always celebrated on 14 Nisan, which was Thursday, April 10, in A.D. 32 (Royal Observatory). So the Lord came to Bethany April 4 (6 days before Passover) which was a Friday. The meal with Lazarus at Bethany must have been a Sabbath dinner. The "next day" could not have been Saturday (the Sabbath still in effect, Jesus and the Jews would have rested) so the Lord made His triumphal entry on Sunday, April 6 A.D. 32.

To recap all that, Anderson says (1) that Daniel foresaw that there would be 173,880 days between the issuing of Artaxerxes' decree and the coming of the Messiah; (2) that the decree was issued March 14, 445 B.C.; (3) that the Messiah came officially on April 6, A.D. 32.

If Daniel is correct to the exact day, there should have been 173,880 days between those two dates. Anderson works it out this way: From March 14, 445 B.C to April 6 A.D. 32 is 477 years and 24 days. But we must deduct one year because 1 B.C. to A.D. 1 is only one year. So we have 476 years and 24 days. 476 years x 365 days (in our Julian calendar) = 173,740 days. Adding in the extra 24 days = 173,764 days.

That doesn't quite do it. But peculiarities of our calendar, the Julian calendar, must also be considered. We have leap year every four years; therefore, there were 119 leap years during the period (476 years divided by 4 =119). So, adding in the extra 119 days, = 173,883 days.

That's too many days. But Anderson went so far as to calculate the slight inaccuracy of our Julian year as compared with the true solar year. The figures, from the Royal Observatory, show that our year is about $1/128^{th}$ of a day longer than the true solar year.

APPENDIX 1

We therefore skip leap year every 128 years on our calendar. Three such leap years must be skipped during Daniel's prophetic period of 483 years. Thus we subtract 3 days and arrive at 173,880 days.

And we see that Daniel was accurate to the exact day.

APPENDIX 2

Overview of Daniel's Visions

Reference	Purpose	Title
King's statue a. 2:38-40	a. Geographical makeup of As-Sufyani's kingdom	a. The iron legs
b. 2:41-45	b. Mahdi's reign as foundation of Islamic Empire	b. Feet of clay mixed with iron having 10 toes
Beasts from the sea a. 7:3-7, 23	a. Manner in which As-Sufyani's kingdom is consolidated	a. Iron beast
b. 7:8-14, 24-28	b. Rise and demise of Al Mahdi	b. Eleventh horn out of the iron beast
Ram and goat a. 8:3-22	a. Origin of As-Sufyani, motivation for specific activities	a. horn out of the horn
b. 8:23-26	b. Deception of Mahdi as manner of gaining power	b. Insolent king

Seventy weeks a. 9:26b-27a	a. As-Sufyani in context of prophetic timeline	a. The one whose covenant the *Nagid* to Come strengthens with the Many
b. 9:27b	b. Mahdi in context of prophecy	b. The one who Makes Desolate
Antiochus a. 11:21-45	a. As-Sufyani in type—details of his military campaigns	a. The Despicable person
b. 12:1-13	b. The time of distress at the end of age	b. None. Reference to Michael matches Rev 12 after which Mahdi arises in Rev 13 as beast out of sea

APPENDIX 3

Parallels of the As-Sufyani/Mahdi pair in Daniel, Revelation and Matthew

Reference	As-Sufyani	Reference	Al Mahdi
Daniel 7:7	<ul><li>A dreadful fourth beast</li><li>Devours, crushes, tramples</li><li>Ten horns.</li></ul>	Daniel 7:8	<ul><li>Eleventh horn</li><li>Pulls out three horns</li><li>Mouth uttering great boasts</li></ul>
Daniel 7:23	<ul><li>Fourth kingdom on the earth</li><li>Devours, crushes, tramples whole earth</li><li>Out of the kingdom ten kings will arise</li></ul>	Daniel 7:24-25	<ul><li>Eleventh king</li><li>Subdues three kings</li><li>Speaks out against God, wears down saints for a time, times and half a time</li><li>Makes alterations in times and in law</li></ul>
Daniel 8:8-14	<ul><li>Horn comes out of one of the four horns of Alexander's kingdom (Syro-Babylonia)</li><li>Conquers toward south, east, and Israel</li><li>Causes some of host and stars to fall and tramples them</li><li>Throws down the sanctuary</li><li>Because of transgression, Host and regular sacrifice given over to him, for 2300 evenings and mornings</li></ul>	Daniel 8:23-26	<ul><li>Insolent king arises in latter period of their rule, when the transgressors are done</li><li>HE WILL BE MIGHTY, BUT NOT BY HIS OWN POWER.</li><li>Destroys/corrupts the holy people.</li><li>Opposes Prince of Princes.</li><li>Will be broken without human agency.</li><li>The vision about the 2300 evenings and mornings is true...</li></ul>
Daniel 9:27a	<ul><li>Associated with *nagid's* covenant with the many for 7 years</li></ul>	Daniel 9:27b	<ul><li>Comes on the wing of abominations</li><li>Makes desolate</li></ul>

Daniel 11:3-45	<ul><li>Despicable Person abolishes regular sacrifice, sets up abomination of desolation.</li><li>Corrupts those opposed to the covenant</li><li>Those who know their God will take action</li><li>Those with insight give understanding to the many, yet some will fall to refine, purge, make them pure until the end time</li><li>Those given understanding will fall for many days by sword, flame, plunder and captivity</li><li>King does as he pleases, and claims to be above every god</li><li>At end of time, kings of south and north battle him</li><li>He enters Israel</li><li>He goes out to destroy because of rumors from east and north</li><li>Pitches his royal pavilion between the seas and Temple Mount</li><li>Comes to his end with no one to help him.</li></ul>	Daniel 12:1	<ul><li>At that time Michael stands up</li><li>A time of distress such as never occurred since there was a nation until that time</li><li>At that time your people, everyone who is found written in the book, will be rescued.</li></ul>

Revelation 12:3, 4; 7-9; 13-17	<ul><li>Red dragon with seven heads and ten horns,</li><li>**Each *head* has a diadem**</li><li>Tail sweeps away 1/3 stars and throws them to the earth</li><li>Waits to devour woman's child</li><li>dragon wars with Michael</li><li>dragon is thrown down</li><li>Persecutes woman</li><li>Woman flees to wilderness for 1260 days</li><li>Serpent pours water out of mouth to destroy woman</li><li>dragon goes to war with saints</li><li>Stands on seashore</li></ul>	Revelation 13:1-8	<ul><li>Best comes out of the sea, has ten horns and seven heads</li><li>**Each *horn* has a diadem** and on his heads are blasphemous names</li><li>Body of leopard, feet like bear, mouth like lion.</li><li>DRAGON GIVES HIM HIS POWER AND THRONE AND AUTHORITY.</li><li>One of his heads slain, and fatal wound healed.</li><li>Blasphemes God, and those who tabernacle in heaven.</li><li>Makes war with the saints and overcomes them</li><li>Has authority over every tribe and people and tongue and nation</li></ul>
Revelation 17:8, 9-12	<ul><li>The beast was and is not and will come again</li><li>Seven heads=seven kings; five have fallen, one is, the other has not yet come; and when he comes, he must remain a little while.</li><li>Beast is one of the seven kings, but also an eighth, and he goes to destruction.</li><li>The ten horns are ten kings, who have not yet received a kingdom</li></ul>	Revelation 17:12-14, 16	<ul><li>Ten kings receive authority as kings with the beast for one hour. These have one purpose: to give their power and authority to the beast.</li><li>They wage war against the Lamb…</li><li>They make the city desolate</li></ul>
Matthew 24:4-10	<ul><li>Many come in my name saying, 'I am the Christ', and mislead many.</li><li>Wars and rumors of wars, nation rises against nation and kingdom against kingdom; famines and earthquakes</li><li>They deliver you to tribulation, kill you and all nations hate you on account of My name.</li><li>Many fall away and deliver up one another and hate one another.</li><li>And many false prophets arise and mislead many</li><li>Then the end shall come.</li></ul>	Matthew 24:15, 21, 31	<ul><li>Therefore, when you see the Abomination of Desolation in the holy place, there will be a great tribulation such as has not occurred since the beginning of the world until now</li><li>After the tribulation the sun and moon will grow dark</li><li>He will come on the clouds to gather together His elect</li></ul>

APPENDIX 4

Summary of the Letters and their Corresponding Seals

Seals (parallel verses in Matthew 24)	Letter	Comment
1. **White horse**: conquering and to conquer (5-6: Birth Pangs: False Christs mislead many, wars and rumors of wars)	1. **Ephesus**: test the apostles and find them to be false; left first love; hate the Nicolaitans. *Overcomers*: tree of life	1. *Nagid* to Come confirms association with As-Sufyani which appears to usher in the Messianic age with a promise of peace
2. **Red horse**: takes peace from earth and receives magistrate's sword (6: Wars and civil wars)	2. **Smyrna**: devil puts in prison; suffers tribulation by those who say they are Jews but are a synagogue of Satan. *Overcomers*: not hurt by second death	2. Civil war breaks out in "Muhammad's nation," in Medina but perhaps all over Middle East (and the West?) As-Sufyani continues to conquer
3. **Black horse**: famine (7: famines and earthquakes)	3. **Pergamos**: live where Satan's throne is; hold fast my name; some hold to the teaching of Balaam and Nicolaitans. *Overcomers*: hidden manna	3. Deprivation and persecution lead to compromise within the Church.
4. **Ashen horse**: Death and Hades kill with sword, famine, death and the beasts of the earth (9-10: Persecution of the Church, apostasy; 11-13: False prophets arise, lawlessness increases; 14: gospel preached to whole earth; 15-22: Abomination of Desolation, persecution of Judea	4. **Thyatira**: love and perseverance, deeds greater than at first; tolerates Jezebel but she and her children will be killed with death; those who fornicate with her suffer great tribulation; the rest of the Church Jesus places no other burden on. *Overcomers*: shall rule the nations with a rod of iron	4. As-Sufyani installs Abomination of Desolation and persecutes Church who is raptured as male child "who will rule nations with rod of iron" (Rev 12:5); persecution of the Jews; army swallowed up by earth (sign of Al Mahdi)

5. **Martyrs**: ask for vengeance	5. **Sardis**: dead; "wake up and strengthen what remains"; just a few people with clean garments. *Overcomers*: clothed in white garments, name not blotted out, name confessed before Father	5. Martyrs are the result of false Jews and As-Sufyani's attack; just a few in Sardis wear clean garments because Thyatira is gone; some who are left repent; some become Christians after rapture.
6. **Earthquake, moon turns red, sun turns black, stars fall** (24-29: False Christs and prophets perform wonders; sun and moon will darken, stars fall from sky; powers shaken)	6. **Philadelphia**: Jesus calls self "He who is holy, true, has key of David, opens and shuts" (Is 22:22); have open door and a little power; Jesus will guard in the hour of testing. *Overcomers*: pillar in temple with name of God and New Jerusalem	6. 2nd sign of Mahdi; rise of the beast out of the sea: Mahdi establishes his kingdom with Jerusalem as its capital; 144,000 are sealed, John sees the multitude of gentiles before God's throne. Great Distress begins; wars with the witnesses and the "rest of the woman's offspring"; hour of testing is the coming 7trumpets.
7. **Silence for 30 minutes; seven trumpets and seven bowls** (30: Christ comes in the clouds to reap harvest. 33: when you see these things, recognize that He is right at the door)	7. **Laodicea**: neither hot nor cold, spit out of Jesus' mouth; materially wealthy but spiritually poor, blind, naked; advised to buy purified gold and white garments to hide nakedness; Jesus knocks on door	5th trumpet: 144,000 protected against the 5 month plague of the scorpion locusts. 6th trumpet: Prophet Jesus appears to defeat witnesses and saints. 7th trumpet: campaign of the mark; 144,000 raptured (Rev 14:3-4), rest of Philadelphian church raptured in harvest (Rev 14:16). 6th bowl: Jesus says, "Keep your garments lest men see your shame." 7th bowl: destruction of Babylon ("the great city").

CPSIA information can be obtained at www.ICGtesting.com
Printed in the USA
BVOW071327290712

296420BV00002B/11/P